MIGRATION AND REMITTANCES FACTBOOK 2008

MIGRATION AND REMITTANCES FACTBOOK 2008

THE WORLD BANK

© 2008 The International Bank for Reconstruction and Development / The World Bank
1818 H Street NW
Washington DC 20433
Telephone: 202-473-1000
Internet: www.worldbank.org
E-mail: feedback@worldbank.org

1 2 3 4 5 11 10 09 08

This volume is a product of the staff of the International Bank for Reconstruction and Development / The World Bank. The findings, interpretations, and conclusions expressed in this volume do not necessarily reflect the views of the Executive Directors of The World Bank or the governments they represent.

The World Bank does not guarantee the accuracy of the data included in this work. The boundaries, colors, denominations, and other information shown on any map in this work do not imply any judgement on the part of The World Bank concerning the legal status of any territory or the endorsement or acceptance of such boundaries.

ISBN: 978-0-8213-7413-9
eISBN: 978-0-8213-7414-6
DOI: 10.1596/978-0-8213-7413-9

Library of Congress Cataloging-in-Publication data has been applied for.

Cover and interior design by Auras Design.

Contents

Acknowledgments

The *Migration and Remittances Factbook 2008* was compiled by Dilip Ratha and Zhimei Xu of the Development Prospects Group of the Development Economics Vice Presidency, under the direction of Uri Dadush. The authors extend a special thanks to Sanket Mohapatra for his contributions and many discussions. They gratefully acknowledge the constructive comments and advice from Susan Martin, Changqing Sun, K. M. Vijayalakshmi, and Piyasiri Wickramasekara and offer many thanks to Nigar Farhad Aliyeva and Sarah Crow for their assistance in creating the online version of the *Factbook*.

Production of this volume (including design, editing, and layout) was coordinated by Stephen McGroarty and Susan Graham of the Office of the Publisher at the World Bank; the printing was managed by Denise Bergeron (also of the World Bank).

Foreword

The *Migration and Remittances Factbook 2008* attempts to present numbers and facts behind the stories of international migration and remittances, drawing on authoritative, publicly available data. It provides a snapshot of statistics on immigration, emigration, skilled emigration, and remittance flows for 194 countries and 13 regional and income groups. Some interesting facts emerge:

- Nearly 200 million people, or 3 percent of the world population, live outside their countries of birth. Current migration flows, relative to population, are weaker than those of the last decades of the nineteenth century.

- The top migrant destination countries are the United States, the Russian Federation, Germany, Ukraine, and France. The top immigration countries, relative to population, are Qatar (78 percent), the United Arab Emirates (71 percent), Kuwait (62 percent), Singapore (43 percent), Israel (40 percent), and Jordan (39 percent).

- The volume of South–South migration is almost as large as that of South–North migration, which accounts for 47 percent of the total emigration from developing countries. South–South migration is larger than South–North migration in Sub-Saharan Africa (72 percent), Europe and Central Asia (64 percent), and South Asia (54 percent).

- The Mexico–United States corridor is the largest migration corridor in the world, accounting for 10.4 million migrants by 2005. Migration corridors in the Former Soviet Union—Russia–Ukraine, and Ukraine–Russia—are the next largest, followed by Bangladesh–India. In these corridors, natives became migrants without moving when new international boundaries were drawn.

- Smaller countries tend to have higher rates of skilled emigration. Almost all the physicians trained in Grenada and Dominica have emigrated abroad. St. Lucia, Cape Verde, Fiji, São Tomé and Principe, and Liberia are also among the countries with the highest emigration rates of physicians.

- Refugees and asylum seekers made up 13.5 million or just over 7 percent of international migrants in 2005. The share of refugees in the population was 14.3 percent in the low-income countries— more than five times larger than the share of 2.6 percent in the high-income OECD countries. The Middle East and North Africa had the largest share of refugees and asylum seekers among immigrants (60 percent), followed by Sub-Saharan Africa (17 percent), East Asia and Pacific (11 percent), and South Asia (11 percent).

- Worldwide remittance flows are estimated to have exceeded $318 billion in 2007, of which developing countries received $240 billion. The true size, including unrecorded flows through formal and informal channels, is believed to be significantly larger. Recorded remittances are more than twice as large as official aid and nearly two-thirds of FDI flows to developing countries.

- In 2007, the top recipient countries of recorded remittances were India, China, Mexico, the Philippines, and France. As a share of GDP, however, smaller countries such as Tajikistan (36 percent), Moldova (36 percent), Tonga (32 percent), the Kyrgyz Republic (27 percent), and Honduras (26 percent) were the largest recipients in 2006.

- Rich countries are the main source of remittances. The United States is by far the largest, with $42 billion in recorded outward flows in 2006. Saudi Arabia ranks as the second largest, followed by Switzerland and Germany.

The authors have attempted to present the best possible data in the *Factbook,* drawing on authoritative sources. However, the user is advised to take note of the pitfalls of using currently available migration and remittances data. Remittance flows and the stock of migrants may be underestimated due to the use of informal remittance channels, irregular migration, and ambiguity in the definition of migrants (foreign born versus foreigner, seasonal versus permanent). Considerably more effort is needed to improve the quality of data.

We hope the *Factbook* serves as a stepping stone toward a more concrete understanding of migration and remittance trends in the world.

Uri Dadush
Director, Development Prospects Group
and International Trade Department
Chair, Migration Working Group
The World Bank

Data Notes

The reader is advised to note the pitfalls of using the data on international migration and remittances, which are often missing, lagging, or lacking in cross-country comparability. Capturing data on irregular movements of migrants and remittances remains a big challenge.

Data on Migration

According to the Recommendations on Statistics of International Migration by the United Nations, *long-term migrants* are persons who move to a country other than that of his or her usual residence for a period of at least a year—so the country of destination effectively becomes his or her new country of usual residence. And *short-term migrants* are persons who move to a country other than that of their usual residence for a period of at least three months but less than a year, except in cases where the movement to that country is for purposes of recreation, holiday, visits to friends and relatives, business, medical treatment, or religious pilgrimage (UN Statistics Division 1998).

The United Nations Population Division (UNPD) database is the most comprehensive source of information on international migrant stock for the period 1960–2005 (UNPD 2005). For 165 countries, the data are based on foreign-born statistics, and for 50 countries on foreign nationality. For Côte d'Ivoire and the Democratic Republic of Congo, a combination of the two types of data is used. For thirteen countries, migrant stock data are estimated indirectly using various assumptions. Time series data on migrant stocks are generated assuming certain growth rates.

The duration threshold that identifies migrants varies across countries (Lemaitre and others 2006). For example, under the UN definition, international students who study in the receiving country for more than a year would be considered as migrants. The *International Migration Outlook* (OECD 2006) made a first attempt to characterize migrants by "reasons for movement" and to harmonize statistics among OECD countries.

Data on bilateral migrant stock are available for only a few selected OECD countries. For the vast majority of countries, bilateral migration data do not exist. Preliminary efforts to estimate bilateral migration data include Harrison and others (2004); the University of Sussex data originally constructed for the Global Trade Analysis Project (GTAP) trade modeling; and the Development Prospects Group, World Bank data used for estimating South-South migration and remittance flows (Ratha and Shaw 2007). The quality of data on bilateral migration are as good (or poor) as the quality of the population censuses of different countries, but in a significant number of countries, they are just missing.

Data on Remittances[1]

The remittance tables in the country pages and in the world and regional tables report officially recorded remittances. The true size of remittances, including unrecorded flows through formal and informal channels, is believed to be larger. Total flows may not always equal the sum of the components as they may have been taken from alternative sources.

Migrant remittances are defined as the sum of workers' remittances, compensation of employees, and migrants' transfers.

Workers' remittances, as defined in the International Monetary Fund (IMF) Balance of Payments manual, are current private transfers from migrant workers who are considered residents of the host country to recipients in their country of origin.[2] If the migrants live in the host country for a year or longer, they are considered residents, regardless of their immigration status. If the migrants have lived in the host country for less than a year, their entire income in the host country should be classified as compensation of employees.

Although the residence guideline in the manual is clear, this rule is often not followed for various reasons. Many countries compile data based on the citizenship of migrant workers rather than on their residency status. Further, data are shown entirely as either compensation of employees or as worker remittances, although they should be split between the two categories if the guidelines were correctly followed.[3] The distinction between these two categories appears to be entirely arbitrary, depending on country preference, convenience, and tax laws or data availability.[4]

---

[1] This part is excerpted from *Global Economic Prospects 2006.*

[2] Official statistics on remittances tend to underestimate the size of remittance flows. Following a request from the G7 nations in June 2004, the World Bank, together with the IMF and UN, led an international working group to improve remittance statistics. This working group, now functioning as the "Luxembourg Group," has recommended that three new items—personal remittances, total remittances, and total remittances and transfers to nonprofit institutions serving households—be added to the *Balance of Payments Manual,* 6th edition.

[3] For example, India shows very little compensation of employees, but large workers' remittances, although it is well known that India supplies a large number of temporary IT workers to the United States and European countries. On the other hand, the Philippines shows large compensation of employees and very few migrants' transfers.

[4] Due to the difficulty in classifications, countries have often classified workers' remittances either as other current transfers or as transfers from other sectors. In some countries, notably China, remittances may have been misclassified as foreign direct investment. In the case of India and many other countries, remittances may have been classified as nonresident deposits, especially those in local currency terms.

Migrants' transfers are the net worth of migrants that are transferred from one country to another at the time of migration (for a period of at least one year). As the number of temporary workers increases, the importance of migrants' transfers may increase. Therefore, in order to get a complete picture of the resource flow, one has to consider these three items together.

Many countries do not report data on remittances in the IMF balance of payment statistics, even though it is known that emigration from those countries took place. Several developing countries (for example, Lebanon) do not report to the IMF. Some high-income countries (notably Canada, Singapore, and the United Arab Emirates) also do not report remittance data. A survey of central banks reveals widespread problems with remittance data collection methodology (de Luna Martinez 2005). Most of the central banks use remittance data reported by commercial banks, but leave out flows through money transfer operators and informal channels. Even when data are available and properly classified, in many cases, these data are often weak or out of date. Also, the methodology for preparing estimates is not the same in all countries, and it is not always described in the country notes in the publicly available balance of payments data. It is hoped that the increased awareness about the importance of remittances and the shortcomings in both the remittance and migrant workers' data will result in efforts to improve the data transmission.

Perhaps the most difficult aspect of remittance data is estimating informal flows. One way to estimate the true size of remittances is to undertake surveys of remittance senders and recipients. Unless new, adequately randomized and representative surveys of recipients and senders are carried out, evidence from existing household surveys would only be indicative rather than comprehensive.

Sources of Data

Data on immigration and emigration are from UNPD (2005) and Ratha and Shaw (2007). Data on the emigration rate of the tertiary educated are from Docquier and Marfouk (2004). Data on the emigration of physicians and nurses are from Docquier and Bhargava (2006), while supplementary data from Clemens and Pettersson (2006) are used for Sub-Saharan African countries. Remittances data are from the IMF (2007).

Data on the following variables are from the World Bank (2007): population, population growth, population density, labor force, urban population, age dependency ratio, surface area, gross national income (GNI), GNI per capita, GDP growth, and poverty headcount ratio at national poverty line.

In the tables, we use . . to indicate that data are not available.

Bibliography

Bilsborrow, R.E., Hugo Graeme, A. S. Oberai, and Hania Zlotnik. 1997. *International Migration Statistics, Guidelines for Improving Data Collection Systems.* Geneva: International Labor Office.

Clemens, Michael A., and Gunilla Pettersson. 2006. "New Data on African Health Professionals Abroad." Working Paper 95, Center for Global Development, Washington, DC.

de Luna Martinez, Jose. 2005. "Workers' Remittances to Developing Countries: A Survey with Central Banks on Selected Public Policy Issues." Policy Research Working Paper 3638, World Bank, Washington, DC.

Docquier, Frédéric, and Alok Bhargava. 2006. "The Medical Brain Drain: A New Panel Data-set on Physicians' Emigration Rates (1991–2004)." World Bank, Washington, DC.

Docquier, Frédéric, and Abdeslam Marfouk. 2004. "Measuring the International Mobility of Skilled Workers (1990–2000)—Release 1.0." Policy Research Working Paper 3381, World Bank, Washington, DC.

Harrison, Anne, assisted by Tolani Britton and Annika Swanson. 2004. "Working Abroad—The Benefits Flowing from Nationals Working in Other Countries." Paper prepared for the OECD Round Table on Sustainable Development, Paris.

IMF (International Monetary Fund). 2007. *IMF Balance of Payments Statistics Yearbook.* Washington, DC: IMF.

Lemaitre, Georges, Thomas Liebig, and Cécile Thoreau. 2006. "Harmonised statistics on immigrant inflows—preliminary results, sources and methods." OECD.

OECD (Organisation for Economic Co-operation and Development). 2006. *International Migration Outlook.* Paris: OECD.

Parsons, Christopher R., Ronald Skeldon, Terrie L. Walmsley, and L. Alan Winters. 2007. "Quantifying International Migration: A Database of Bilateral Migrant Stocks." Policy Research Working Paper 4165, World Bank, Washington, DC.

Ratha, Dilip, and William Shaw. 2007. "South-South Migration and Remittances." World Bank Working Paper No. 102. Washington, D.C.

World Bank. 2005. *Global Economic Prospects 2006: Economic Implications of Remittances and Migration.* Washington, DC: World Bank.

_____. 2007. *World Development Indicators.* Washington, DC: World Bank.

United Nations Population Division. 2005. Trends in Total Migrant Stock: The 2005 Revision. (online database) United Nations, New York.

United Nations Statistics Division. 1998. "Recommendations on Statistics of International Migration." United Nations Statistical Papers Series M, No. 58, Rev. 1. New York.

Migration and Remittances: Top 10 Countries

Top Immigration Countries, 2005

number of immigrants, millions

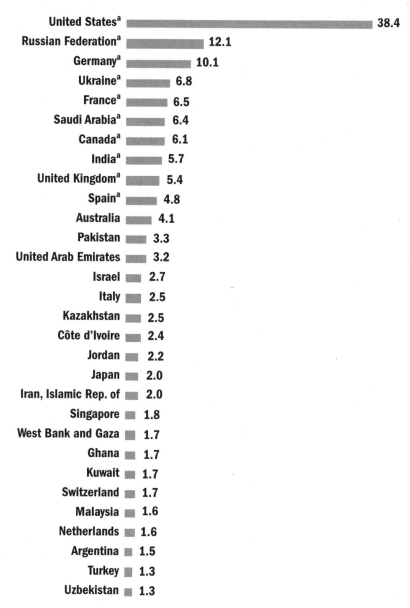

United States[a]	38.4
Russian Federation[a]	12.1
Germany[a]	10.1
Ukraine[a]	6.8
France[a]	6.5
Saudi Arabia[a]	6.4
Canada[a]	6.1
India[a]	5.7
United Kingdom[a]	5.4
Spain[a]	4.8
Australia	4.1
Pakistan	3.3
United Arab Emirates	3.2
Israel	2.7
Italy	2.5
Kazakhstan	2.5
Côte d'Ivoire	2.4
Jordan	2.2
Japan	2.0
Iran, Islamic Rep. of	2.0
Singapore	1.8
West Bank and Gaza	1.7
Ghana	1.7
Kuwait	1.7
Switzerland	1.7
Malaysia	1.6
Netherlands	1.6
Argentina	1.5
Turkey	1.3
Uzbekistan	1.3

Source: UN Population Division.
a. Top 10 countries.

Top Immigration Countries, 2005
percent of population

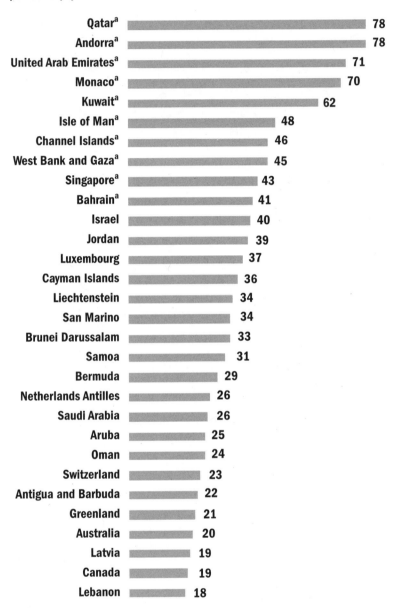

Country	Percent
Qatar[a]	78
Andorra[a]	78
United Arab Emirates[a]	71
Monaco[a]	70
Kuwait[a]	62
Isle of Man[a]	48
Channel Islands[a]	46
West Bank and Gaza[a]	45
Singapore[a]	43
Bahrain[a]	41
Israel	40
Jordan	39
Luxembourg	37
Cayman Islands	36
Liechtenstein	34
San Marino	34
Brunei Darussalam	33
Samoa	31
Bermuda	29
Netherlands Antilles	26
Saudi Arabia	26
Aruba	25
Oman	24
Switzerland	23
Antigua and Barbuda	22
Greenland	21
Australia	20
Latvia	19
Canada	19
Lebanon	18

Source: UN Population Division.
a. Top 10 countries.

Migration and Remittances Factbook 2008

Top Emigration Countries, 2005
number of emigrants, millions

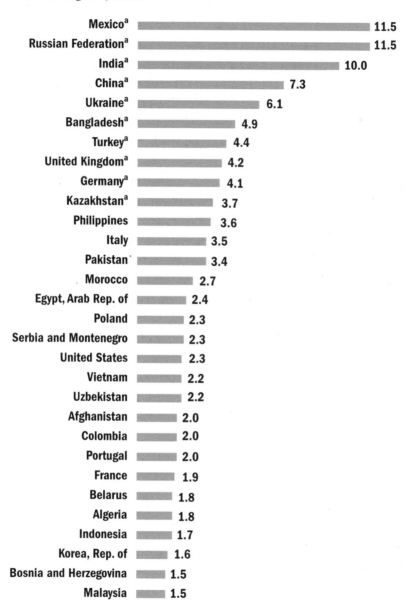

Mexico[a]	11.5
Russian Federation[a]	11.5
India[a]	10.0
China[a]	7.3
Ukraine[a]	6.1
Bangladesh[a]	4.9
Turkey[a]	4.4
United Kingdom[a]	4.2
Germany[a]	4.1
Kazakhstan[a]	3.7
Philippines	3.6
Italy	3.5
Pakistan	3.4
Morocco	2.7
Egypt, Arab Rep. of	2.4
Poland	2.3
Serbia and Montenegro	2.3
United States	2.3
Vietnam	2.2
Uzbekistan	2.2
Afghanistan	2.0
Colombia	2.0
Portugal	2.0
France	1.9
Belarus	1.8
Algeria	1.8
Indonesia	1.7
Korea, Rep. of	1.6
Bosnia and Herzegovina	1.5
Malaysia	1.5

Sources: Development Prospects Group, World Bank.
a. Top 10 countries.

Top Emigration Countries, 2005

percent of population

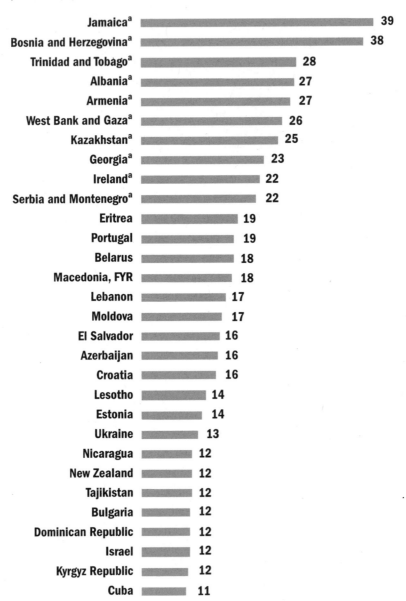

Jamaica[a]	39
Bosnia and Herzegovina[a]	38
Trinidad and Tobago[a]	28
Albania[a]	27
Armenia[a]	27
West Bank and Gaza[a]	26
Kazakhstan[a]	25
Georgia[a]	23
Ireland[a]	22
Serbia and Montenegro[a]	22
Eritrea	19
Portugal	19
Belarus	18
Macedonia, FYR	18
Lebanon	17
Moldova	17
El Salvador	16
Azerbaijan	16
Croatia	16
Lesotho	14
Estonia	14
Ukraine	13
Nicaragua	12
New Zealand	12
Tajikistan	12
Bulgaria	12
Dominican Republic	12
Israel	12
Kyrgyz Republic	12
Cuba	11

Sources: Development Prospects Group, World Bank.
Note: Countries with less than 1 million population excluded.
a. Top 10 countries.

Migration and Remittances Factbook 2008

Top Migration Corridors, 2005
number of migrants, millions

Mexico–United States[a]	10.3
Russian Federation–Ukraine[a]	4.8
Ukraine–Russian Federation[a]	3.6
Bangladesh–India[a]	3.5
Turkey–Germany[a]	2.7
Kazakhstan–Russian Federation[a]	2.6
India–United Arab Emirates[a]	2.2
Russian Federation–Kazakhstan[a]	1.8
Philippines–United States[a]	1.6
Afghanistan–Islamic Rep. of Iran[a]	1.6
Germany–United States	1.4
Algeria–France	1.4
India–Saudi Arabia	1.3
Arab Rep. of Egypt–Saudi Arabia	1.2
Pakistan–India	1.2
India–United States	1.1
China–United States	1.1
Vietnam–United States	1.1
Canada–United States	1.0
United States–Australia	1.0
India–Bangladesh	1.0
Malaysia–Singapore	1.0
Burkina Faso–Côte d'Ivoire	1.0
Cuba–United States	1.0
Belarus–Russian Federation	0.9
Uzbekistan–Russian Federation	0.9
El Salvador–United States	0.9
United Kingdom–United States	0.9
Serbia and Montenegro–Germany	0.9
Italy–Germany	0.9

Sources: Development Prospects Group, World Bank.
a. Top 10 countries.

Top Migration Corridors (excluding Former Soviet Union), 2005

number of migrants, millions

Mexico–United States[a]	10.3
Bangladesh–India[a]	3.5
Turkey–Germany[a]	2.7
India–United Arab Emirates[a]	2.2
Philippines–United States[a]	1.6
Afghanistan–Islamic Rep. of Iran[a]	1.6
Germany–United States[a]	1.4
Algeria–France[a]	1.4
India–Saudi Arabia[a]	1.3
Arab Rep. of Egypt–Saudi Arabia[a]	1.2
Pakistan–India	1.2
India–United States	1.1
China–United States	1.1
Vietnam–United States	1.1
Canada–United States	1.0
United Kingdom–Australia	1.0
India–Bangladesh	1.0
Malaysia–Singapore	1.0
Burkina Faso–Côte d'Ivoire	1.0
Cuba–United States	1.0
El Salvador–United States	0.9
United Kingdom–United States	0.9
Serbia and Montenegro–Germany	0.9
Italy–Germany	0.9
Pakistan–Saudi Arabia	0.8
Morocco–France	0.8
Dominican Republic–United States	0.8
Rep. of Korea–United States	0.7
India–Nepal	0.7
Indonesia–Malaysia	0.7

Sources: Development Prospects Group, World Bank.
a. Top 10 countries.

Top Destination Countries for Refugees, 2005
number of refugees, millions

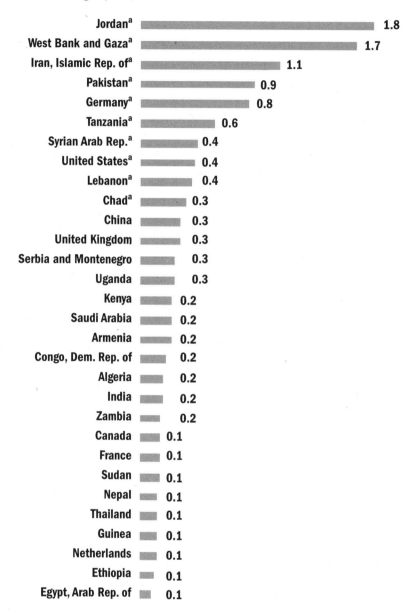

Jordan[a]	1.8
West Bank and Gaza[a]	1.7
Iran, Islamic Rep. of[a]	1.1
Pakistan[a]	0.9
Germany[a]	0.8
Tanzania[a]	0.6
Syrian Arab Rep.[a]	0.4
United States[a]	0.4
Lebanon[a]	0.4
Chad[a]	0.3
China	0.3
United Kingdom	0.3
Serbia and Montenegro	0.3
Uganda	0.3
Kenya	0.2
Saudi Arabia	0.2
Armenia	0.2
Congo, Dem. Rep. of	0.2
Algeria	0.2
India	0.2
Zambia	0.2
Canada	0.1
France	0.1
Sudan	0.1
Nepal	0.1
Thailand	0.1
Guinea	0.1
Netherlands	0.1
Ethiopia	0.1
Egypt, Arab Rep. of	0.1

Source: UN Population Division.
a. Top 10 countries.

Top Destination Countries for Refugees, 2005

percent of immigrants

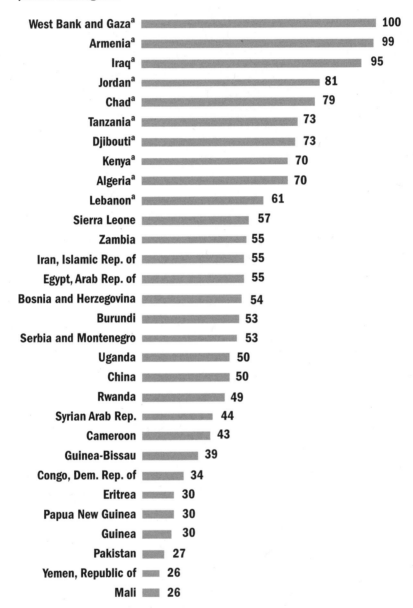

West Bank and Gaza[a]	100
Armenia[a]	99
Iraq[a]	95
Jordan[a]	81
Chad[a]	79
Tanzania[a]	73
Djibouti[a]	73
Kenya[a]	70
Algeria[a]	70
Lebanon[a]	61
Sierra Leone	57
Zambia	55
Iran, Islamic Rep. of	55
Egypt, Arab Rep. of	55
Bosnia and Herzegovina	54
Burundi	53
Serbia and Montenegro	53
Uganda	50
China	50
Rwanda	49
Syrian Arab Rep.	44
Cameroon	43
Guinea-Bissau	39
Congo, Dem. Rep. of	34
Eritrea	30
Papua New Guinea	30
Guinea	30
Pakistan	27
Yemen, Republic of	26
Mali	26

Source: UN Population Division.
a. Top 10 countries.

Migration and Remittances Factbook 2008

Top Emigration Countries of Tertiary Educated, 2000

percent of total tertiary educated in the country

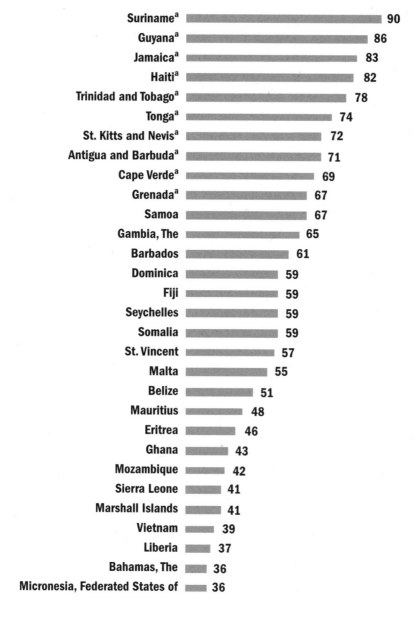

Suriname[a]	90
Guyana[a]	86
Jamaica[a]	83
Haiti[a]	82
Trinidad and Tobago[a]	78
Tonga[a]	74
St. Kitts and Nevis[a]	72
Antigua and Barbuda[a]	71
Cape Verde[a]	69
Grenada[a]	67
Samoa	67
Gambia, The	65
Barbados	61
Dominica	59
Fiji	59
Seychelles	59
Somalia	59
St. Vincent	57
Malta	55
Belize	51
Mauritius	48
Eritrea	46
Ghana	43
Mozambique	42
Sierra Leone	41
Marshall Islands	41
Vietnam	39
Liberia	37
Bahamas, The	36
Micronesia, Federated States of	36

Source: Docquier and Marfouk 2004.
a. Top 10 countries.

Top Emigration Countries of Physicians, 2000
number of emigrated physicians, thousands

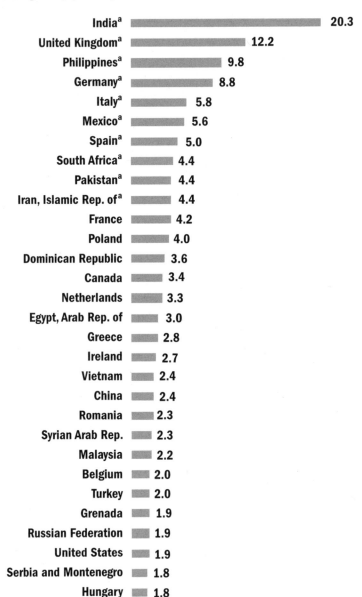

India[a]	20.3
United Kingdom[a]	12.2
Philippines[a]	9.8
Germany[a]	8.8
Italy[a]	5.8
Mexico[a]	5.6
Spain[a]	5.0
South Africa[a]	4.4
Pakistan[a]	4.4
Iran, Islamic Rep. of[a]	4.4
France	4.2
Poland	4.0
Dominican Republic	3.6
Canada	3.4
Netherlands	3.3
Egypt, Arab Rep. of	3.0
Greece	2.8
Ireland	2.7
Vietnam	2.4
China	2.4
Romania	2.3
Syrian Arab Rep.	2.3
Malaysia	2.2
Belgium	2.0
Turkey	2.0
Grenada	1.9
Russian Federation	1.9
United States	1.9
Serbia and Montenegro	1.8
Hungary	1.8

Source: Docquier and Bhargava 2006.
a. Top 10 countries.

Migration and Remittances Factbook 2008

Top Emigration Countries of Physicians, 2000
percent of total physicians trained in the country

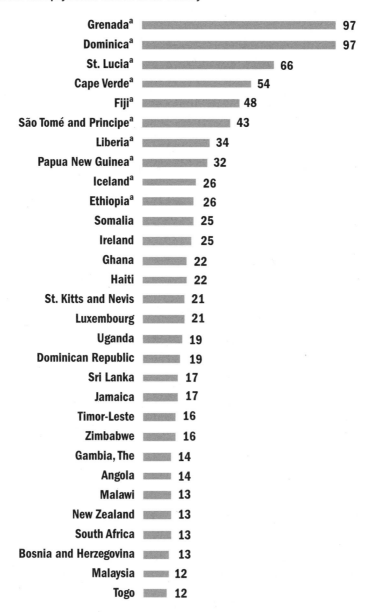

Country	Percent
Grenada[a]	97
Dominica[a]	97
St. Lucia[a]	66
Cape Verde[a]	54
Fiji[a]	48
São Tomé and Principe[a]	43
Liberia[a]	34
Papua New Guinea[a]	32
Iceland[a]	26
Ethiopia[a]	26
Somalia	25
Ireland	25
Ghana	22
Haiti	22
St. Kitts and Nevis	21
Luxembourg	21
Uganda	19
Dominican Republic	19
Sri Lanka	17
Jamaica	17
Timor-Leste	16
Zimbabwe	16
Gambia, The	14
Angola	14
Malawi	13
New Zealand	13
South Africa	13
Bosnia and Herzegovina	13
Malaysia	12
Togo	12

Source: Docquier and Bhargava 2006.
a. Top 10 countries.

Top Remittance-Receiving Countries, 2007
US$ billions

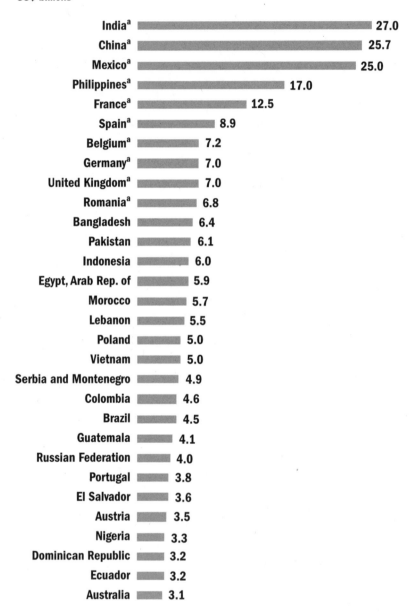

India[a]	27.0
China[a]	25.7
Mexico[a]	25.0
Philippines[a]	17.0
France[a]	12.5
Spain[a]	8.9
Belgium[a]	7.2
Germany[a]	7.0
United Kingdom[a]	7.0
Romania[a]	6.8
Bangladesh	6.4
Pakistan	6.1
Indonesia	6.0
Egypt, Arab Rep. of	5.9
Morocco	5.7
Lebanon	5.5
Poland	5.0
Vietnam	5.0
Serbia and Montenegro	4.9
Colombia	4.6
Brazil	4.5
Guatemala	4.1
Russian Federation	4.0
Portugal	3.8
El Salvador	3.6
Austria	3.5
Nigeria	3.3
Dominican Republic	3.2
Ecuador	3.2
Australia	3.1

Sources: Development Prospects Group, World Bank.
a. Top 10 countries.

Top Remittance-Receiving Countries, 2006
percent of GDP

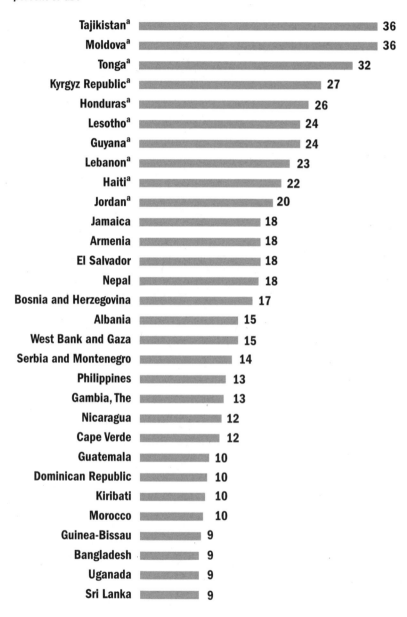

Tajikistan[a]	36
Moldova[a]	36
Tonga[a]	32
Kyrgyz Republic[a]	27
Honduras[a]	26
Lesotho[a]	24
Guyana[a]	24
Lebanon[a]	23
Haiti[a]	22
Jordan[a]	20
Jamaica	18
Armenia	18
El Salvador	18
Nepal	18
Bosnia and Herzegovina	17
Albania	15
West Bank and Gaza	15
Serbia and Montenegro	14
Philippines	13
Gambia, The	13
Nicaragua	12
Cape Verde	12
Guatemala	10
Dominican Republic	10
Kiribati	10
Morocco	10
Guinea-Bissau	9
Bangladesh	9
Uganada	9
Sri Lanka	9

Sources: Development Prospects Group, World Bank.
a. Top 10 countries.

Top Remittance-Sending Countries, 2006

US$ billions

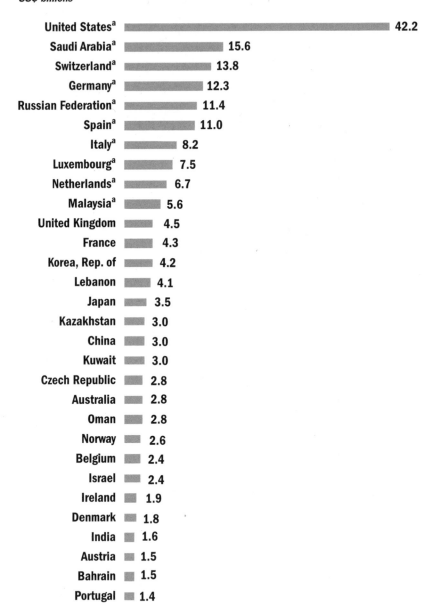

United States[a]	42.2
Saudi Arabia[a]	15.6
Switzerland[a]	13.8
Germany[a]	12.3
Russian Federation[a]	11.4
Spain[a]	11.0
Italy[a]	8.2
Luxembourg[a]	7.5
Netherlands[a]	6.7
Malaysia[a]	5.6
United Kingdom	4.5
France	4.3
Korea, Rep. of	4.2
Lebanon	4.1
Japan	3.5
Kazakhstan	3.0
China	3.0
Kuwait	3.0
Czech Republic	2.8
Australia	2.8
Oman	2.8
Norway	2.6
Belgium	2.4
Israel	2.4
Ireland	1.9
Denmark	1.8
India	1.6
Austria	1.5
Bahrain	1.5
Portugal	1.4

Sources: Development Prospects Group, World Bank.
a. Top 10 countries.

Top Remittance-Sending Countries, 2006
percent of GDP

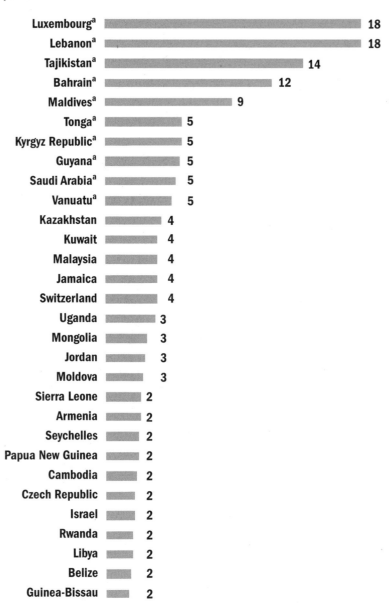

Luxembourg[a]	18
Lebanon[a]	18
Tajikistan[a]	14
Bahrain[a]	12
Maldives[a]	9
Tonga[a]	5
Kyrgyz Republic[a]	5
Guyana[a]	5
Saudi Arabia[a]	5
Vanuatu[a]	5
Kazakhstan	4
Kuwait	4
Malaysia	4
Jamaica	4
Switzerland	4
Uganda	3
Mongolia	3
Jordan	3
Moldova	3
Sierra Leone	2
Armenia	2
Seychelles	2
Papua New Guinea	2
Cambodia	2
Czech Republic	2
Israel	2
Rwanda	2
Libya	2
Belize	2
Guinea-Bissau	2

Sources: Development Prospects Group, World Bank.
a. Top 10 countries.

World

Population (millions, 2006)	6,518
Population growth (avg. annual %, 1997-2006)	1.3
Population density (people per sq. km, 2006)	50
Labor force (millions, 2006)	3,071
Urban population (% of pop., 2006)	49.2
Age dependency ratio (2006)	0.56
Surface area (1000 sq. km, 2006)	133,841
GNI ($ billions, 2006)	48,188
GNI per capita, Atlas method ($, 2006)	7,439
GDP growth (avg. annual %, 2002-06)	3.2
Poverty headcount ratio at national poverty line (% of pop., 2004)	..

Migration

MIGRATION, 2005

- Stock of immigrants: **190.6** million or **3.0** percent of population (UN). Current migration flows, relative to population, are weaker than during the last decades of the nineteenth century.
- Females as percentage of immigrants: **49.6** percent
- Refugees: **13.5** million or **7.1** percent of the total immigrants
- South-South migration is nearly as large as South-North migration. Over **47** percent of the migrants from developing countries are believed to be residing in other developing countries.
- Top 10 destination countries: the United States, Russia, Germany, Ukraine, France, Saudi Arabia, Canada, India, the United Kingdom, Spain. But as a share of population, top immigration countries include Qatar (78.3 percent), the United Arab Emirates (71.4 percent), Kuwait (62.1 percent), Singapore (42.6 percent), Bahrain (40.7 percent), Israel (39.6 percent), Jordan (39.0 percent), Brunei Darussalam (33.2 percent), Saudi Arabia (25.9 percent), Oman (24.4 percent)
- Top 10 emigration countries: Mexico, Russia, India, China, Ukraine, Bangladesh, Turkey, the United Kingdom, Germany, Kazakhstan
- Top 10 migration corridors: Mexico–the United States, Russia–Ukraine, Ukraine–Russia, Bangladesh–India, Turkey–Germany, Kazakhstan–Russia, India–the United Arab Emirates, Russia–Kazakhstan, the Philippines–the United States, Afghanistan–the Islamic Republic of Iran

SKILLED EMIGRATION, 2000

- Emigration rate of tertiary educated (top 10 countries): Suriname (89.9 percent), Guyana (85.9 percent), Jamaica (82.5 percent), Haiti (81.6 percent), Trinidad and Tobago (78.4 percent), Tonga (74.2 percent), St. Kitts and Nevis (71.8 percent), Antigua and Barbuda (70.9 percent), Cape Verde (69.1 percent), Grenada (66.7 percent)
- Emigration of physicians: **182,397** or **2.1** percent of physicians trained in the world

Remittances

US$ billions	1995	2000	2001	2002	2003	2004	2005	2006	2007
Inward									
remittance flows	**101.6**	**131.5**	**146.8**	**169.5**	**205.6**	**231.3**	**262.7**	**297.1ᵃ**	**317.7**
All developing									
countries	*57.5*	*84.5*	*95.6*	*115.9*	*143.6*	*161.3*	*191.2*	*221.3*	*239.7*
Outward									
remittance flows	**98.6**	**110.1**	**118.8**	**131.3**	**146.8**	**166.2**	**183.4**	**207.0ᵇ**	
All developing									
countries	*12.4*	*11.5*	*13.6*	*20.4*	*23.8*	*30.9*	*36.0*	*44.2*	

a. 0.7% of GDP in 2006.
b. 0.5% of GDP in 2006.

- Top 10 remittance recipients in 2007: India ($27.0 bn), China ($25.7 bn), Mexico ($25.0 bn), the Philippines ($17.0 bn), France ($12.5 bn), Spain ($8.9 bn), Belgium ($7.2 bn), United Kingdom ($7.0 bn), Germany ($7.0 bn), Romania ($6.8 bn).
- Top 10 remittance recipients in 2006 (percentage of GDP): Tajikistan (36.2%), Moldova (36.2%), Tonga (32.3%), the Kyrgyz Republic (27.4%), Honduras (25.6%), Lesotho (24.5%), Guyana (24.3%), Lebanon (22.8%), Haiti (21.6%), Jordan (20.3%).
- Top 10 remittance senders in 2006: the United States ($42.2 bn), Saudi Arabia ($15.6 bn), Switzerland ($13.8 bn), Germany ($12.3 bn), Russia ($11.4 bn), Spain ($11 bn), Italy ($8.2 bn), Luxembourg ($7.5 bn), the Netherlands ($6.7 bn), Malaysia ($5.6 bn).
- Top 10 remittance senders in 2006 (percentage of GDP): Luxembourg (18.2%), Lebanon (18.2%), Tajikistan (14.0%), Bahrain (11.9%), Maldives (9.1%), Tonga (5.4%), the Kyrgyz Republic (5.4%), Guyana (5.4%), Saudi Arabia (5.0%), Vanuatu (4.6%).

Developing Countries

Population (millions, 2006)	5,489
Population growth (avg. annual %, 1997–2006)	1.4
Population density (people per sq. km, 2006)	57
Labor force (millions, 2006)	2,569
Urban population (% of pop., 2006)	43.9
Age dependency ratio (2006)	0.57
Surface area (1,000 sq. km, 2006)	99,224
GNI ($ billions, 2006)	11,568
GNI per capita, Atlas method ($, 2006)	2,000
GDP growth (avg. annual %, 2002-06)	6.1
Poverty headcount ratio at national poverty line (% of pop., 2004)	..

Migration

EMIGRATION, 2005

- Stock of emigrants: **145.0** million or **2.7** percent of population
- Top 10 emigration countries: Mexico, Russia, India, China, Ukraine, Bangladesh, Turkey, Kazakhstan, the Philippines, Pakistan
- Identified destinations: high-income OECD countries (41.5 percent), high-income non-OECD countries (11.5 percent), low-income countries (12.1 percent), middle-income countries (26.3 percent), unidentified (8.5 percent).
- Top 10 migration corridors: Mexico–the United States, Russia–Ukraine, Ukraine–Russia, Bangladesh–India, Turkey–Germany, Kazakhstan–Russia, India–the United Arab Emirates, Russia–Kazakhstan, the Philippines–the United States, Afghanistan–the Islamic Republic of Iran
- Top 10 migration corridors excluding the Former Soviet Union: Mexico–the United States, Bangladesh–India, Turkey–Germany, India–the United Arab Emirates, the Philippines–the United States, Afghanistan–the Islamic Republic of Iran, Algeria–France, India–Saudi Arabia, Egypt–Saudi Arabia, Pakistan–India

SKILLED EMIGRATION, 2000

- Emigration rate of tertiary educated (top 10 countries): Suriname (89.9 percent), Guyana (85.9 percent), Jamaica (82.5 percent), Haiti (81.6 percent), Tonga (74.2 percent), St. Kitts and Nevis (71.8 percent), Cape Verde (69.1 percent), Grenada (66.7 percent), Samoa (66.6 percent), The Gambia (64.7)
- Emigration of physicians: **111,433** or **2.0** percent of physicians trained in the region

IMMIGRATION, 2005

- Stock of immigrants: **77.2** million or **1.4** percent of population (compared to 190.6 million or 3.0 percent for the world)
- Females as percentage of immigrants: **50.8** percent (compared to 49.6 percent for the world)
- Refugees as percentage of immigrants: **14.1** percent (compared to 7.1 percent for the world)
- Top 10 immigration countries: Russia, Ukraine, India, Pakistan, Kazakhstan, Côte d'Ivoire, Jordan, the Islamic Republic of Iran, West Bank and Gaza, Ghana

Remittances

US$ billions	1995	2000	2001	2002	2003	2004	2005	2006	2007
Inward									
remittance flows	**57.5**	**84.5**	**95.6**	**115.9**	**143.6**	**161.3**	**191.2**	**221.3**[a]	**239.7**
World	*101.6*	*131.5*	*146.8*	*169.5*	*205.6*	*231.3*	*262.7*	*297.1*	*317.7*
Outward									
remittance flows	**12.4**	**11.5**	**13.6**	**20.4**	**23.8**	**30.9**	**36.0**	**44.2**[b]	
World	*98.6*	*110.1*	*118.8*	*131.3*	*146.8*	*166.2*	*183.4*	*207.0*	

a. 1.9% of GDP in 2006.
b. 0.4% of GDP in 2006.

- Top 10 remittance recipients in 2007: India ($27.0 bn), China ($25.7 bn), Mexico ($25.0 bn), the Philippines ($17.0 bn), Romania ($6.8 bn), Bangladesh ($6.4 bn), Pakistan ($6.1 bn), Indonesia ($6.0 bn), Egypt ($5.9 bn), Morocco ($5.7 bn).
- Top 10 remittance recipients in 2006 (percentage of GDP): Tajikistan (36.2%), Moldova (36.2%), Tonga (32.3%), the Kyrgyz Republic (27.4%), Honduras (25.6%), Lesotho (24.5%), Guyana (24.3%), Lebanon (22.8%), Haiti (21.6%), Jordan (20.3%).
- Top 10 remittance senders in 2006: Russia ($11.4 bn), Malaysia ($5.6 bn), Lebanon ($4.1 bn), Kazakhstan ($3.0 bn), China ($3.0 bn), Oman ($2.8 bn), India ($1.6 bn), Indonesia ($1.4 bn), South Africa ($1.1 bn), Libya ($0.9 bn).
- Top 10 remittance senders in 2006 (percentage of GDP): Lebanon (18.2%), Tajikistan (14.0%), Maldives (9.1%), Tonga (5.4%), the Kyrgyz Republic (5.4%), Guyana (5.4%), Vanuatu (4.6%), Kazakhstan (3.9%), Malaysia (3.7%), Jamaica (3.7%).

Regional Tables

The country composition of regions is based on the World Bank's analytical regions and may differ from common geographic usage.

East Asia and Pacific (developing only: 23)

American Samoa, Cambodia, China, the Democratic People's Republic of Korea, Fiji, Indonesia, Kiribati, Lao People's Democratic Republic, Malaysia, the Marshall Islands, Federated States of Micronesia, Mongolia, Myanmar, Palau, Papua New Guinea, the Philippines, Samoa, the Solomon Islands, Thailand, Timor-Leste, Tonga, Vanuatu, Vietnam

Europe and Central Asia (developing only: 26)

Albania, Armenia, Azerbaijan, Belarus, Bosnia and Herzegovina, Bulgaria, Croatia, Georgia, Hungary, Kazakhstan, the Kyrgyz Republic, Latvia, Lithuania, former Yugoslav Republic of Macedonia, Moldova, Montenegro,[1] Poland, Romania, Russia, Serbia,[1] the Slovak Republic, Tajikistan, Turkey, Turkmenistan, Ukraine, Uzbekistan

Latin America and the Caribbean (developing only: 29)

Argentina, Belize, Bolivia, Brazil, Chile, Colombia, Costa Rica, Cuba, Dominica, the Dominican Republic, Ecuador, El Salvador, Grenada, Guatemala, Guyana, Haiti, Honduras, Jamaica, Mexico, Nicaragua, Panama, Paraguay, Peru, St. Kitts and Nevis, St. Lucia, St. Vincent and the Grenadines, Suriname, Uruguay, República Bolivariana de Venezuela

Middle East and North Africa (developing only: 14)

Algeria, Djibouti, Egypt, Iraq, the Islamic Republic of Iran, Jordan, Lebanon, Libya, Morocco, Oman, Syria, Tunisia, West Bank and Gaza, the Republic of Yemen

South Asia (8)

Afghanistan, Bangladesh, Bhutan, India, Maldives, Nepal, Pakistan, Sri Lanka

Sub-Saharan Africa (47)

Angola, Benin, Botswana, Burkina Faso, Burundi, Cameroon, Cape Verde, the Central African Republic, Chad, Comoros, the Democratic Republic of Congo, the Republic of Congo, Côte d'Ivoire, Equatorial Guinea, Eritrea, Ethiopia, Gabon, The Gambia, Ghana, Guinea, Guinea-Bissau, Kenya, Lesotho, Liberia, Madagascar, Malawi, Mali, Mauritania, Mauritius, Mozambique, Namibia, Niger, Nigeria, Rwanda, São Tomé and Principe, Senegal, Seychelles, Sierra Leone, Somalia, South Africa, Sudan, Swaziland, Tanzania, Togo, Uganda, Zambia, Zimbabwe

---

[1]Serbia and Montenegro became separate countries in 2006; however, we report them jointly in this *Factbook* since the historical statistics of the two countries were combined.

Migration and Remittances Factbook 2008

East Asia and Pacific

Population (millions, 2006)	1,900
Population growth (avg. annual %, 1997–2006)	0.9
Population density (people per sq. km, 2006)	120
Labor force (millions, 2006)	1,076
Urban population (% of pop., 2006)	42.3
Age dependency ratio (2006)	0.44
Surface area (1,000 sq. km, 2006)	16,300
GNI ($ billions, 2006)	3,647
GNI per capita, Atlas method ($, 2006)	1,863
GDP growth (avg. annual %, 2002–06)	8.8
Poverty headcount ratio at national poverty line (% of pop., 2004)	9.1

Migration

EMIGRATION, 2005

- Stock of emigrants: **19.3** million or **1.0** percent of population
- Top 10 emigration countries: China, the Philippines, Vietnam, Indonesia, Malaysia, Thailand, the Democratic People's Republic of Korea, Myanmar, Lao PDR, Cambodia
- Identified destinations: high-income OECD countries (50.0 percent), high-income non-OECD countries (27.3 percent), intra-regional (13.1 percent), other developing countries (1.1 percent); unidentified (8.5 percent)
- Top 10 migration corridors: the Philippines–the United States, China–the United States, Vietnam–the United States, Malaysia–Singapore, Indonesia–Malaysia, China–Singapore, the Philippines–Saudi Arabia, China–Japan, China–Canada, Indonesia–Saudi Arabia

SKILLED EMIGRATION, 2000

- Emigration rate of tertiary educated (top 10 countries): Tonga (74.2 percent), Samoa (66.6 percent), Fiji (58.7 percent), the Marshall Islands (41.0 percent), Vietnam (39.0 percent), the Federated States of Micronesia (36.4 percent), Palau (30.0 percent), Papua New Guinea (28.2 percent), Kiribati (24.9 percent), the Philippines (14.8 percent)
- Emigration of physicians: **19,071** or **0.8** percent of physicians trained in the region

IMMIGRATION, 2005

- Stock of immigrants: **4.4** million or **0.2** percent of population (compared to 190.6 million or 3.0 percent for the world)
- Females as percentage of immigrants: **48.1** percent (compared to 49.6 percent for the world)
- Refugees as percentage of immigrants: **10.8** percent (compared to 7.1 percent for the world)
- Top 10 immigration countries: Malaysia, Thailand, China, the Philippines, Cambodia, Indonesia, Myanmar, the Democratic People's Republic of Korea, Papua New Guinea, Lao PDR

Remittances

US$ billions	1995	2000	2001	2002	2003	2004	2005	2006	2007
Inward remittance flows	**9.7**	**16.7**	**20.1**	**29.5**	**35.4**	**39.1**	**46.6**	**52.8**[a]	**58.0**
All developing countries	*57.5*	*84.5*	*95.6*	*115.9*	*143.6*	*161.3*	*191.2*	*221.3*	*239.7*
Outward remittance flows	**1.6**	**1.7**	**2.0**	**5.4**	**5.5**	**8.4**	**9.9**	**10.4**[b]	
All developing countries	*12.4*	*11.5*	*13.6*	*20.4*	*23.8*	*30.9*	*36.0*	*44.2*	

a. **1.5% of GDP in 2006.**
b. **0.3% of GDP in 2006.**

- Top 10 remittance recipients in 2007: China ($25.7 bn), the Philippines ($17.0 bn), Indonesia ($6.0 bn), Vietnam ($5.0 bn), Thailand ($1.7 bn), Malaysia ($1.7 bn), Cambodia ($0.3 bn), Mongolia ($0.2 bn), Fiji ($0.2 bn), Myanmar ($0.1 bn).
- Top 10 remittance recipients in 2006 (percentage of GDP): Tonga (32.3%), the Philippines (13.0%), Kiribati (9.9%), Vietnam (7.9%), Mongolia (6.8%), the Solomon Islands (6.3%), Fiji (5.8%), Cambodia (4.1%), Vanuatu (2.8%), Indonesia (1.6%).

Europe and Central Asia

Population (millions, 2006)	460
Population growth (avg. annual %, 1997-2006)	0.2
Population density (people per sq. km, 2006)	20
Labor force (millions, 2006)	210
Urban population (% of pop., 2006)	63.8
Age dependency ratio (2006)	0.46
Surface area (1,000 sq. km, 2006)	24,114
GNI ($ billions, 2006)	2,421
GNI per capita, Atlas method ($, 2006)	4,796
GDP growth (avg. annual %, 2002-06)	6.2
Poverty headcount ratio at national poverty line (% of pop., 2004)	1.0

Migration

EMIGRATION, 2005

- Stock of emigrants: **47.6** million or **10.0** percent of population
- Top 10 emigration countries: Russia, Ukraine, Turkey, Kazakhstan, Poland, Serbia and Montenegro, Uzbekistan, Belarus, Bosnia and Herzegovina, Azerbaijan.
- Identified destinations: high-income OECD countries (28.5 percent), high-income non-OECD countries (5.3 percent), intra-regional (57.6 percent), other developing countries (0.2 percent); unidentified (8.5 percent)
- Top 10 migration corridors: Russia–Ukraine, Ukraine–Russia, Turkey–Germany, Kazakhstan–Russia, Russia–Kazakhstan, Belarus–Russia, Uzbekistan–Russia, Serbia and Montenegro–Germany, Azerbaijan–Russia, Russia–Belarus

SKILLED EMIGRATION, 2000

- Emigration rate of tertiary educated (top 10 countries): Croatia (29.4 percent), Bosnia and Herzegovina (28.6 percent), FYR Macedonia (20.9 percent), Albania (20.0 percent), Serbia and Montenegro (17.4 percent), the Slovak Republic (15.3 percent), Romania (14.1 percent), Estonia (13.9 percent), Poland (12.3 percent), Hungary (12.1 percent)
- Emigration of physicians: 19,555 or 1.3 percent of physicians trained in the region

IMMIGRATION, 2005

- Stock of immigrants: **31.1** million or **6.5** percent of population (compared to 190.6 million or 3.0 percent for the world)
- Females as percentage of immigrants: **57.2** percent (compared to 49.6 percent for the world)
- Refugees as percentage of immigrants: **2.2** percent (compared to 7.1 percent for the world)
- Top 10 immigration countries: Russia, Ukraine, Kazakhstan, Turkey, Uzbekistan, Belarus, Poland, Croatia, Serbia and Montenegro, the Czech Republic

Remittances

US$ billions	1995	2000	2001	2002	2003	2004	2005	2006	2007
Inward remittance flows	**7.9**	**13.1**	**12.7**	**14.0**	**16.7**	**21.1**	**29.5**	**35.1**[a]	**38.6**
All developing countries	*57.5*	*84.5*	*95.6*	*115.9*	*143.6*	*161.3*	*191.2*	*221.3*	*239.7*
Outward remittance flows	**4.9**	**2.4**	**3.3**	**3.9**	**5.2**	**8.1**	**11.0**	**17.4**[b]	
All developing countries	*12.4*	*11.5*	*13.6*	*20.4*	*23.8*	*30.9*	*36.0*	*44.2*	

a. 1.4% of GDP in 2006.
b. 0.7% of GDP in 2006.

- Top 10 remittance recipients in 2007: Romania ($6.8 bn), Poland ($5.0 bn), Serbia and Montenegro ($4.9 bn), Russia ($4.0 bn), Bosnia and Herzegovina ($1.9 bn), Bulgaria ($1.9 bn), Croatia ($1.8 bn), Albania ($1.5 bn), Armenia ($1.3 bn), Tajikistan ($1.3 bn).
- Top 10 remittance recipients in 2006 (percentage of GDP): Tajikistan (36.2%), Moldova (36.2%), the Kyrgyz Republic (27.4%), Armenia (18.3%), Bosnia and Herzegovina (17.2%), Albania (14.9%), Serbia and Montenegro (13.8%), Georgia (6.4%), Romania (5.5%), Bulgaria (5.4%).

Migration and Remittances Factbook 2008

Latin America and the Caribbean

Population (millions, 2006)	556
Population growth (avg. annual %, 1997-2006)	1.4
Population density (people per sq. km, 2006)	28
Labor force (millions, 2006)	257
Urban population (% of pop., 2006)	77.7
Age dependency ratio (2006)	0.56
Surface area (1,000 sq. km, 2006)	20,415
GNI ($ billions, 2006)	2,860
GNI per capita, Atlas method ($, 2006)	4,767
GDP growth (avg. annual %, 2002-06)	3.6
Poverty headcount ratio at national poverty line (% of pop., 2004)	8.6

Migration

EMIGRATION, 2005

- Stock of emigrants: **28.3** million or **5.1** percent of population
- Top 10 emigration countries: Mexico, Colombia, Cuba, Brazil, El Salvador, the Dominican Republic, Jamaica, Ecuador, Peru, Haiti
- Identified destinations: high-income OECD countries (79.0 percent), high-income non-OECD countries (0.6 percent), intra-regional (11.9 percent), other developing countries (0.05 percent); unidentified (8.5 percent)
- Top 10 migration corridors: Mexico–the United States, Cuba–the United States, El Salvador–the United States, the Dominican Republic–the United States, Jamaica–the United States, Colombia–República Bolivariana de Venezuela, Colombia–the United States, Guatemala–the United States, Ecuador–Spain, Haiti–the United States

SKILLED EMIGRATION, 2000

- Emigration rate of tertiary educated (top 10 countries): Suriname (89.9 percent), Guyana (85.9 percent), Jamaica (82.5 percent), Haiti (81.6 percent), Trinidad and Tobago (78.4 percent), St. Kitts and Nevis (71.8 percent), Grenada (66.7 percent), Barbados (61.4 percent), Dominica (58.9 percent), St. Vincent (56.8 percent)
- Emigration of physicians: **21,208** or **2.4** percent of physicians trained in the region

IMMIGRATION, 2005

- Stock of immigrants: **5.8** million or **1.0** percent of population (compared to 190.6 million or 3.0 percent for the world)
- Females as percentage of immigrants: **50.0** percent (compared to 49.6 percent for the world)
- Refugees as percentage of immigrants: **0.6** percent (compared to 7.1 percent for the world)
- Top 10 immigration countries: Argentina, República Bolivariana de Venezuela, Mexico, Brazil, Costa Rica, Chile, Paraguay, the Dominican Republic, Colombia, Bolivia

Remittances

US$ billions	1995	2000	2001	2002	2003	2004	2005	2006	2007
Inward remittance flows	**13.3**	**20.0**	**24.2**	**27.9**	**34.8**	**41.3**	**48.6**	**56.5**[a]	**59.9**
All developing countries	*57.5*	*84.5*	*95.6*	*115.9*	*143.6*	*161.3*	*191.2*	*221.3*	*239.7*
Outward remittance flows	**1.1**	**2.0**	**2.4**	**1.9**	**1.8**	**2.0**	**2.3**	**2.6**[b]	
All developing countries	*12.4*	*11.5*	*13.6*	*20.4*	*23.8*	*30.9*	*36.0*	*44.2*	

a. 1.9% of GDP in 2006.
b. 0.1% of GDP in 2006.

- Top 10 remittance recipients in 2007: Mexico ($25.0 bn), Colombia ($4.6 bn), Brazil ($4.5 bn), Guatemala ($4.1 bn), El Salvador ($3.6 bn), the Dominican Republic ($3.2 bn), Ecuador ($3.2 bn), Honduras ($2.6 bn), Jamaica ($2.0 bn), Peru ($2.0 bn).
- Top 10 remittance recipients in 2006 (percentage of GDP): Honduras (25.6%), Guyana (24.3%), Haiti (21.6%), Jamaica (18.5%), El Salvador (18.2%), Nicaragua (12.2%), Guatemala (10.3%), the Dominican Republic (10.0%), Ecuador (7.2%), Bolivia (5.5%).

Middle East and North Africa

Population (millions, 2006)	311
Population growth (avg. annual %, 1997–2006)	1.9
Population density (people per sq. km, 2006)	35
Labor force (millions, 2006)	112
Urban population (% of pop., 2006)	57.4
Age dependency ratio (2006)	0.60
Surface area (1,000 sq. km, 2006)	8,990
GNI ($ billions, 2006)	811
GNI per capita, Atlas method ($, 2006)	2,481
GDP growth (avg. annual %, 2002–06)	4.3
Poverty headcount ratio at national poverty line (% of pop., 2004)	1.5

Migration

EMIGRATION, 2005

- Stock of emigrants: **12.9** million or **4.2** percent of population
- Top 10 emigration countries: Morocco, Egypt, Algeria, Iraq, the Islamic Republic of Iran, West Bank and Gaza, Jordan, Tunisia, Lebanon, the Republic of Yemen
- Identified destinations: high-income OECD countries (52.2 percent), high-income non-OECD countries (21.3 percent), intra-regional (16.3 percent), other developing countries (1.7 percent); unidentified (8.5 percent)
- Top 10 migration corridors: Afghanistan–the Islamic Republic of Iran, Algeria–France, Egypt–Saudi Arabia, Morocco–France, Morocco–Spain, West Bank and Gaza–Syria, Israel–West Bank and Gaza, the Republic of Yemen–Saudi Arabia, Tunisia–France, Egypt–Libya

SKILLED EMIGRATION, 2000

- Emigration rate of tertiary educated (top 10 countries): Lebanon (29.7 percent), Djibouti (17.8 percent), the Islamic Republic of Iran (13.1 percent), Morocco (10.3 percent), Tunisia (9.6 percent), Iraq (9.1 percent), Algeria (6.5 percent), Jordan (6.4 percent), the Republic of Yemen, (5.7 percent), Syria (5.2 percent)
- Emigration of physicians: **15,974** or **4.7** percent of physicians trained in the region

IMMIGRATION, 2005

- Stock of immigrants: **9.6** million or **3.1** percent of population (compared to 190.6 million or 3.0 percent for the world)
- Females as percentage of immigrants: **43.4** percent (compared to 49.6 percent for the world)
- Refugees as percentage of immigrants: **59.9** percent (compared to 7.1 percent for the world)
- Top 10 immigration countries: Jordan, the Islamic Republic of Iran, West Bank and Gaza, Syria, Lebanon, Oman, Libya, the Republic of Yemen, Algeria, Egypt

Remittances

US$ billions	1995	2000	2001	2002	2003	2004	2005	2006	2007
Inward remittance flows	**13.4**	**12.9**	**14.7**	**15.3**	**20.4**	**23.1**	**24.2**	**26.7**[a]	**28.5**
All developing countries	*57.5*	*84.5*	*95.6*	*115.9*	*143.6*	*161.3*	*191.2*	*221.3*	*239.7*
Outward remittance flows	**2.2**	**2.3**	**2.6**	**5.2**	**6.9**	**7.3**	**7.8**	**8.8**[b]	
All developing countries	*12.4*	*11.5*	*13.6*	*20.4*	*23.8*	*30.9*	*36.0*	*44.2*	

a. 3.9% of GDP in 2006.
b. 2.6% of GDP in 2006.

- Top 10 remittance recipients in 2007: Egypt ($5.9 bn), Morocco ($5.7 bn), Lebanon ($5.5 bn), Jordan ($2.9 bn), Algeria ($2.9 bn), Tunisia ($1.7 bn), the Republic of Yemen ($1.3 bn), the Islamic Republic of Iran ($1.1 bn), Syria ($0.8 bn), West Bank and Gaza ($0.6 bn).
- Top 10 remittance recipients in 2006 (percentage of GDP): Lebanon (22.8%), Jordan (20.3%), West Bank and Gaza (14.7%), Morocco (9.5%), the Republic of Yemen (6.7%), Tunisia (5.0%), Egypt (5.0%), Djibouti (3.8%), Syria (2.3%), Algeria (2.2%).

Migration and Remittances Factbook 2008

South Asia

Population (millions, 2006)	1,493
Population growth (avg. annual %, 1997–2006)	1.7
Population density (people per sq. km, 2006)	312
Labor force (millions, 2006)	597
Urban population (% of pop., 2006)	28.8
Age dependency ratio (2006)	0.61
Surface area (1,000 sq. km, 2006)	5,140
GNI ($ billions, 2006)	1,138
GNI per capita, Atlas method ($, 2006)	766
GDP growth (avg. annual %, 2002–06)	7.3
Poverty headcount ratio at national poverty line (% of pop., 2004)	30.8

Migration

EMIGRATION, 2005

- Stock of emigrants: **22.1** million or **1.5** percent of population
- Top 5 emigration countries: India, Bangladesh, Pakistan, Afghanistan, Sri Lanka
- Identified destinations: high-income OECD countries (20.3 percent), high-income non-OECD countries (25.3 percent), intra-regional (34.5 percent), other developing countries (11.4 percent); unidentified (8.5 percent)
- Top 5 migration corridors: Bangladesh–India, India–the United Arab Emirates, Afghanistan–the Islamic Republic of Iran, India–Saudi Arabia, Pakistan–India

SKILLED EMIGRATION, 2000

- Emigration rate of tertiary educated (top 5 countries): Sri Lanka (27.5 percent), Afghanistan (13.2 percent), Pakistan (9.2 percent), Bangladesh (4.7 percent), India (4.2 percent)
- Emigration of physicians: **27,508** or **4.1** percent of physicians trained in the region

IMMIGRATION, 2005

- Stock of immigrants: **11.2** million or **0.8** percent of population (compared to 190.6 million or 3.0 percent for the world)
- Females as percentage of immigrants: **45.3** percent (compared to 49.6 percent for the world)
- Refugees as percentage of immigrants: **10.7** percent (compared to 7.1 percent for the world)
- Top 5 immigration countries: India, Pakistan, Bangladesh, Nepal, Sri Lanka

Remittances

US$ billions	1995	2000	2001	2002	2003	2004	2005	2006	2007
Inward remittance flows	**10.0**	**17.2**	**19.2**	**24.1**	**30.4**	**28.7**	**33.1**	**39.8**[a]	**43.8**
All developing countries	*57.5*	*84.5*	*95.6*	*115.9*	*143.6*	*161.3*	*191.2*	*221.3*	*239.7*
Outward remittance flows	**0.5**	**0.6**	**1.0**	**1.5**	**1.6**	**2.0**	**1.7**	**2.0**[b]	
All developing countries	*12.4*	*11.5*	*13.6*	*20.4*	*23.8*	*30.9*	*36.0*	*44.2*	

a. **3.5% of GDP in 2006.**
b. **0.2% of GDP in 2006.**

- Top 5 remittance recipients in 2007: India ($27.0 bn), Bangladesh ($6.4 bn), Pakistan ($6.1 bn), Sri Lanka ($2.7 bn), Nepal ($1.6 bn).
- Top 5 remittance recipients in 2006 (percentage of GDP): Nepal (18.0%), Bangladesh (8.8%), Sri Lanka (8.7%), Pakistan (4.0%), India (2.8%).

Sub-Saharan Africa

Population (millions, 2006)	770
Population growth (avg. annual %, 1997–2006)	2.5
Population density (people per sq. km, 2006)	33
Labor force (millions, 2006)	317
Urban population (% of pop., 2006)	35.9
Age dependency ratio (2006)	0.88
Surface area (1,000 sq. km, 2006)	24,265
GNI ($ billions, 2006)	668
GNI per capita, Atlas method ($, 2006)	842
GDP growth (avg. annual %, 2002–06)	4.9
Poverty headcount ratio at national poverty line (% of pop., 2004)	41.1

Migration

EMIGRATION, 2005

- Stock of emigrants: **15.9** million or **2.1** percent of population
- Top 10 emigration countries: Mali, Burkina Faso, Ghana, Eritrea, Nigeria, Mozambique, Zimbabwe, South Africa, Sudan, the Democratic Republic of Congo
- Identified destinations: high-income OECD countries (25.2 percent), high-income non-OECD countries (2.9 percent), intra-regional (63.2 percent), other developing countries (0.2 percent); unidentified (8.5 percent)
- Top 10 migration corridors: Burkina Faso–Côte d'Ivoire, Zimbabwe–South Africa, Mali–Côte d'Ivoire, Eritrea–Sudan, Ghana–Côte d'Ivoire, Mali–Burkina Faso, Eritrea–Ethiopia, Mozambique–South Africa, Sudan–Saudi Arabia, Lesotho–South Africa

SKILLED EMIGRATION, 2000

- Emigration rate of tertiary educated (top 10 countries): Cape Verde (69.1 percent), The Gambia (64.7 percent), Seychelles (58.6 percent), Somalia (58.6 percent), Mauritius (48.0 percent), Eritrea (45.8 percent), Ghana (42.9 percent), Mozambique (42.0 percent), Sierra Leone (41.0 percent), Liberia (37.4 percent)
- Emigration of physicians:
  a) **9,425** or **8.8** percent of physicians trained in the region *(Source: Docquier and Bhargava 2006)*
  b) **36,653** or **28** percent of physicians trained in the region *(Source: Clemens and Pettersson 2006)*
- Emigration of nurses: **53,298** or **11** percent of nurses trained in the region

IMMIGRATION, 2005

- Stock of immigrants: **15.7** million or **2.1** percent of population (compared to 190.6 million or 3.0 percent for the world)
- Females as percentage of immigrants: **47.9** percent (compared to 49.6 percent for the world)
- Refugees as percentage of immigrants: **17.4** percent (compared to 7.1 percent for the world)
- Top 10 immigration countries: Côte d'Ivoire, Ghana, South Africa, Nigeria, Tanzania, Burkina Faso, Sudan, Ethiopia, the Democratic Republic of Congo, Uganda

Remittances

US$ billions	1995	2000	2001	2002	2003	2004	2005	2006	2007
Inward remittance flows	**3.2**	**4.6**	**4.7**	**5.0**	**6.0**	**8.0**	**9.3**	**10.3**[a]	**10.8**
All developing countries	*57.5*	*84.5*	*95.6*	*115.9*	*143.6*	*161.3*	*191.2*	*221.3*	*239.7*
Outward remittance flows	**2.0**	**2.5**	**2.3**	**2.5**	**2.8**	**3.0**	**3.3**	**2.9**[b]	
All developing countries	*12.4*	*11.5*	*13.6*	*20.4*	*23.8*	*30.9*	*36.0*	*44.2*	

a. 1.6% of GDP in 2006.
b. 0.4% of GDP in 2006.

- Top 10 remittance recipients in 2007: Nigeria ($3.3 bn), Kenya ($1.3 bn), Sudan ($1.2 bn), Senegal ($0.9 bn), Uganda ($0.9 bn), South Africa ($0.7 bn), Lesotho ($0.4 bn), Mauritius ($0.2 bn), Togo ($0.2 bn), Mali ($0.2 bn).
- Top 10 remittance recipients in 2006 (percentage of GDP): Lesotho (24.5%), Gambia, The (12.5%), Cape Verde (12.0%), Guinea-Bissau (9.2%), Uganda (8.7%), Togo (8.7%), Senegal (7.1%), Kenya (5.3%), Swaziland (3.7%), Benin (3.6%).

Migration and Remittances Factbook 2008

Income-Group Tables

Low-income countries (53)

Afghanistan, Bangladesh, Benin, Burkina Faso, Burundi, Cambodia, the Central African Republic, Chad, Comoros, the Democratic Republic of Congo, Côte d'Ivoire, Eritrea, Ethiopia, The Gambia, Ghana, Guinea, Guinea-Bissau, Haiti, India, Kenya, the Democratic People's Republic of Korea, the Kyrgyz Republic, Lao PDR, Liberia, Madagascar, Malawi, Mali, Mauritania, Mongolia, Mozambique, Myanmar, Nepal, Niger, Nigeria, Pakistan, Papua New Guinea, Rwanda, São Tomé and Principe, Senegal, Sierra Leone, the Solomon Islands, Somalia, Sudan, Tajikistan, Tanzania, Timor-Leste, Togo, Uganda, Uzbekistan, Vietnam, the Republic of Yemen, Zambia, Zimbabwe

Lower-middle-income countries (55)

Albania, Algeria, Angola, Armenia, Azerbaijan, Belarus, Bhutan, Bolivia, Bosnia and Herzegovina, Cameroon, Cape Verde, China, Colombia, the Republic of Congo, Cuba, Djibouti, the Dominican Republic, Ecuador, Egypt, El Salvador, Fiji, Georgia, Guatemala, Guyana, Honduras, Indonesia, Iraq, the Islamic Republic of Iran, Jamaica, Jordan, Kiribati, Lesotho, FYR Macedonia, Maldives, the Marshall Islands, the Federated States of Micronesia, Moldova, Morocco, Namibia, Nicaragua, Paraguay, Peru, the Philippines, Samoa, Sri Lanka, Suriname, Swaziland, Syria, Thailand, Tonga, Tunisia, Turkmenistan, Ukraine, Vanuatu, West Bank and Gaza

Upper-middle-income countries (41)

American Samoa, Argentina, Belize, Botswana, Brazil, Bulgaria, Chile, Costa Rica, Croatia, Dominica, Equatorial Guinea, Gabon, Grenada, Hungary, Kazakhstan, Latvia, Lebanon, Libya, Lithuania, Malaysia, Mauritius, Mayotte, Mexico, Montenegro, Northern Mariana Islands, Oman, Palau, Panama, Poland, Romania, Russia, Serbia, Seychelles, the Slovak Republic, South Africa, St. Kitts and Nevis, St. Lucia, St. Vincent, Turkey, Uruguay, República Bolivariana de Venezuela

High-income countries and economies (60)

Andorra, Antigua and Barbuda, Aruba, Australia, Austria, The Bahamas, Bahrain, Barbados, Belgium, Bermuda, Brunei Darussalam, Canada, Cayman Islands, Channel Islands, Cyprus, the Czech Republic, Denmark, Estonia, Faeroe Islands, Finland, France, French Polynesia, Germany, Greece, Greenland, Guam, Hong Kong (China), Iceland, Ireland, Isle of Man, Israel, Italy, Japan, the Republic of Korea, Kuwait, Liechtenstein, Luxembourg, Macao (China), Malta, Monaco, the Netherlands, Netherlands Antilles, New Caledonia, New Zealand, Norway, Portugal, Puerto Rico, Qatar, San Marino, Saudi Arabia, Singapore, Slovenia, Spain, Sweden, Switzerland, Trinidad and Tobago, the United Arab Emirates, the United Kingdom, the United States, Virgin Islands (U.S.)

High-income OECD members (25)

Australia, Austria, Belgium, Canada, the Czech Republic, Denmark, Finland, France, Germany, Greece, Iceland, Ireland, Italy, Japan, the Republic of Korea, Luxembourg, the Netherlands, New Zealand, Norway, Portugal, Spain, Sweden, Switzerland, the United Kingdom, the United States

Low-Income Countries

Population (millions, 2006)	2,403
Population growth (avg. annual %, 1997–2006)	1.9
Population density (people per sq. km, 2006)	85
Labor force (millions, 2006)	991
Urban population (% of pop., 2006)	30.4
Age dependency ratio (2006)	0.69
Surface area (1,000 sq. km, 2006)	29,215
GNI ($ billions, 2006)	1,580
GNI per capita, Atlas method ($, 2006)	650
GDP growth (avg. annual %, 2002–06)	6.8
Poverty headcount ratio at national poverty line (% of pop., 2004)	..

Migration

EMIGRATION, 2005

- Stock of emigrants: **43.5** million or **1.8** percent of population
- Top 10 emigration countries: India, Bangladesh, Pakistan, Vietnam, Uzbekistan, Afghanistan, Mali, Burkina Faso, Ghana, Eritrea
- Identified destinations: high-income OECD countries (24.4 percent), high-income non-OECD countries (15.1 percent), low-income countries (35.9 percent), middle-income countries (16.1 percent); unidentified (8.5 percent)
- Top 10 migration corridors: Bangladesh–India, India–the United Arab Emirates, Afghanistan–the Islamic Republic of Iran, India–Saudi Arabia, Pakistan–India, India–the United States, Vietnam–the United States, India–Bangladesh, Burkina Faso–Côte d'Ivoire, Uzbekistan–Russia

SKILLED EMIGRATION, 2000

- Emigration rate of tertiary educated (top 10 countries): Haiti (81.6 percent), The Gambia (64.7 percent), Somalia (58.6 percent), Eritrea (45.8 percent), Ghana (42.9 percent), Mozambique (42.0 percent), Sierra Leone (41.0 percent), Vietnam (39.0 percent), Liberia (37.4 percent), Nigeria (36.1 percent)
- Emigration of physicians: **34,269** or **3.9** percent of physicians trained in the region

IMMIGRATION, 2005

- Stock of immigrants: **27.1** million or **1.1** percent of population (compared to 190.6 million or 3.0 percent for the world)
- Females as percentage of immigrants: **47.6** percent (compared to 49.6 percent for the world)
- Refugees as percentage of immigrants: **14.3** percent (compared to 7.1 percent for the world)
- Top 10 immigration countries: India, Pakistan, Côte d'Ivoire, Ghana, Uzbekistan, Bangladesh, Nigeria, Nepal, Tanzania, Burkina Faso

Remittances

US$ billions	1995	2000	2001	2002	2003	2004	2005	2006	2007
Inward									
remittance flows	**12.8**	**21.8**	**25.9**	**32.1**	**39.0**	**40.0**	**46.3**	**55.5**[a]	**60.2**
All developing									
countries	*57.5*	*84.5*	*95.6*	*115.9*	*143.6*	*161.3*	*191.2*	*221.3*	*239.7*
Outward									
remittance flows	**1.3**	**2.0**	**2.2**	**2.9**	**3.2**	**3.8**	**3.8**	**3.8**[b]	
All developing									
countries	*12.4*	*11.5*	*13.6*	*20.4*	*23.8*	*30.9*	*36.0*	*44.2*	

a. 3.6% of GDP in 2006.
b. 0.3% of GDP in 2006.

- Top 10 remittance recipients in 2007: India ($27.0 bn), Bangladesh ($6.4 bn), Pakistan ($6.1 bn), Vietnam ($5 bn), Nigeria ($3.3 bn), Nepal ($1.6 bn), Kenya ($1.3 bn), the Republic of Yemen ($1.3 bn), Tajikistan ($1.3 bn), Haiti ($1.2 bn).

- Top 10 remittance recipients in 2006 (percentage of GDP): Tajikistan (36.2%), the Kyrgyz Republic (27.4%), Haiti (21.6%), Nepal (18.0%), The Gambia (12.5%), Guinea-Bissau (9.2%), Bangladesh (8.8%), Uganda (8.7%), Togo (8.7%), Vietnam (7.9%).

Middle-Income Countries

Population (millions, 2006)	3,086
Population growth (avg. annual %, 1997–2006)	1.0
Population density (people per sq. km, 2006)	45
Labor force (millions, 2006)	1,579
Urban population (% of pop., 2006)	54.5
Age dependency ratio (2006)	0.48
Surface area (1,000 sq. km, 2006)	70,009
GNI ($ billions, 2006)	9,988
GNI per capita, Atlas method ($, 2006)	3,051
GDP growth (avg. annual %, 2002–06)	6.0
Poverty headcount ratio at national poverty line (% of pop., 2004)	..

Migration

EMIGRATION, 2005

- Stock of emigrants: **101.5** million or **3.3** percent of population
- Top 10 emigration countries: Mexico, Russia, China, Ukraine, Turkey, Kazakhstan, the Philippines, Morocco, Egypt, Poland
- Identified destinations: high-income OECD countries (48.9 percent), high-income non-OECD countries (10.0 percent), low-income countries (1.9 percent), middle-income countries (30.7 percent); unidentified (8.5 percent)
- Top 10 migration corridors: Mexico–the United States, Russia–Ukraine, Ukraine–Russia, Turkey–Germany, Kazakhstan–Russia, Russia–Kazakhstan, the Philippines–the United States, Afghanistan–the Islamic Republic of Iran, Algeria–France, Egypt–Saudi Arabia
- Top 10 migration corridors excluding the Former Soviet Union: Mexico–the United States, Turkey–Germany, the Philippines–the United States, Afghanistan–the Islamic Republic of Iran, Algeria–France, Egypt–Saudi Arabia, China–the United States, Malaysia–Singapore, Cuba–the United States, El Salvador–the United States

SKILLED EMIGRATION, 2000

- Emigration rate of tertiary educated (top 10 countries): Suriname (89.9 percent), Guyana (85.9 percent), Jamaica (82.5 percent), Tonga (74.2 percent), St. Kitts and Nevis (71.8 percent), Cape Verde (69.1 percent), Grenada (66.7 percent), Samoa (66.6 percent), Dominica (58.9 percent), Fiji (58.7 percent)
- Emigration of physicians: **77,164** or **1.6** percent of physicians trained in the region

IMMIGRATION, 2005

- Stock of immigrants: **50.1** million or **1.6** percent of population (compared to 190.6 million or 3.0 percent for the world)
- Females as percentage of immigrants: **52.5** percent (compared to 49.6 percent for the world)
- Refugees as percentage of immigrants: **14.0** percent (compared to 7.1 percent for the world)
- Top 10 immigration countries: Russia, Ukraine, Kazakhstan, Jordan, the Islamic Republic of Iran, West Bank and Gaza, Malaysia, Argentina, Turkey, Belarus

Remittances

US$ billions	1995	2000	2001	2002	2003	2004	2005	2006	2007
Inward									
remittance flows	**44.7**	**62.7**	**69.6**	**83.8**	**104.6**	**121.3**	**144.9**	**165.8**[a]	**179.5**
All developing									
countries	*57.5*	*84.5*	*95.6*	*115.9*	*143.6*	*161.3*	*191.2*	*221.3*	*239.7*
Outward									
remittance flows	**11.0**	**9.5**	**11.4**	**17.5**	**20.6**	**27.1**	**32.2**	**40.4**[b]	
All developing									
countries	*12.4*	*11.5*	*13.6*	*20.4*	*23.8*	*30.9*	*36.0*	*44.2*	

a. 1.7% of GDP in 2006.
b. 0.5% of GDP in 2006.

- Top 10 remittance recipients in 2007: China ($25.7 bn), Mexico ($25.0 bn), the Philippines ($17.0 bn), Romania ($6.8 bn), Indonesia ($6.0 bn), Egypt ($5.9 bn), Morocco ($5.7 bn), Lebanon ($5.5 bn), Poland ($5.0 bn), Serbia and Montenegro ($4.9 bn).

- Top 10 remittance recipients in 2006 (percentage of GDP): Moldova (36.2%), Tonga (32.3%), Honduras (25.6%), Lesotho (24.5%), Guyana (24.3%), Lebanon (22.8%), Jordan (20.3%), Jamaica (18.5%), Armenia (18.3%), El Salvador (18.2%).

High-Income OECD Countries

Population (millions, 2006)	942
Population growth (avg. annual %, 1997–2006)	0.6
Population density (people per sq. km, 2006)	31
Labor force (millions, 2006)	475
Urban population (% of pop., 2006)	77.2
Age dependency ratio (2006)	0.49
Surface area (1,000 sq. km, 2006)	31,896
GNI ($ billions, 2006)	35,027
GNI per capita, Atlas method ($, 2006)	38,120
GDP growth (avg. annual %, 2002–06)	2.4
Poverty headcount ratio at national poverty line (% of pop., 2004)	..

Migration

IMMIGRATION, 2005

- Stock of immigrants: **90.9** million or **9.8** percent of population (compared to 190.6 million or 3.0 percent for the world)
- Females as percentage of immigrants: **50.8** percent (compared to 49.6 percent for the world)
- Refugees as percentage of immigrants: **2.6** percent (compared to 7.1 percent for the world)
- Top 10 immigration countries: The United States, Germany, France, Canada, the United Kingdom, Spain, Australia, Italy, Japan, Switzerland
- Identified sources: high-income OECD countries (27.7 percent), high-income non-OECD countries (4.8 percent), low-income countries (11.6 percent), middle-income countries (54.4 percent); unidentified (1.5 percent)
- Top 10 migration corridors: Mexico–the United States, Turkey–Germany, the Philippines–the United States, Germany–the United States, Algeria–France, India–the United States, China–the United States, Vietnam–the United States, Canada–the United States, the United Kingdom–Australia

EMIGRATION, 2005

- Stock of emigrants: **29.5** million or **3.2** percent of population
- Top 10 emigration countries: The United Kingdom, Germany, Italy, the United States, Portugal, France, the Republic of Korea, Canada, Spain, Greece

SKILLED EMIGRATION, 2000

- Emigration rate of tertiary educated (top 10 countries): Ireland (34.4 percent), the United Kingdom (16.7 percent), Iceland (16.3 percent), New Zealand (15.0 percent), Greece (14.0 percent), Portugal (13.8 percent), Austria (11.1 percent), Switzerland (9.1 percent), the Netherlands (8.9 percent), Germany (8.8 percent)
- Emigration of physicians: **64,093** or **2.3** percent of physicians trained in the group

Remittances

US$ billions	1995	2000	2001	2002	2003	2004	2005	2006	2007
Inward remittance flows	**42.7**	**45.8**	**49.8**	**52.2**	**59.2**	**65.8**	**66.6**	**70.3**[a]	**72.4**
All developing countries	*57.5*	*84.5*	*95.6*	*115.9*	*143.6*	*161.3*	*191.2*	*221.3*	*239.7*
Outward remittance flows	**66.1**	**76.1**	**82.6**	**87.8**	**100.4**	**113.4**	**123.9**	**135.8**[b]	
All developing countries	*12.4*	*11.5*	*13.6*	*20.4*	*23.8*	*30.9*	*36.0*	*44.2*	

a. 0.2% of GDP in 2006.
b. 0.4% of GDP in 2006.

- Top 10 remittance recipients in 2007: France ($12.5 bn), Spain ($8.9 bn), Belgium ($7.2 bn), the United Kingdom ($7.0 bn), Germany ($7.0 bn), Portugal ($3.8 bn), Austria ($3.5 bn), Australia ($3.1 bn), the United States ($3.0 bn), Italy ($2.6 bn).

- Top 10 remittance recipients in 2006 (percentage of GDP): Luxembourg (3.1%), Belgium (1.8%), Portugal (1.7%), Austria (1.0%), Spain (0.7%), Greece (0.6%), New Zealand (0.6%), France (0.6%), Iceland (0.5%), Switzerland (0.5%).

- Top 10 remittance senders in 2006: the United States ($42.2 bn), Switzerland ($13.8 bn), Germany ($12.3 bn), Spain ($11.0 bn), Italy ($8.2 bn), Luxembourg ($7.5 bn), the Netherlands ($6.7 bn), the United Kingdom ($4.5 bn), France ($4.3 bn), the Republic of Korea ($4.2 bn).

- Top 10 remittance senders in 2006 (percentage of GDP): Luxembourg (18.2%), Switzerland (3.6%), the Netherlands (1.0%), Spain (0.9%), Ireland (0.9%), Norway (0.8%), New Zealand (0.8%), Portugal (0.7%), Belgium (0.7%), Denmark (0.7%).

High-Income Non-OECD Countries and Economies

Population (millions, 2006)	87
Population growth (avg. annual %, 1997–2006)	1.6
Population density (people per sq. km, 2006)	32
Labor force (millions, 2006)	27
Urban population (% of pop., 2006)	84.4
Age dependency ratio (2006)	0.52
Surface area (1,000 sq. km, 2006)	2,721
GNI ($ billions, 2006)	1,546
GNI per capita, Atlas method ($, 2006)	18,014
GDP growth (avg. annual %, 2002–06)	5.1
Poverty headcount ratio at national poverty line (% of pop., 2004)	..

Migration

IMMIGRATION, 2005

- Stock of immigrants: **21.6** million or **33.6** percent of population (compared to 190.6 million or 3.0 percent for the world)
- Females as percentage of immigrants: **39.9** percent (compared to 49.6 percent for the world)
- Refugees as percentage of immigrants: **1.1** percent (compared to 7.1 percent for the world)
- Top 10 immigration countries: Saudi Arabia, the United Arab Emirates, Israel, Singapore, Kuwait, Qatar, Bahrain, Estonia, Slovenia, Brunei Darussalam
- Identified sources: high-income OECD countries (3.7 percent), high-income non-OECD countries (1.3 percent), low-income countries (30.8 percent), middle-income countries (47.6 percent); unidentified (16.7 percent)
- Top 10 migration corridors: India–the United Arab Emirates, India–Saudi Arabia, Egypt–Saudi Arabia, Malaysia–Singapore, Pakistan–Saudi Arabia, Russia–Israel, China–Singapore, the Philippines–Saudi Arabia, Bangladesh–Saudi Arabia, the Republic of Yemen–Saudi Arabia

EMIGRATION, 2005

- Stock of emigrants: **5.3** million or **8.2** percent of population
- Top 10 emigration countries: Israel, Trinidad and Tobago, Singapore, Kuwait, Estonia, Cyprus, Slovenia, Barbados, Malta, Saudi Arabia

SKILLED EMIGRATION, 2000

- Emigration rate of tertiary educated (top 10 countries): Trinidad and Tobago (78.4 percent), Antigua and Barbuda (70.9 percent), Barbados (61.4 percent), Malta (55.2 percent), The Bahamas (36.4 percent), San Marino (29.9 percent), Brunei Darussalam (21.0 percent), Cyprus (17.9 percent), Liechtenstein (16.9 percent), Monaco (15.3 percent)
- Emigration of physicians: **5,371** or **4.2** percent of physicians trained in the group

Remittances

US$ billions	1995	2000	2001	2002	2003	2004	2005	2006	2007
Inward remittance flows	**1.3**	**1.2**	**1.4**	**1.4**	**2.8**	**4.2**	**4.8**	**5.4**[a]	**5.6**
All developing countries	*57.5*	*84.5*	*95.6*	*115.9*	*143.6*	*161.3*	*191.2*	*221.3*	*239.7*
Outward remittance flows	**20.1**	**22.5**	**22.6**	**23.0**	**22.7**	**21.9**	**23.6**	**27.0**[b]	
All developing countries	*12.4*	*11.5*	*13.6*	*20.4*	*23.8*	*30.9*	*36.0*	*44.2*	

a. 1.0% of GDP in 2006.
b. 2.9% of GDP in 2006.

- Top 5 remittance recipients in 2007: the Czech Republic ($1.3 bn), Israel ($1.1 bn), French Polynesia ($0.6 bn), New Caledonia ($0.5 bn), Estonia ($0.4 bn).
- Top 5 remittance recipients in 2006 (percentage of GDP): Barbados (4.5%), Estonia (2.4%), Antigua and Barbuda (1.1%), Israel (0.9%), the Czech Republic (0.8%).
- Top 5 remittance senders in 2006: Saudi Arabia ($15.6 bn), Kuwait ($3.0 bn), the Czech Republic ($2.8 bn), Israel ($2.4 bn), Bahrain ($1.5 bn).
- Top 5 remittance senders in 2006 (percentage of GDP): Bahrain (11.9%), Saudi Arabia (5.0%), Kuwait (3.7%), the Czech Republic (2.0%), Israel (2.0%).

Least-Developed Countries (UN Classification)

Population (millions, 2006)	768
Population growth (avg. annual %, 1997–2006)	2.4
Population density (people per sq. km, 2006)	38
Labor force (millions, 2006)	331
Urban population (% of pop., 2006)	27.3
Age dependency ratio (2006)	0.83
Surface area (1,000 sq. km, 2006)	20,802
GNI ($ billions, 2006)	349
GNI per capita, Atlas method ($, 2006)	436
GDP growth (avg. annual %, 2002–06)	6.0
Poverty headcount ratio at national poverty line (% of pop., 2004)	..

Migration

EMIGRATION, 2005

- Stock of emigrants: **21.8** million or **2.9** percent of population
- Top 10 emigration countries: Bangladesh, Afghanistan, Mali, Burkina Faso, Eritrea, Haiti, Mozambique, Nepal, the Republic of Yemen, Sudan
- Identified destinations: high-income OECD countries (19.9 percent), high-income non-OECD countries (6.7 percent), least developed countries (19.8 percent), other developing countries (45.1 percent); unidentified (8.5 percent)
- Top 10 migration corridors: Bangladesh–India, Afghanistan–the Islamic Republic of Iran, India–Bangladesh, Burkina Faso–Côte d'Ivoire, India–Nepal, Nepal–India, Mali–Côte d'Ivoire, Haiti–the United States, Bangladesh–Saudi Arabia, the Republic of Yemen–Saudi Arabia

SKILLED EMIGRATION, 2000

- Emigration rate of tertiary educated (top 10 countries): Haiti (81.6 percent), Cape Verde (69.1 percent), Samoa (66.6 percent), The Gambia (64.7 percent), Somalia (58.6 percent), Eritrea (45.8 percent), Mozambique (42.0 percent), Sierra Leone (41.0 percent), Liberia (37.4 percent), Madagascar (36.0 percent)
- Emigration of physicians: **4,835** or **5.7** percent of physicians trained in the group

IMMIGRATION, 2005

- Stock of immigrants: **10.5** million or **1.4** percent of population (compared to 190.6 million or 3.0 percent for the world)
- Females as percentage of immigrants: **46.5** percent (compared to 49.6 percent for the world)
- Refugees as percentage of immigrants: **23.2** percent (compared to 7.1 percent for the world)
- Top 10 immigration countries: Bangladesh, Nepal, Tanzania, Burkina Faso, Sudan, Ethiopia, the Democratic Republic of Congo, Uganda, Chad, Mozambique

Remittances

US$ billions	1995	2000	2001	2002	2003	2004	2005	2006	2007
Inward remittance flows	**4.1**	**6.2**	**6.7**	**8.4**	**9.6**	**10.8**	**11.9**	**14.0ᵃ**	**15.6**
All developing countries	*57.5*	*84.5*	*95.6*	*115.9*	*143.6*	*161.3*	*191.2*	*221.3*	*239.7*
Outward remittance flows	**0.7**	**1.4**	**1.3**	**1.3**	**1.3**	**1.5**	**1.7**	**2.0ᵇ**	
All developing countries	*12.4*	*11.5*	*13.6*	*20.4*	*23.8*	*30.9*	*36.0*	*44.2*	

a. 5.6% of GDP in 2006.
b. 0.7% of GDP in 2006.

- Top 10 remittance recipients in 2007: Bangladesh ($6.4 bn), Nepal ($1.6 bn), the Republic of Yemen ($1.3 bn), Haiti ($1.2 bn), Sudan ($1.2 bn), Senegal ($0.9 bn), Uganda ($0.9 bn), Lesotho ($0.4 bn), Cambodia ($0.3 bn), Togo ($0.2 bn).
- Top 10 remittance recipients in 2006 (percentage of GDP): Lesotho (24.5%), Haiti (21.6%), Nepal (18.0%), The Gambia (12.5%), Cape Verde (12.0%), Kiribati (9.9%), Guinea-Bissau (9.2%), Bangladesh (8.8%), Uganda (8.7%), Togo (8.7%).

Country Tables

Afghanistan

LOW INCOME

Population (millions, 2006)	..
Population growth (avg. annual %, 1997-2006)	..
Population density (people per sq. km, 2006)	..
Labor force (millions, 2006)	..
Urban population (% of pop., 2006)	23.3
Age dependency ratio	..
Surface area (1,000 sq. km, 2006)	652
GNI ($ billions, 2006)	8.4
GNI per capita, Atlas method ($, 2006)	..
GDP growth (avg. annual %, 2002-06)	10.8
Poverty headcount ratio at national poverty line (% of pop., 2004)	..

Migration

EMIGRATION, 2005
- Stock of emigrants: **2,031,678**
- Stock of emigrants as percentage of population: **6.8%**
- Top 10 destination countries: the Islamic Republic of Iran, Germany, the United States, the Netherlands, Canada, the United Kingdom, Saudi Arabia, Australia, Turkey, India

SKILLED EMIGRATION, 2000
- Emigration rate of tertiary educated: **13.2%**
- Emigration of physicians: **445** or **9.1%** of physicians trained in the country

IMMIGRATION, 2005
- Stock of immigrants: **43,165**
- Stock of immigrants as percentage of population: **0.1%**
- Females as percentage of immigrants: **44.8%**
- Refugees as percentage of immigrants: **0.1%**

Remittances
Remittance data are currently not available for this country.

Albania

　　　　　　　　　　　　　　　　　　LOWER MIDDLE INCOME

Population (millions, 2006)	3.1
Population growth (avg. annual %, 1997–2006)	0.1
Population density (people per sq. km, 2006)	115
Labor force (millions, 2006)	1.4
Urban population (% of pop., 2006)	46.1
Age dependency ratio	0.53
Surface area (1,000 sq. km, 2006)	29
GNI ($ billions, 2006)	9.3
GNI per capita, Atlas method ($, 2006)	2,960
GDP growth (avg. annual %, 2002–06)	5.0
Poverty headcount ratio at national poverty line (% of pop., 2004)	0.3

Migration

EMIGRATION, 2005
- Stock of emigrants: **860,485**
- Stock of emigrants as percentage of population: **27.5%**
- Top 10 destination countries: Greece, Italy, FYR Macedonia, the United States, Germany, Canada, Turkey, France, the United Kingdom, Austria

SKILLED EMIGRATION, 2000
- Emigration rate of tertiary educated: **20.0%**
- Emigration of physicians: **61** or **1.4%** of physicians trained in the country

IMMIGRATION, 2005
- Stock of immigrants: **82,668**
- Stock of immigrants as percentage of population: **2.6%**
- Females as percentage of immigrants: **50.8%**
- Refugees as percentage of immigrants: **0.1%**
- Top source countries: Greece, FYR Macedonia, the Czech Republic, Serbia and Montenegro, Israel, Italy, Russia

Remittances

US$ millions	2000	2001	2002	2003	2004	2005	2006	2007
Inward remittance flows	598	699	734	889	1,160	1,290	1,360[a]	1,481
of which								
Workers' remittances	531	615	643	778	1,028	1,161	1,176	..
Compensation of employees	67	84	90	111	132	129	184	..
Migrants' transfer	..	..	..	..	..	..	..	..
Outward remittance flows	..	..	..	4	5	7	27[b]	..
of which								
Workers' remittances	..	..	..	0	0	..	0	..
Compensation of employees	..	..	..	4	5	7	27	..
Migrants' transfer	..	..	..	..	..	..	..	..

a. 14.9% of GDP in 2006.
b. 0.3% of GDP in 2006.

Algeria

LOWER MIDDLE INCOME

Population (millions, 2006)	33
Population growth (avg. annual %, 1997–2006)	1.5
Population density (people per sq. km, 2006)	14
Labor force (millions, 2006)	14
Urban population (% of pop., 2006)	63.9
Age dependency ratio	0.5
Surface area (1,000 sq. km, 2006)	2,382
GNI ($ billions, 2006)	107
GNI per capita, Atlas method ($, 2006)	3,030
GDP growth (avg. annual %, 2002–06)	5.0
Poverty headcount ratio at national poverty line (% of pop., 2004)	0.6

Migration

EMIGRATION, 2005
- Stock of emigrants: **1,783,476**
- Stock of emigrants as percentage of population: **5.4%**
- Top 10 destination countries: France, Spain, Israel, Italy, Germany, Canada, Tunisia, the United States, the United Kingdom, Belgium

SKILLED EMIGRATION, 2000
- Emigration rate of tertiary educated: **6.5%**
- Emigration of physicians:
  a) **905** or **2.9%** of physicians trained in the country *(Source: Docquier and Bhargava 2006)*
  b) **10,860** or **44.3%** of physicians trained in the country *(Source: Clemens and Pettersson 2006)*
- Emigration of nurses: **8,245** or **9.0%** of nurses trained in the country

IMMIGRATION, 2005
- Stock of immigrants: **242,446**
- Stock of immigrants as percentage of population: **0.7%**
- Females as percentage of immigrants: **45.2%**
- Refugees as percentage of immigrants: **69.7%**

Remittances

US$ millions	2000	2001	2002	2003	2004	2005	2006	2007
Inward remittance flows	790	670	1,070	1,750	2,460	1,950	2,527[a]	2,906
of which								
Workers' remittances	..	..	..	..	..	..	..	..
Compensation of employees	..	..	..	..	..	..	..	..
Migrants' transfer	..	..	..	..	..	..	..	..
Outward remittance flows	..	..	..	..	..	..	..	..
of which								
Workers' remittances	..	..	..	..	..	..	..	..
Compensation of employees	..	..	..	..	..	..	..	..
Migrants' transfer	..	..	..	..	..	..	..	..

a. 2.2% of GDP in 2006.

American Samoa

	UPPER MIDDLE INCOME
Population (thousands, 2006)	60
Population growth (avg. annual %, 1997-2006)	..
Population density (people per sq. km, 2006)	298
Labor force (millions, 2006)	..
Urban population (% of pop., 2006)	91.6
Age dependency ratio	..
Surface area (sq. km, 2006)	200
GNI ($ millions, 2006)	..
GNI per capita, Atlas method ($, 2006)	..
GDP growth (avg. annual %, 2002-06)	..
Poverty headcount ratio at national poverty line (% of pop., 2004)	..

Migration

EMIGRATION, 2005

- Stock of emigrants: **44,650**
- Stock of emigrants as percentage of population: **68.8%**
- Top 10 destination countries: the United States, Samoa, New Zealand, Australia, Fiji, Kiribati, Canada, the United Kingdom, the Czech Republic, Greece

SKILLED EMIGRATION, 2000

- Skilled emigration data are currently not available for this country.

IMMIGRATION, 2005

- Stock of immigrants: **20,382**
- Stock of immigrants as percentage of population: **31.4%**
- Females as percentage of immigrants: **49.0%**
- Refugees as percentage of immigrants: **0.0%**
- Top source countries: Samoa, the United States, Tonga, the Philippines, New Zealand, Vietnam, the Republic of Korea, China, Fiji

Remittances

Remittance data are currently not available for this country.

Angola

Population (millions, 2006)	16
Population growth (avg. annual %, 1997–2006)	2.6
Population density (people per sq. km, 2006)	13
Labor force (millions, 2006)	7.3
Urban population (% of pop., 2006)	54
Age dependency ratio	0.95
Surface area (1,000 sq. km, 2006)	1,247
GNI ($ billions, 2006)	39
GNI per capita, Atlas method ($, 2006)	1,980
GDP growth (avg. annual %, 2002–06)	12.8
Poverty headcount ratio at national poverty line (% of pop., 2004)	..

Migration

EMIGRATION, 2005
- Stock of emigrants: **522,964**
- Stock of emigrants as percentage of population: **3.3%**
- Top 10 destination countries: Portugal, Zambia, Namibia, the Republic of Congo, Germany, France, the United Kingdom, Brazil, Spain, the United States

SKILLED EMIGRATION, 2000
- Emigration rate of tertiary educated: **25.6%**
- Emigration of physicians:
  a) **155** or **13.5%** of physicians trained in the country *(Source: Docquier and Bhargava 2006)*
  b) **2,102** or **70.5%** of physicians trained in the country *(Source: Clemens and Pettersson 2006)*
- Emigration of nurses: **1,841** or **12.3%** of nurses trained in the country

IMMIGRATION, 2005
- Stock of immigrants: **56,351**
- Stock of immigrants as percentage of population: **0.4%**
- Females as percentage of immigrants: **48.9%**
- Refugees as percentage of immigrants: **25.3%**

Remittances

US$ millions	2000	2001	2002	2003	2004	2005	2006	2007
Inward remittance flows	..	..	..	..	..	..	..	..
of which								
Workers' remittances	..	..	..	..	..	..	..	..
Compensation of employees	..	..	..	..	..	..	..	..
Migrants' transfer	..	..	..	..	..	..	..	..
Outward remittance flows	266	216	224	230	296	215	413[a]	..
of which								
Workers' remittances	76	98	100	88	117	117	172	..
Compensation of employees	190	118	123	142	179	98	241	..
Migrants' transfer	..	..	..	..	..	..	..	..

a. 0.9% of GDP in 2006.

Argentina

Population (millions, 2006)	39
Population growth (avg. annual %, 1997–2006)	1.0
Population density (people per sq. km, 2006)	14
Labor force (millions, 2006)	19
Urban population (% of pop., 2006)	90.3
Age dependency ratio	0.57
Surface area (1,000 sq. km, 2006)	2,780
GNI ($ billions, 2006)	209
GNI per capita, Atlas method ($, 2006)	5,150
GDP growth (avg. annual %, 2002–06)	4.9
Poverty headcount ratio at national poverty line (% of pop., 2004)	..

Migration

EMIGRATION, 2005
- Stock of emigrants: **806,369**
- Stock of emigrants as percentage of population: **2.1%**
- Top 10 destination countries: Spain, the United States, Paraguay, Chile, Israel, Bolivia, Brazil, Uruguay, Canada, Italy

SKILLED EMIGRATION, 2000
- Emigration rate of tertiary educated: **2.5%**
- Emigration of physicians: **1,210** or **1.1%** of physicians trained in the country

IMMIGRATION, 2005
- Stock of immigrants: **1,500,142**
- Stock of immigrants as percentage of population: **3.9%**
- Females as percentage of immigrants: **53.4%**
- Refugees as percentage of immigrants: **0.2%**
- Top 10 source countries: Paraguay, Bolivia, Italy, Chile, Spain, Uruguay, Peru, Brazil, Poland, Germany

Remittances

US$ millions	2000	2001	2002	2003	2004	2005	2006	2007
Inward remittance flows	86	190	189	274	312	432	542[a]	542
of which								
Workers' remittances	50	156	171	236	270	381	486	..
Compensation of employees	36	34	18	38	42	51	56	..
Migrants' transfer	..	..	..	..	..	..	..	..
Outward remittance flows	268	256	99	180	235	314	367[b]	..
of which								
Workers' remittances	240	226	59	117	154	212	253	..
Compensation of employees	28	30	40	63	81	102	114	..
Migrants' transfer	..	..	..	..	..	..	..	..

a. 0.3% of GDP in 2006.
b. 0.2% of GDP in 2006.

Armenia

Population (millions, 2006)	3.0
Population growth (avg. annual %, 1997-2006)	-0.6
Population density (people per sq. km, 2006)	107
Labor force (millions, 2006)	1.3
Urban population (% of pop., 2006)	64
Age dependency ratio	0.47
Surface area (1,000 sq. km, 2006)	30
GNI ($ billions, 2006)	6.5
GNI per capita, Atlas method ($, 2006)	1,930
GDP growth (avg. annual %, 2002-06)	13
Poverty headcount ratio at national poverty line (% of pop., 2004)	1.7

Migration

EMIGRATION, 2005

- Stock of emigrants: **812,700**
- Stock of emigrants as percentage of population: **26.9%**
- Top 10 destination countries: Russia, the United States, Ukraine, Georgia, Germany, Israel, Turkmenistan, Greece, Spain, Belarus

SKILLED EMIGRATION, 2000

- Emigration rate of tertiary educated: **11.2%**
- Emigration of physicians: **8** or **0.1%** of physicians trained in the country

IMMIGRATION, 2005

- Stock of immigrants: **235,235**
- Stock of immigrants as percentage of population: **7.8%**
- Females as percentage of immigrants: **58.9%**
- Refugees as percentage of immigrants: **99.1%**
- Top 10 source countries: Azerbaijan, Georgia, Russia, the Islamic Republic of Iran, Syria, Ukraine, Turkey, Greece, Uzbekistan, Lebanon

Remittances

US$ millions	2000	2001	2002	2003	2004	2005	2006	2007
Inward remittance flows	87	94	131	686	813	940	1,175ª	1,273
of which								
Workers' remittances	9	10	10	9	31	47	77	..
Compensation of employees	78	84	121	153	295	337	575	..
Migrants' transfer	..	..	..	6	10	11	8	..
Outward remittance flows	5	21	24	27	127	146	155ᵇ	..
of which								
Workers' remittances	2	6	7	6	5	14	19	..
Compensation of employees	1	12	15	19	116	129	130	..
Migrants' transfer	1	2	2	2	6	3	6	..

a. **18.3% of GDP in 2006.**
b. **2.4% of GDP in 2006.**

Aruba

Population (thousands, 2006)	101
Population growth (avg. annual %, 1997–2006)	..
Population density (people per sq. km, 2006)	533
Labor force (millions, 2006)	..
Urban population (% of pop., 2006)	46.7
Age dependency ratio	..
Surface area (sq. km, 2006)	190
GNI ($ millions, 2006)	..
GNI per capita, Atlas method ($, 2006)	..
GDP growth (avg. annual %, 2002–06)	-0.5
Poverty headcount ratio at national poverty line (% of pop., 2004)	..

Migration

IMMIGRATION, 2005
- Stock of immigrants: **24,464**
- Stock of immigrants as percentage of population: **24.6%**
- Females as percentage of immigrants: **56.5%**
- Refugees as percentage of immigrants: **0.0%**
- Top source countries: Colombia, República Bolivariana de Venezuela, the Dominican Republic, the United States, Portugal, Dominica

EMIGRATION, 2005
- Stock of emigrants: **11,681**
- Stock of emigrants as percentage of population: **11.7%**
- Top 10 destination countries: the United States, Netherlands Antilles, the Netherlands, Canada, República Bolivariana de Venezuela, the Dominican Republic, Greece, Colombia, the Philippines, Australia

SKILLED EMIGRATION, 2000
Skilled emigration data are currently not available for this country.

Remittances

US$ millions	2000	2001	2002	2003	2004	2005	2006	2007
Inward remittance flows	8	9	10	11	14	14	19	19
of which								
Workers' remittances	1	1	1	1	1	2	7	..
Compensation of employees	0	0	1	0	1	1	1	..
Migrants' transfer	7	8	8	10	12	11	11	..
Outward remittance flows	43	44	52	61	61	72	81	..
of which								
Workers' remittances	43	38	45	47	48	63	68	..
Compensation of employees	0	1	1	1	1	1	5	..
Migrants' transfer	5	10	6	13	12	8	8	..

Australia

Population (millions, 2006)	21
Population growth (avg. annual %, 1997-2006)	1.1
Population density (people per sq. km, 2006)	3
Labor force (millions, 2006)	10
Urban population (% of pop., 2006)	88.4
Age dependency ratio	0.47
Surface area (1,000 sq. km, 2006)	7,741
GNI ($ billions, 2006)	737
GNI per capita, Atlas method ($, 2006)	35,990
GDP growth (avg. annual %, 2002-06)	3.0
Poverty headcount ratio at national poverty line (% of pop., 2004)	..

Migration

IMMIGRATION, 2005
- Stock of immigrants: **4,097,204**
- Stock of immigrants as percentage of population: **20.3%**
- Females as percentage of immigrants: **51.6%**
- Refugees as percentage of immigrants: **1.6%**
- Top 10 source countries: the United Kingdom, New Zealand, Italy, Vietnam, China, Greece, Germany, the Philippines, India, the Netherlands

EMIGRATION, 2005
- Stock of emigrants: **415,270**
- Stock of emigrants as percentage of population: **2.1%**
- Top 10 destination countries: the United Kingdom, the United States, New Zealand, Canada, Greece, Papua New Guinea, Germany, Japan, the Netherlands, Ireland

SKILLED EMIGRATION, 2000
- Emigration rate of tertiary educated: **2.3%**
- Emigration of physicians: **1,195** or **2.3%** of physicians trained in the country

Remittances

US$ millions	2000	2001	2002	2003	2004	2005	2006	2007
Inward remittance flows	**1,903**	**1,783**	**1,795**	**2,326**	**2,837**	**2,990**	**3,119**[a]	**3,119**
of which								
Workers' remittances	..	..	..	..	..	..	..	..
Compensation of employees	504	472	479	695	868	982	1,007	..
Migrants' transfer	1,399	1,311	1,294	1,631	1,969	2,008	2,112	..
Outward remittance flows	**1,053**	**1,059**	**1,219**	**1,779**	**2,253**	**2,375**	**2,815**[b]	..
of which								
Workers' remittances	..	..	..	..	..	..	..	..
Compensation of employees	578	599	734	1,192	1,530	1,686	2,190	..
Migrants' transfer	475	460	485	587	723	689	625	..

a. 0.4% of GDP in 2006.
b. 0.4% of GDP in 2006.

Austria

Population (millions, 2006)	8.2
Population growth (avg. annual %, 1997–2006)	0.3
Population density (people per sq. km, 2006)	100
Labor force (millions, 2006)	4.0
Urban population (% of pop., 2006)	66.1
Age dependency ratio	0.48
Surface area (1,000 sq. km, 2006)	84
GNI ($ billions, 2006)	319
GNI per capita, Atlas method ($, 2006)	39,590
GDP growth (avg. annual %, 2002–06)	1.9
Poverty headcount ratio at national poverty line (% of pop., 2004)	..

Migration

IMMIGRATION, 2005

- Stock of immigrants: **1,233,546**
- Stock of immigrants as percentage of population: **15.1%**
- Females as percentage of immigrants: **51.9%**
- Refugees as percentage of immigrants: **1.5%**
- Top 10 source countries: Serbia and Montenegro, Germany, Bosnia and Herzegovina, Turkey, the Czech Republic, Poland, Romania, Croatia, Hungary, Italy

EMIGRATION, 2005

- Stock of emigrants: **576,953**
- Stock of emigrants as percentage of population: **7.0%**
- Top 10 destination countries: Germany, the United States, Switzerland, Canada, the United Kingdom, Australia, Italy, Turkey, France, Spain

SKILLED EMIGRATION, 2000

- Emigration rate of tertiary educated: **11.1%**
- Emigration of physicians: **1,320** or **5.0%** of physicians trained in the country

Remittances

US$ millions	2000	2001	2002	2003	2004	2005	2006	2007
Inward remittance flows	1,441	1,519	1,711	2,310	2,480	2,941	3,084[a]	3,492
of which								
Workers' remittances	305	315	354	499	641	802	802	..
Compensation of employees	911	950	979	1,263	1,566	1,846	1,989	..
Migrants' transfer	225	255	378	548	273	293	293	..
Outward remittance flows	858	950	1,095	1,466	2,014	2,543	1,533[b]	..
of which								
Workers' remittances	280	260	373	541	765	954	954	..
Compensation of employees	383	428	461	601	932	1,142	1,533	..
Migrants' transfer	196	262	261	324	317	447	447	..

a. 1.0% of GDP in 2006.
b. 0.5% of GDP in 2006.

Azerbaijan

LOWER MIDDLE INCOME

Population (millions, 2006)	8.5
Population growth (avg. annual %, 1997–2006)	0.9
Population density (people per sq. km, 2006)	103
Labor force (millions, 2006)	4.2
Urban population (% of pop., 2006)	51.6
Age dependency ratio	0.47
Surface area (1,000 sq. km, 2006)	87
GNI ($ billions, 2006)	17
GNI per capita, Atlas method ($, 2006)	1,850
GDP growth (avg. annual %, 2002–06)	18.6
Poverty headcount ratio at national poverty line (% of pop., 2004)	0.7

Migration

EMIGRATION, 2005
- Stock of emigrants: **1,365,004**
- Stock of emigrants as percentage of population: **16.2%**
- Top 10 destination countries: Russia, Ukraine, Armenia, Israel, Kazakhstan, Germany, Turkey, the United States, Georgia, Turkmenistan

SKILLED EMIGRATION, 2000
- Emigration rate of tertiary educated: **2.6%**
- Emigration of physicians: **5** or **0.02%** of physicians trained in the country

IMMIGRATION, 2005
- Stock of immigrants: **181,818**
- Stock of immigrants as percentage of population: **2.2%**
- Females as percentage of immigrants: **57.8%**
- Refugees as percentage of immigrants: **24.3%**

Remittances

US$ millions	2000	2001	2002	2003	2004	2005	2006	2007
Inward remittance flows	57	104	181	171	227	693	812[a]	993
of which								
Workers' remittances	57	104	163	154	191	490	662	..
Compensation of employees	..	..	..	2	12	133	128	..
Migrants' transfer	..	..	18	15	24	70	22	..
Outward remittance flows	101	142	235	170	201	268	300[b]	..
of which								
Workers' remittances	54	95	149	78	65	127	149	..
Compensation of employees	47	47	39	54	108	112	125	..
Migrants' transfer	..	..	47	38	28	29	26	..

a. 4.0% of GDP in 2006.
b. 1.5% of GDP in 2006.

Bahamas, The

Population (thousands, 2006)	327
Population growth (avg. annual %, 1997-2006)	1.4
Population density (people per sq. km, 2006)	33
Labor force (thousands, 2006)	158
Urban population (% of pop., 2006)	90.6
Age dependency ratio	0.52
Surface area (1,000 sq. km, 2006)	14
GNI ($ millions, 2006)	..
GNI per capita, Atlas method ($, 2006)	..
GDP growth (avg. annual %, 2002-06)	0.7
Poverty headcount ratio at national poverty line (% of pop., 2004)	..

Migration

IMMIGRATION, 2005
- Stock of immigrants: **31,632**
- Stock of immigrants as percentage of population: **9.8%**
- Females as percentage of immigrants: **48.5%**
- Refugees as percentage of immigrants: **0.0%**
- Top 10 source countries: Haiti, the United States, Jamaica, the United Kingdom, Canada, Guyana, Trinidad and Tobago, India, Germany, Switzerland

EMIGRATION, 2005
- Stock of emigrants: **38,716**
- Stock of emigrants as percentage of population: **12.0%**
- Top 10 destination countries: the United States, the United Kingdom, Canada, Australia, Netherlands Antilles, Cayman Islands, Switzerland, Germany, Spain, Barbados

SKILLED EMIGRATION, 2000
- Emigration rate of tertiary educated: **36.4%**
- Emigration of physicians: **2** or **0.7%** of physicians trained in the country

Remittances

US$ millions	2000	2001	2002	2003	2004	2005	2006	2007
Inward remittance flows	..	..	..	..	..	..	..	..
of which								
Workers' remittances	..	..	..	..	..	..	..	..
Compensation of employees	..	..	..	..	..	..	..	..
Migrants' transfer	-	..	..	..	..	..	..	..
Outward remittance flows	73	75	83	99	119	144	164	..
of which								
Workers' remittances	5	5	8	6	8	11	7	..
Compensation of employees	51	49	50	56	63	73	93	..
Migrants' transfer	16	21	25	37	48	60	64	..

Bahrain

Population (thousands, 2006)	740
Population growth (avg. annual %, 1997–2006)	2.0
Population density (people per sq. km, 2006)	1,042
Labor force (thousands, 2006)	344
Urban population (% of pop., 2006)	96.7
Age dependency ratio	0.42
Surface area (sq. km, 2006)	710
GNI ($ billions, 2006)	10
GNI per capita, Atlas method ($, 2006)	14,370
GDP growth (avg. annual %, 2002–06)	6.2
Poverty headcount ratio at national poverty line (% of pop., 2004)	..

Migration

IMMIGRATION, 2005
- Stock of immigrants: **295,461**
- Stock of immigrants as percentage of population: **40.7%**
- Females as percentage of immigrants: **30.9%**
- Refugees as percentage of immigrants: **0.0%**
- Top 10 source countries: India, Saudi Arabia, Egypt, the Islamic Republic of Iran, Sudan, Algeria, Morocco, Iraq, the Republic of Yemen, Syria

EMIGRATION, 2005
- Stock of emigrants: **20,090**
- Stock of emigrants as percentage of population: **2.8%**
- Top 10 destination countries: the Philippines, the United Kingdom, the United States, Canada, Australia, Ireland, New Zealand, Sudan, the Netherlands, Denmark

SKILLED EMIGRATION, 2000
- Emigration rate of tertiary educated: **3.4%**
- Emigration of physicians: **14** or **1.3%** of physicians trained in the country

Remittances

US$ millions	2000	2001	2002	2003	2004	2005	2006	2007
Inward remittance flows	..	..	..	..	..	..	..	..
of which								
Workers' remittances	..	..	..	..	..	..	..	..
Compensation of employees	..	..	..	..	..	..	..	..
Migrants' transfer	..	..	..	..	..	..	..	..
Outward remittance flows	1,013	1,287	872	1,082	1,120	1,223	1,531[a]	..
of which								
Workers' remittances	1,013	1,287	872	1,082	1,120	1,223	1,531	..
Compensation of employees	..	..	..	..	..	..	..	..
Migrants' transfer	..	..	..	..	..	..	..	..

a. 11.9% of GDP in 2006.

Bangladesh

Population (millions, 2006)	144
Population growth (avg. annual %, 1997-2006)	1.9
Population density (people per sq. km, 2006)	1,109
Labor force (millions, 2006)	65
Urban population (% of pop., 2006)	25.5
Age dependency ratio	0.63
Surface area (1,000 sq. km, 2006)	144
GNI ($ billions, 2006)	65
GNI per capita, Atlas method ($, 2006)	480
GDP growth (avg. annual %, 2002-06)	5.7
Poverty headcount ratio at national poverty line (% of pop., 2004)	32.6

Migration

EMIGRATION, 2005
- Stock of emigrants: **4,885,704**
- Stock of emigrants as percentage of population: **3.4%**
- Top 10 destination countries: India, Saudi Arabia, the United Kingdom, the United States, Oman, Italy, Canada, Singapore, the Republic of Korea, Malaysia

SKILLED EMIGRATION, 2000
- Emigration rate of tertiary educated: **4.7%**
- Emigration of physicians: **702** or **2.5%** of physicians trained in the country

IMMIGRATION, 2005
- Stock of immigrants: **1,031,850**
- Stock of immigrants as percentage of population: **0.7%**
- Females as percentage of immigrants: **13.9%**
- Refugees as percentage of immigrants: **2.0%**
- Top source countries: India, Pakistan

Remittances

US$ millions	2000	2001	2002	2003	2004	2005	2006	2007
Inward remittance flows	1,968	2,105	2,858	3,192	3,584	4,314	5,428[a]	6,400
of which								
Workers' remittances	1,958	2,094	2,848	3,180	3,572	4,302	5,418	..
Compensation of employees	9	10	10	12	12	12	10	..
Migrants' transfer	..	..	..	..	..	..	..	..
Outward remittance flows	4	4	6	7	8	6	3[b]	..
of which								
Workers' remittances	3	2	3	4	5	3	2	..
Compensation of employees	2	2	3	3	3	3	1	..
Migrants' transfer	..	..	..	..	..	..	..	..

a. **8.8% of GDP in 2006.**
b. **0.005% of GDP in 2006.**

Barbados

Population (thousands, 2006)	270
Population growth (avg. annual %, 1997–2006)	0.3
Population density (people per sq. km, 2006)	628
Labor force (thousands, 2006)	156
Urban population (% of pop., 2006)	53.3
Age dependency ratio	0.4
Surface area (sq. km, 2006)	430
GNI ($ billions, 2006)	2.9
GNI per capita, Atlas method ($, 2006)	..
GDP growth (avg. annual %, 2002–06)	..
Poverty headcount ratio at national poverty line (% of pop., 2004)	..

Migration

EMIGRATION, 2005
- Stock of emigrants: **113,628**
- Stock of emigrants as percentage of population: **42.2%**
- Top 10 destination countries: the United States, the United Kingdom, Canada, Trinidad and Tobago, Netherlands Antilles, Jamaica, Australia, Germany, Antigua and Barbuda, Dominica

SKILLED EMIGRATION, 2000
- Emigration rate of tertiary educated: **61.4%**
- Emigration of physicians: **5** or **1.5%** of physicians trained in the country

IMMIGRATION, 2005
- Stock of immigrants: **26,234**
- Stock of immigrants as percentage of population: **9.7%**
- Females as percentage of immigrants: **60.1%**
- Refugees as percentage of immigrants: **0.0%**
- Top 10 source countries: the United Kingdom, Guyana, Trinidad and Tobago, the United States, Canada, Jamaica, Grenada, Dominica, India, the Bahamas

Remittances

US$ millions	2000	2001	2002	2003	2004	2005	2006	2007
Inward remittance flows	102	118	109	114	109	140[a]	140	140
of which								
Workers' remittances	84	100	93	97	100	131	..	..
Compensation of employees	16	16	16	17	9	9	..	..
Migrants' transfer	2	1	..	..	..	..	..	..
Outward remittance flows	16	18	17	19	19	40[b]	40	..
of which								
Workers' remittances	14	15	15	16	16	37	..	..
Compensation of employees	2	2	3	3	3	3	..	..
Migrants' transfer	..	..	..	..	..	..	..	..

a. 4.5% of GDP in 2005.
b. 1.3% of GDP in 2005.

Belarus

Population (millions, 2006)	9.7
Population growth (avg. annual %, 1997–2006)	-0.4
Population density (people per sq. km, 2006)	47
Labor force (millions, 2006)	4.8
Urban population (% of pop., 2006)	72.7
Age dependency ratio	0.42
Surface area (1,000 sq. km, 2006)	208
GNI ($ billions, 2006)	36
GNI per capita, Atlas method ($, 2006)	3,380
GDP growth (avg. annual %, 2002–06)	8.6
Poverty headcount ratio at national poverty line (% of pop., 2004)	0

Migration

EMIGRATION, 2005
- Stock of emigrants: **1,799,790**
- Stock of emigrants as percentage of population: **18.4%**
- Top 10 destination countries: Russia, Ukraine, Poland, Lithuania, Kazakhstan, the United States, Israel, Germany, Latvia, Estonia

SKILLED EMIGRATION, 2000
- Emigration rate of tertiary educated: **3.0%**
- Emigration of physicians: **18** or **0.04%** of physicians trained in the country

IMMIGRATION, 2005
- Stock of immigrants: **1,190,944**
- Stock of immigrants as percentage of population: **12.2%**
- Females as percentage of immigrants: **57.8%**
- Refugees as percentage of immigrants: **0.1%**
- Top 10 source countries: Russia, Poland, Ukraine, Armenia, Lithuania, Azerbaijan, Germany, Moldova, Georgia, Latvia

Remittances

US$ millions	2000	2001	2002	2003	2004	2005	2006	2007
Inward remittance flows	139	149	141	222	256	370	334[a]	334
of which								
Workers' remittances	..	..	..	..	..	..	..	..
Compensation of employees	14	17	21	89	126	235	173	..
Migrants' transfer	126	132	120	133	130	135	161	..
Outward remittance flows	58	77	68	65	82	94	93[b]	..
of which								
Workers' remittances	..	..	..	..	..	..	..	..
Compensation of employees	2	1	1	1	1	0	3	..
Migrants' transfer	56	76	67	64	81	94	90	..

a. 0.9% of GDP in 2006.
b. 0.3% of GDP in 2006.

Belgium

Population (millions, 2006)	10
Population growth (avg. annual %, 1997–2006)	0.3
Population density (people per sq. km, 2006)	347
Labor force (millions, 2006)	4.5
Urban population (% of pop., 2006)	97.2
Age dependency ratio	0.52
Surface area (1,000 sq. km, 2006)	31
GNI ($ billions, 2006)	396
GNI per capita, Atlas method ($, 2006)	38,600
GDP growth (avg. annual %, 2002–06)	1.9
Poverty headcount ratio at national poverty line (% of pop., 2004)	..

Migration

IMMIGRATION, 2005
- Stock of immigrants: **719,276**
- Stock of immigrants as percentage of population: **6.9%**
- Females as percentage of immigrants: **49.1%**
- Refugees as percentage of immigrants: **1.9%**
- Top 10 source countries: France, Italy, Morocco, the Netherlands, Germany, Turkey, the Democratic Republic of Congo, Spain, the United Kingdom, Portugal

EMIGRATION, 2005
- Stock of emigrants: **454,599**
- Stock of emigrants as percentage of population: **4.4%**
- Top 10 destination countries: France, Spain, the Netherlands, the United States, Germany, the United Kingdom, Canada, Luxembourg, Switzerland, Turkey

SKILLED EMIGRATION, 2000
- Emigration rate of tertiary educated: **5.9%**
- Emigration of physicians: **2,048** or **4.6%** of physicians trained in the country

Remittances

US$ millions	2000	2001	2002	2003	2004	2005	2006	2007
Inward remittance flows	**4,005**	**3,811**	**4,674**	**5,871**	**6,863**	**7,164**	**7,220ᵃ**	**7,220**
of which								
Workers' remittances	..	..	40	20	19	20	28	..
Compensation of employees	..	..	4,490	5,754	6,536	6,790	6,970	..
Migrants' transfer	..	..	144	216	308	354	222	..
Outward remittance flows	**3,588**	**3,958**	**1,846**	**2,329**	**2,617**	**2,755**	**2,570ᵇ**	..
of which								
Workers' remittances	..	..	264	333	343	416	429	..
Compensation of employees	..	..	1,363	1,763	1,997	2,012	2,005	..
Migrants' transfer	..	..	218	233	277	327	136	..

a. 1.8% of GDP in 2006.
b. 0.7% of GDP in 2006.

Belize

Latin America and the Caribbean	UPPER MIDDLE INCOME
Population (thousands, 2006)	297
Population growth (avg. annual %, 1997-2006)	2.9
Population density (people per sq. km, 2006)	13
Labor force (thousands, 2006)	120
Urban population (% of pop., 2006)	48.5
Age dependency ratio	0.68
Surface area (1,000 sq. km, 2006)	23
GNI ($ billions, 2006)	1.1
GNI per capita, Atlas method ($, 2006)	3,650
GDP growth (avg. annual %, 2002-06)	5.2
Poverty headcount ratio at national poverty line (% of pop., 2004)	..

Migration

EMIGRATION, 2005
- Stock of emigrants: **59,110**
- Stock of emigrants as percentage of population: **21.9%**
- Top 10 destination countries: the United States, Canada, Mexico, the United Kingdom, Bolivia, Guatemala, Honduras, Cayman Islands, Jamaica, Costa Rica

SKILLED EMIGRATION, 2000
- Emigration rate of tertiary educated: **51.0%**
- Emigration of physicians: **5** or **1.9%** of physicians trained in the country

IMMIGRATION, 2005
- Stock of immigrants: **40,537**
- Stock of immigrants as percentage of population: **15.0%**
- Females as percentage of immigrants: **50.5%**
- Refugees as percentage of immigrants: **1.7%**
- Top 10 source countries: Guatemala, El Salvador, Honduras, Mexico, the United States, China, Canada, Jamaica, Nicaragua, India

Remittances

US$ millions	2000	2001	2002	2003	2004	2005	2006	2007
Inward remittance flows	22	30	29	34	34	46	66[a]	66
of which								
Workers' remittances	23	26	25	30	31	41	58	..
Compensation of employees	2	2	2	2	2	4	6	..
Migrants' transfer	2	2	2	2	1	1	2	..
Outward remittance flows	11	17	17	20	19	20	22[b]	..
of which								
Workers' remittances	1	11	12	14	12	13	15	..
Compensation of employees	6	5	4	5	6	6	6	..
Migrants' transfer	4	1	1	1	1	1	1	..

a. 5.4% of GDP in 2006.
b. 1.8% of GDP in 2006.

Benin

Population (millions, 2006)	8.7
Population growth (avg. annual %, 1997–2006)	3.1
Population density (people per sq. km, 2006)	79
Labor force (millions, 2006)	3.4
Urban population (% of pop., 2006)	40.5
Age dependency ratio	0.88
Surface area (1,000 sq. km, 2006)	113
GNI ($ billions, 2006)	4.7
GNI per capita, Atlas method ($, 2006)	540
GDP growth (avg. annual %, 2002–06)	3.7
Poverty headcount ratio at national poverty line (% of pop., 2004)	30.8

Migration

EMIGRATION, 2005

- Stock of emigrants: **508,640**
- Stock of emigrants as percentage of population: **6.0%**
- Top 10 destination countries: Nigeria, Togo, Côte d'Ivoire, Burkina Faso, Gabon, France, the Republic of Congo, Niger, Germany, Italy

SKILLED EMIGRATION, 2000

- Emigration rate of tertiary educated: **7.5%**
- Emigration of physicians:
  a) **10** or **2.7%** of physicians trained in the country *(Source: Docquier and Bhargava 2006)*
  b) **224** or **35.6%** of physicians trained in the country *(Source: Clemens and Pettersson 2006)*
- Emigration of Nurses: **187** or **12.5%** of nurses trained in the country

IMMIGRATION, 2005

- Stock of immigrants: **174,726**
- Stock of immigrants as percentage of population: **2.1%**
- Females as percentage of immigrants: **46.0%**
- Refugees as percentage of immigrants: **2.7%**
- Top source countries: Nigeria, Togo, Niger, Côte d'Ivoire, Ghana

Remittances

US$ millions	2000	2001	2002	2003	2004	2005	2006	2007
Inward remittance flows	87	84	76	55	63	173	173[a]	173
of which								
Workers' remittances	80	78	70	49	54	137	..	..
Compensation of employees	5	5	6	6	9	10	..	..
Migrants' transfer	1	1	0	0	0	26	..	..
Outward remittance flows	9	10	7	5	7	39	39[b]	..
of which								
Workers' remittances	7	7	5	4	3	30	..	..
Compensation of employees	2	3	1	1	3	3	..	..
Migrants' transfer	..	..	..	0	1	6	..	..

a. 3.6% of GDP in 2006.
b. 0.8% of GDP in 2006.

Bermuda

Population (thousands, 2006)	64
Population growth (avg. annual %, 1997–2006)	0.3
Population density (people per sq. km, 2006)	1,276
Labor force (millions, 2006)	..
Urban population (% of pop., 2006)	100
Age dependency ratio	..
Surface area (sq. km, 2006)	50
GNI ($ millions, 2006)	..
GNI per capita, Atlas method ($, 2006)	..
GDP growth (avg. annual %, 2002–06)	..
Poverty headcount ratio at national poverty line (% of pop., 2004)	..

Migration

IMMIGRATION, 2005
- Stock of immigrants: **18,829**
- Stock of immigrants as percentage of population: **29.3%**
- Females as percentage of immigrants: **51.7%**
- Refugees as percentage of immigrants: **0.0%**
- Top source countries: the United Kingdom, the United States, Canada, Portugal

EMIGRATION, 2005
- Stock of emigrants: **24,281**
- Stock of emigrants as percentage of population: **37.8%**
- Top 10 destination countries: the United States, the United Kingdom, Canada, Australia, Portugal, New Zealand, Ireland, France, the Netherlands, Cayman Islands

SKILLED EMIGRATION, 2000
Skilled emigration data are currently not available for this country.

Remittances
Remittance data are currently not available for this country.

Bhutan

Population (thousands, 2006)	647
Population growth (avg. annual %, 1997–2006)	2.4
Population density (people per sq. km, 2006)	14
Labor force (thousands, 2006)	259
Urban population (% of pop., 2006)	11.4
Age dependency ratio	0.74
Surface area (1,000 sq. km, 2006)	47
GNI ($ millions, 2006)	925
GNI per capita, Atlas method ($, 2006)	1,410
GDP growth (avg. annual %, 2002–06)	7.7
Poverty headcount ratio at national poverty line (% of pop., 2004)	..

Migration

EMIGRATION, 2005
- Stock of emigrants: **39,109**
- Stock of emigrants as percentage of population: **1.8%**
- Top 10 destination countries: Nepal, India, Germany, the United States, France, the United Kingdom, Switzerland, Australia, Belgium, Japan

SKILLED EMIGRATION, 2000
- Emigration rate of tertiary educated: **1.2%**
- Emigration of physicians: **3** or **7.4%** of physicians trained in the country

IMMIGRATION, 2005
- Stock of immigrants: **9,775**
- Stock of immigrants as percentage of population: **0.5%**
- Females as percentage of immigrants: **44.8%**
- Refugees as percentage of immigrants: **0.0%**

Remittances

Remittance data are currently not available for this country.

Bolivia

Population (millions, 2006)	9.3
Population growth (avg. annual %, 1997–2006)	2.0
Population density (people per sq. km, 2006)	9
Labor force (millions, 2006)	4.3
Urban population (% of pop., 2006)	64.7
Age dependency ratio	0.73
Surface area (1,000 sq. km, 2006)	1,099
GNI ($ billions, 2006)	11
GNI per capita, Atlas method ($, 2006)	1,100
GDP growth (avg. annual %, 2002–06)	3.6
Poverty headcount ratio at national poverty line (% of pop., 2004)	23.9

Migration

EMIGRATION, 2005
- Stock of emigrants: **417,956**
- Stock of emigrants as percentage of population: **4.6%**
- Top 10 destination countries: Argentina, the United States, Spain, Brazil, Chile, Japan, Canada, Sweden, Peru, Germany

SKILLED EMIGRATION, 2000
- Emigration rate of tertiary educated: **6.0%**
- Emigration of physicians: **221** or **3.0%** of physicians trained in the country

IMMIGRATION, 2005
- Stock of immigrants: **116,306**
- Stock of immigrants as percentage of population: **1.3%**
- Females as percentage of immigrants: **48.2%**
- Refugees as percentage of immigrants: **0.4%**
- Top 10 source countries: Argentina, Brazil, Mexico, Peru, Chile, the United States, Paraguay, Canada, Spain, Japan

Remittances

US$ millions	2000	2001	2002	2003	2004	2005	2006	2007
Inward remittance flows	127	135	113	159	210	347	611[a]	758
of which								
Workers' remittances	101	107	83	127	178	304	569	..
Compensation of employees	26	28	30	32	32	34	33	..
Migrants' transfer	..	..	..	..	..	9	9	..
Outward remittance flows	37	36	38	46	50	66	73[b]	..
of which								
Workers' remittances	31	30	31	39	43	59	66	..
Compensation of employees	6	6	7	7	7	7	7	..
Migrants' transfer	..	..	..	..	..	..	..	..

a. 5.5% of GDP in 2006.
b. 0.7% of GDP in 2006.

Bosnia and Herzegovina

Europe and Central Asia	LOWER MIDDLE INCOME
Population (millions, 2006)	3.9
Population growth (avg. annual %, 1997–2006)	1.4
Population density (people per sq. km, 2006)	76
Labor force (millions, 2006)	2.1
Urban population (% of pop., 2006)	46.3
Age dependency ratio	0.44
Surface area (1,000 sq. km, 2006)	51
GNI ($ billions, 2006)	12
GNI per capita, Atlas method ($, 2006)	2,980
GDP growth (avg. annual %, 2002–06)	5.2
Poverty headcount ratio at national poverty line (% of pop., 2004)	..

Migration

EMIGRATION, 2005

- Stock of emigrants: **1,471,594**
- Stock of emigrants as percentage of population: **37.7%**
- Top 10 destination countries: Croatia, Germany, Austria, the United States, Slovenia, Sweden, Switzerland, Canada, France, Australia

SKILLED EMIGRATION, 2000

- Emigration rate of tertiary educated: **28.6%**
- Emigration of physicians: **821** or **12.7%** of physicians trained in the country

IMMIGRATION, 2005

- Stock of immigrants: **40,814**
- Stock of immigrants as percentage of population: **1.0%**
- Females as percentage of immigrants: **50.8%**
- Refugees as percentage of immigrants: **54.1%**
- Top 10 source countries: Serbia and Montenegro, Croatia, Albania, Ukraine, Slovenia, FYR Macedonia, Hungary, Italy, the Czech Republic, Poland

Remittances

US$ millions	2000	2001	2002	2003	2004	2005	2006	2007
Inward remittance flows	1,595	1,521	1,526	1,749	1,941	1,931	1,943[a]	1,943
of which								
Workers' remittances	950	919	956	1,143	1,343	1,347	1,383	..
Compensation of employees	631	581	540	595	579	570	560	..
Migrants' transfer	26	25	30	11	19	14	..	..
Outward remittance flows	2	11	14	21	62	40	55[b]	..
of which								
Workers' remittances	..	5	7	10	49	28	41	..
Compensation of employees	2	6	7	11	13	12	14	..
Migrants' transfer	..	..	..	..	..	..	..	..

a. 17.2% of GDP in 2006.
b. 0.5% of GDP in 2006.

Botswana

UPPER MIDDLE INCOME

Population (millions, 2006)	1.8
Population growth (avg. annual %, 1997–2006)	0.6
Population density (people per sq. km, 2006)	3
Labor force (thousands, 2006)	613
Urban population (% of pop., 2006)	58.2
Age dependency ratio	0.69
Surface area (1,000 sq. km, 2006)	582
GNI ($ billions, 2006)	9.7
GNI per capita, Atlas method ($, 2006)	5,900
GDP growth (avg. annual %, 2002–06)	5.2
Poverty headcount ratio at national poverty line (% of pop., 2004)	20.4

Migration

EMIGRATION, 2005
- Stock of emigrants: **37,840**
- Stock of emigrants as percentage of population: **2.1%**
- Top 10 destination countries: South Africa, Namibia, the United Kingdom, the United States, Australia, Tanzania, Zambia, Canada, France, the Netherlands

SKILLED EMIGRATION, 2000
- Emigration rate of tertiary educated: **2.1%**
- Emigration of physicians:
  a) **31** or **6.1%** of physicians trained in the country *(Source: Docquier and Bhargava 2006)*
  b) **68** or **11.4%** of physicians trained in the country *(Source: Clemens and Pettersson 2006)*
- Emigration of nurses: **80** or **2.2%** of nurses trained in the country

IMMIGRATION, 2005
- Stock of immigrants: **80,064**
- Stock of immigrants as percentage of population: **4.5%**
- Females as percentage of immigrants: **44.3%**
- Refugees as percentage of immigrants: **3.5%**

Remittances

US$ millions	2000	2001	2002	2003	2004	2005	2006	2007
Inward remittance flows	26	26	27	39	93	125	118[a]	118
of which								
Workers' remittances	0	0	0	0	51	82	79	..
Compensation of employees	18	18	19	27	29	30	26	..
Migrants' transfer	8	7	8	12	13	13	13	..
Outward remittance flows	147	139	144	205	120	123	118[b]	..
of which								
Workers' remittances	79	72	72	103	10	10	10	..
Compensation of employees	55	55	58	82	89	91	87	..
Migrants' transfer	13	13	14	20	21	22	21	..

a. 1.1% of GDP in 2006.
b. 1.1% of GDP in 2006.

Brazil

Latin America and the Caribbean	UPPER MIDDLE INCOME
Population (millions, 2006)	189
Population growth (avg. annual %, 1997–2006)	1.4
Population density (people per sq. km, 2006)	22
Labor force (millions, 2006)	93
Urban population (% of pop., 2006)	84.7
Age dependency ratio	0.51
Surface area (1,000 sq. km, 2006)	8,515
GNI ($ billions, 2006)	1,038
GNI per capita, Atlas method ($, 2006)	4,730
GDP growth (avg. annual %, 2002–06)	3.2
Poverty headcount ratio at national poverty line (% of pop., 2004)	7.6

Migration

EMIGRATION, 2005
- Stock of emigrants: **1,135,060**
- Stock of emigrants as percentage of population: **0.6%**
- Top 10 destination countries: Japan, the United States, Paraguay, Spain, Portugal, Germany, Italy, Argentina, France, Bolivia

SKILLED EMIGRATION, 2000
- Emigration rate of tertiary educated: **3.3%**
- Emigration of physicians: **951** or **0.3**% of physicians trained in the country

IMMIGRATION, 2005
- Stock of immigrants: **641,474**
- Stock of immigrants as percentage of population: **0.3%**
- Females as percentage of immigrants: **46.4%**
- Refugees as percentage of immigrants: **0.5%**
- Top 10 source countries: Portugal, Japan, Italy, Spain, Paraguay, Argentina, Uruguay, Bolivia, Germany, Chile

Remittances

US$ millions	2000	2001	2002	2003	2004	2005	2006	2007
Inward remittance flows	**1,649**	**1,775**	**2,449**	**2,822**	**3,576**	**3,540**	**4,253ᵃ**	**4,500**
of which								
Workers' remittances	1,112	1,178	1,711	2,018	2,459	2,480	2,890	..
Compensation of employees	237	270	293	269	354	325	397	..
Migrants' transfer	300	326	445	535	763	735	966	..
Outward remittance flows	**366**	**709**	**361**	**333**	**401**	**498**	**690ᵇ**	..
of which								
Workers' remittances	180	169	138	136	167	263	309	..
Compensation of employees	158	175	191	160	173	111	220	..
Migrants' transfer	28	364	31	37	61	124	161	..

a. 0.4% of GDP in 2006.
b. 0.1% of GDP in 2006.

Brunei Darussalam

Population (thousands, 2006)	381
Population growth (avg. annual %, 1997-2006)	2.3
Population density (people per sq. km, 2006)	72
Labor force (thousands, 2006)	167
Urban population (% of pop., 2006)	73.9
Age dependency ratio	0.48
Surface area (1,000 sq. km, 2006)	6
GNI ($ millions, 2006)	..
GNI per capita, Atlas method ($, 2006)	..
GDP growth (avg. annual %, 2002-06)	2.8
Poverty headcount ratio at national poverty line (% of pop., 2004)	..

Migration

IMMIGRATION, 2005
- Stock of immigrants: **124,193**
- Stock of immigrants as percentage of population: **33.2%**
- Females as percentage of immigrants: **46.8%**
- Refugees as percentage of immigrants: **0.0%**
- Top 10 source countries: Malaysia, the Philippines, Thailand, Nepal, Indonesia, India, the United Kingdom, China, Singapore, Sri Lanka

EMIGRATION, 2005
- Stock of emigrants: **12,623**
- Stock of emigrants as percentage of population: **3.4%**
- Top 10 destination countries: Canada, the United Kingdom, Australia, the Philippines, the United States, the Netherlands, New Zealand, Germany, France, Switzerland

SKILLED EMIGRATION, 2000
- Emigration rate of tertiary educated: **21.0%**
- Emigration of physicians: **37** or **9.9%** of physicians trained in the country

Remittances
Remittance data are currently not available for this country.

Migration and Remittances Factbook 2008

Bulgaria

Population (millions, 2006)	7.7
Population growth (avg. annual %, 1997–2006)	-0.8
Population density (people per sq. km, 2006)	71
Labor force (millions, 2006)	3.1
Urban population (% of pop., 2006)	70.3
Age dependency ratio	0.44
Surface area (1,000 sq. km, 2006)	111
GNI ($ billions, 2006)	32
GNI per capita, Atlas method ($, 2006)	3,990
GDP growth (avg. annual %, 2002–06)	5.8
Poverty headcount ratio at national poverty line (% of pop., 2004)	0

Migration

EMIGRATION, 2005
- Stock of emigrants: **937,341**
- Stock of emigrants as percentage of population: **12.1%**
- Top 10 destination countries: Turkey, Spain, Germany, Moldova, the United States, Greece, Romania, Italy, Israel, Canada

SKILLED EMIGRATION, 2000
- Emigration rate of tertiary educated: **5.8%**
- Emigration of physicians: **647** or **2.3%** of physicians trained in the country

IMMIGRATION, 2005
- Stock of immigrants: **104,076**
- Stock of immigrants as percentage of population: **1.4%**
- Females as percentage of immigrants: **57.9%**
- Refugees as percentage of immigrants: **4.8%**
- Top source country: Turkey

Remittances

US$ millions	2000	2001	2002	2003	2004	2005	2006	2007
Inward remittance flows	58	826	1,177	1,718	1,722	1,613	1,695ª	1,854
of which								
Workers' remittances	..	402	500	681	436	462	407	..
Compensation of employees	58	424	677	1,037	1,286	1,151	1,288	..
Migrants' transfer	..	..	..	..	..	..	..	..
Outward remittance flows	26	27	14	13	29	36	48ᵇ	..
of which								
Workers' remittances	..	..	..	..	18	22	21	..
Compensation of employees	26	27	14	13	11	14	27	..
Migrants' transfer	..	..	..	..	..	..	..	..

a. **5.4% of GDP in 2006.**
b. **0.2% of GDP in 2006.**

Burkina Faso

Population (millions, 2006)	14
Population growth (avg. annual %, 1997-2006)	3.0
Population density (people per sq. km, 2006)	50
Labor force (millions, 2006)	6.0
Urban population (% of pop., 2006)	18.7
Age dependency ratio	0.99
Surface area (1,000 sq. km, 2006)	274
GNI ($ billions, 2006)	6.2
GNI per capita, Atlas method ($, 2006)	460
GDP growth (avg. annual %, 2002-06)	5.7
Poverty headcount ratio at national poverty line (% of pop., 2004)	28.7

Migration

EMIGRATION, 2005
- Stock of emigrants: **1,121,758**
- Stock of emigrants as percentage of population: **8.5%**
- Top 10 destination countries: Côte d'Ivoire, Niger, Nigeria, France, Italy, Germany, the United States, Spain, Canada, Belgium

SKILLED EMIGRATION, 2000
- Emigration rate of tertiary educated: **3.3%**
- Emigration of physicians:
  a) **1** or **0.3%** of physicians trained in the country *(Source: Docquier and Bhargava 2006)*
  b) **78** or **19.9%** of physicians trained in the country *(Source: Clemens and Pettersson 2006)*
- Emigration of nurses: **76** or **2.4%** of nurses trained in the country

IMMIGRATION, 2005
- Stock of immigrants: **772,817**
- Stock of immigrants as percentage of population: **5.8%**
- Females as percentage of immigrants: **51.1%**
- Refugees as percentage of immigrants: **0.1%**
- Top source countries: Mali, Niger, Ghana, Benin, Côte d'Ivoire

Remittances

US$ millions	2000	2001	2002	2003	2004	2005	2006	2007
Inward remittance flows	67	50	50	50	50	50	50[a]	50
of which								
Workers' remittances	62	44	..	..	..	..	..	..
Compensation of employees	5	6	..	..	..	..	..	..
Migrants' transfer	..	..	..	..	..	..	..	..
Outward remittance flows	45	44	44	44	44	44	44[b]	..
of which								
Workers' remittances	37	37	..	..	..	..	..	..
Compensation of employees	7	7	..	..	..	..	..	..
Migrants' transfer	..	..	..	..	..	..	..	..

a. 0.8% of GDP in 2006.
b. 0.7% of GDP in 2006.

Burundi

Sub-Saharan Africa **LOW INCOME**

Population (millions, 2006)	7.8
Population growth (avg. annual %, 1997–2006)	2.3
Population density (people per sq. km, 2006)	305
Labor force (millions, 2006)	4.0
Urban population (% of pop., 2006)	10.3
Age dependency ratio	0.9
Surface area (1,000 sq. km, 2006)	28
GNI ($ millions, 2006)	785
GNI per capita, Atlas method ($, 2006)	100
GDP growth (avg. annual %, 2002–06)	2.8
Poverty headcount ratio at national poverty line (% of pop., 2004)	47.7

Migration

EMIGRATION, 2005
- Stock of emigrants: **315,477**
- Stock of emigrants as percentage of population: **4.2%**
- Top 10 destination countries: Tanzania, Uganda, Rwanda, Canada, Belgium, the United Kingdom, France, the United States, Italy, Germany

SKILLED EMIGRATION, 2000
- Emigration rate of tertiary educated: **19.9%**
- Emigration of physicians:
  a) **24** or **6.5%** of physicians trained in the country *(Source: Docquier and Bhargava 2006)*
  b) **136** or **37.2%** of physicians trained in the country *(Source: Clemens and Pettersson 2006)*
- Emigration of nurses: **134** or **77.9%** of nurses trained in the country

IMMIGRATION, 2005
- Stock of immigrants: **100,189**
- Stock of immigrants as percentage of population: **1.3%**
- Females as percentage of immigrants: **53.6%**
- Refugees as percentage of immigrants: **53.2%**

Remittances

US$ millions	2000	2001	2002	2003	2004	2005	2006	2007
Inward remittance flows	..	..	..	..	..	..	..	..
of which								
Workers' remittances	..	..	..	..	..	..	..	..
Compensation of employees	..	..	..	..	..	..	..	..
Migrants' transfer	..	..	..	..	..	..	..	..
Outward remittance flows	2	2	3	4	1	1	1ª	..
of which								
Workers' remittances	..	..	..	..	0	0	0	..
Compensation of employees	2	2	3	3	..	..	..	..
Migrants' transfer	0	0	0	1	1	0	0	..

a. 0.1% of GDP in 2006.

Cambodia

Population (millions, 2006)	14
Population growth (avg. annual %, 1997–2006)	2.1
Population density (people per sq. km, 2006)	81
Labor force (millions, 2006)	7.0
Urban population (% of pop., 2006)	20.3
Age dependency ratio	0.67
Surface area (1,000 sq. km, 2006)	181
GNI ($ billions, 2006)	6.9
GNI per capita, Atlas method ($, 2006)	480
GDP growth (avg. annual %, 2002–06)	9.7
Poverty headcount ratio at national poverty line (% of pop., 2004)	66

Migration

EMIGRATION, 2005
- Stock of emigrants: **348,710**
- Stock of emigrants as percentage of population: **2.5%**
- Top 10 destination countries: the United States, France, Thailand, Australia, Canada, New Zealand, Japan, Switzerland, Lao PDR, Germany

SKILLED EMIGRATION, 2000
- Emigration rate of tertiary educated: **6.8%**
- Emigration of physicians: **75** or **3.7%** of physicians trained in the country

IMMIGRATION, 2005
- Stock of immigrants: **303,871**
- Stock of immigrants as percentage of population: **2.2%**
- Females as percentage of immigrants: **51.3%**
- Refugees as percentage of immigrants: **0.3%**
- Top 10 source countries: Vietnam, Thailand, China, France, Lao PDR, the United States, Malaysia, the Philippines, Japan, Singapore

Remittances

US$ millions	2000	2001	2002	2003	2004	2005	2006	2007
Inward remittance flows	121	133	140	138	177	200	298[a]	322
of which								
Workers' remittances	100	110	120	125	144	160	180	..
Compensation of employees	3	3	3	3	3	4	4	..
Migrants' transfer	18	20	17	10	30	36	114	..
Outward remittance flows	104	110	133	109	129	144	158[b]	..
of which								
Workers' remittances	7	8	9	10	12	16	20	..
Compensation of employees	53	44	61	46	44	72	85	..
Migrants' transfer	44	58	63	53	73	56	53	..

a. 4.1% of GDP in 2006.
b. 2.2% of GDP in 2006.

Cameroon

Sub-Saharan Africa **LOWER MIDDLE INCOME**

Population (millions, 2006)	17
Population growth (avg. annual %, 1997-2006)	2.0
Population density (people per sq. km, 2006)	36
Labor force (millions, 2006)	6.5
Urban population (% of pop., 2006)	55.5
Age dependency ratio	0.8
Surface area (1,000 sq. km, 2006)	475
GNI ($ billions, 2006)	18
GNI per capita, Atlas method ($, 2006)	1,080
GDP growth (avg. annual %, 2002-06)	3.5
Poverty headcount ratio at national poverty line (% of pop., 2004)	14.9

Migration

EMIGRATION, 2005
- Stock of emigrants: **231,169**
- Stock of emigrants as percentage of population: **1.4%**
- Top 10 destination countries: Chad, France, Gabon, Nigeria, Germany, the United States, the Central African Republic, the Republic of Congo, Italy, the United Kingdom

SKILLED EMIGRATION, 2000
- Emigration rate of tertiary educated: **14.6%**
- Emigration of physicians:
  a) **106** or **8.0%** of physicians trained in the country *(Source: Docquier and Bhargava 2006)*
  b) **845** or **45.6%** of physicians trained in the country *(Source: Clemens and Pettersson 2006)*
- Emigration of nurses: **1,163** or **18.9%** of nurses trained in the country

IMMIGRATION, 2005
- Stock of immigrants: **136,909**
- Stock of immigrants as percentage of population: **0.8%**
- Females as percentage of immigrants: **44.8%**
- Refugees as percentage of immigrants: **43.1%**
- Top 10 source countries: Nigeria, Chad, Gabon, the Republic of Congo, Niger, Benin, Senegal, Mali, Togo, the Democratic Republic of Congo

Remittances

US$ millions	2000	2001	2002	2003	2004	2005	2006	2007
Inward remittance flows	40	20	35	76	103	103	103[a]	103
of which								
Workers' remittances	12	7	14	61	98	..	..	..
Compensation of employees	10	10	15	15	5	..	..	..
Migrants' transfer	18	3	6	0	..	..	..	..
Outward remittance flows	30	42	55	57	43	43	43[b]	..
of which								
Workers' remittances	14	18	27	29	23	..	..	..
Compensation of employees	16	24	28	28	20	..	..	..
Migrants' transfer	..	0	..	0	..	..	..	..

a. **0.6% of GDP in 2006.**
b. **0.2% of GDP in 2006.**

Canada

Population (millions, 2006)	33
Population growth (avg. annual %, 1997-2006)	0.9
Population density (people per sq. km, 2006)	4
Labor force (millions, 2006)	18
Urban population (% of pop., 2006)	80.2
Age dependency ratio	0.44
Surface area (1,000 sq. km, 2006)	9,985
GNI ($ billions, 2006)	1,236
GNI per capita, Atlas method ($, 2006)	36,170
GDP growth (avg. annual %, 2002-06)	2.7
Poverty headcount ratio at national poverty line (% of pop., 2004)	..

Migration

IMMIGRATION, 2005
- Stock of immigrants: **6,105,722**
- Stock of immigrants as percentage of population: **18.9%**
- Females as percentage of immigrants: **52.0%**
- Refugees as percentage of immigrants: **2.4%**
- Top 10 source countries: the United Kingdom, China, India, Italy, the United States, Hong Kong (China), the Philippines, Germany, Poland, Portugal

EMIGRATION, 2005
- Stock of emigrants: **1,340,248**
- Stock of emigrants as percentage of population: **4.2%**
- Top 10 destination countries: the United States, the United Kingdom, Australia, France, Germany, Japan, Greece, the Republic of Korea, Portugal, the Netherlands

SKILLED EMIGRATION, 2000
- Emigration rate of tertiary educated: **4.9%**
- Emigration of physicians: **3,402** or **5.0%** of physicians trained in the country

Remittances
Remittance data are currently not available for this country.

Cape Verde

LOWER MIDDLE INCOME

Population (thousands, 2006)	518
Population growth (avg. annual %, 1997–2006)	2.3
Population density (people per sq. km, 2006)	129
Labor force (thousands, 2006)	169
Urban population (% of pop., 2006)	58
Age dependency ratio	0.76
Surface area (1,000 sq. km, 2006)	4
GNI ($ billions, 2006)	1.1
GNI per capita, Atlas method ($, 2006)	2,130
GDP growth (avg. annual %, 2002–06)	5.6
Poverty headcount ratio at national poverty line (% of pop., 2004)	1.6

Migration

EMIGRATION, 2005
- Stock of emigrants: **181,193**
- Stock of emigrants as percentage of population: **35.8%**
- Top 10 destination countries: Portugal, the United States, Mozambique, Senegal, France, the Netherlands, Italy, Spain, Nigeria, Luxembourg

SKILLED EMIGRATION, 2000
- Emigration rate of tertiary educated: **69.1%**
- Emigration of physicians:
  a) **88** or **54.1%** of physicians trained in the country *(Source: Docquier and Bhargava 2006)*
  b) **211** or **51.1%** of physicians trained in the country *(Source: Clemens and Pettersson 2006)*
- Emigration of nurses: **244** or **40.7%** of nurses trained in the country

IMMIGRATION, 2005
- Stock of immigrants: **11,183**
- Stock of immigrants as percentage of population: **2.2%**
- Females as percentage of immigrants: **50.4%**
- Refugees as percentage of immigrants: **0%**
- Top source countries: São Tomé and Principe, Angola, Portugal, Guinea-Bissau, Italy, Senegal, the Netherlands, Mozambique

Remittances

US$ millions	2000	2001	2002	2003	2004	2005	2006	2007
Inward remittance flows	87	81	85	92	113	137	137[a]	143
of which								
Workers' remittances	86	80	85	108	113	137	136	..
Compensation of employees	1	1	0	0	0	0	1	..
Migrants' transfer	..	..	..	..	..	..	..	..
Outward remittance flows	2	2	2	1	1	5	6[b]	..
of which								
Workers' remittances	0	-	1	7	11	4	5	..
Compensation of employees	0	0	0	1	1	1	1	..
Migrants' transfer	..	..	..	..	..	..	..	..

a. 12.0% of GDP in 2006.
b. 0.5% of GDP in 2006.

Cayman Islands

Population (thousands, 2006)	46
Population growth (avg. annual %, 1997-2006)	..
Population density (people per sq. km, 2006)	177
Labor force (millions, 2006)	..
Urban population (% of pop., 2006)	100
Age dependency ratio	..
Surface area (sq. km, 2006)	260
GNI ($ millions, 2006)	..
GNI per capita, Atlas method ($, 2006)	..
GDP growth (avg. annual %, 2002-06)	..
Poverty headcount ratio at national poverty line (% of pop., 2004)	..

Migration

IMMIGRATION, 2005
- Stock of immigrants: **16,122**
- Stock of immigrants as percentage of population: **35.8%**
- Females as percentage of immigrants: **49.0%**
- Refugees as percentage of immigrants: **0.0%**
- Top 10 source countries: Jamaica, the United States, the United Kingdom, Honduras, Canada, Nicaragua, Cuba, Trinidad and Tobago, Belize, Costa Rica

EMIGRATION, 2005
- Stock of emigrants: **3,633**
- Stock of emigrants as percentage of population: **8.1%**
- Top 10 destination countries: the United States, the United Kingdom, Jamaica, Canada, Virgin Islands (U.S.), Honduras, Ireland, Mexico, Australia, Panama

SKILLED EMIGRATION, 2000
Skilled emigration data are currently not available for this country.

Remittances
Remittance data are currently not available for this country.

Central African Republic, The

Population (millions, 2006)	4.1
Population growth (avg. annual %, 1997–2006)	1.6
Population density (people per sq. km, 2006)	7
Labor force (millions, 2006)	1.9
Urban population (% of pop., 2006)	38.2
Age dependency ratio	0.88
Surface area (1,000 sq. km, 2006)	623
GNI ($ billions, 2006)	1.5
GNI per capita, Atlas method ($, 2006)	360
GDP growth (avg. annual %, 2002–06)	-0.3
Poverty headcount ratio at national poverty line (% of pop., 2004)	63.9

Migration

EMIGRATION, 2005
- Stock of emigrants: **146,557**
- Stock of emigrants as percentage of population: **3.6%**
- Top 10 destination countries: Chad, the Republic of Congo, France, the United Kingdom, the United States, Canada, Germany, Portugal, Switzerland, Sudan

SKILLED EMIGRATION, 2000
- Emigration rate of tertiary educated: **4.7%**
- Emigration of physicians:
  a) **5** or **3.8%** of physicians trained in the country *(Source: Docquier and Bhargava 2006)*
  b) **87** or **42.0%** of physicians trained in the country *(Source: Clemens and Pettersson 2006)*
- Emigration of nurses: **99** or **24.8%** of nurses trained in the country

IMMIGRATION, 2005
- Stock of immigrants: **76,484**
- Stock of immigrants as percentage of population: **1.9%**
- Females as percentage of immigrants: **46.6%**
- Refugees as percentage of immigrants: **24.5%**
- Top 10 source countries: Chad, the Democratic Republic of Congo, Cameroon, France, Sudan, Senegal, Nigeria, the Republic of Congo, Mali, Niger

Remittances
Remittance data are currently not available for this country.

Chad

| LOW INCOME
---|---

Population (millions, 2006)	10
Population growth (avg. annual %, 1997–2006)	3.2
Population density (people per sq. km, 2006)	8
Labor force (millions, 2006)	3.7
Urban population (% of pop., 2006)	25.8
Age dependency ratio	1.01
Surface area (1,000 sq. km, 2006)	1,284
GNI ($ billions, 2006)	5.2
GNI per capita, Atlas method ($, 2006)	480
GDP growth (avg. annual %, 2002–06)	13.3
Poverty headcount ratio at national poverty line (% of pop., 2004)	..

Migration

EMIGRATION, 2005
- Stock of emigrants: **181,442**
- Stock of emigrants as percentage of population: **1.9%**
- Top 10 destination countries: Sudan, the Central African Republic, Cameroon, Nigeria, Saudi Arabia, the Republic of Congo, France, Niger, Canada, the United States

SKILLED EMIGRATION, 2000
- Emigration rate of tertiary educated: **6.9%**
- Emigration of physicians:
  a) **2** or **0.9%** of physicians trained in the country *(Source: Docquier and Bhargava 2006)*
  b) **70** or **22.0%** of physicians trained in the country *(Source: Clemens and Pettersson 2006)*
- Emigration of nurses: **131** or **11.1%** of nurses trained in the country

IMMIGRATION, 2005
- Stock of immigrants: **437,049**
- Stock of immigrants as percentage of population: **4.5%**
- Females as percentage of immigrants: **46.2%**
- Refugees as percentage of immigrants: **79.2%**
- Top 10 source countries: Nigeria, the Central African Republic, Cameroon, Sudan, Niger, Libya, the Republic of Congo, Gabon

Remittances

Remittance data are currently not available for this country.

Chile

Population (millions, 2006)	16
Population growth (avg. annual %, 1997–2006)	1.2
Population density (people per sq. km, 2006)	22
Labor force (millions, 2006)	6.6
Urban population (% of pop., 2006)	87.9
Age dependency ratio	0.48
Surface area (1,000 sq. km, 2006)	757
GNI ($ billions, 2006)	130
GNI per capita, Atlas method ($, 2006)	6,980
GDP growth (avg. annual %, 2002–06)	4.4
Poverty headcount ratio at national poverty line (% of pop., 2004)	0.5

Migration

EMIGRATION, 2005
- Stock of emigrants: **584,869**
- Stock of emigrants as percentage of population: **3.6%**
- Top 10 destination countries: Argentina, the United States, Spain, Sweden, Canada, Australia, Brazil, República Bolivariana de Venezuela, France, Germany

SKILLED EMIGRATION, 2000
- Emigration rate of tertiary educated: **5.3%**
- Emigration of physicians: **392** or **2.2%** of physicians trained in the country

IMMIGRATION, 2005
- Stock of immigrants: **231,496**
- Stock of immigrants as percentage of population: **1.4%**
- Females as percentage of immigrants: **52.3%**
- Refugees as percentage of immigrants: **0.3%**
- Top 10 source countries: Argentina, Peru, Bolivia, Ecuador, Spain, the United States, Brazil, Germany, República Bolivariana de Venezuela, Colombia

Remittances

US$ millions	2000	2001	2002	2003	2004	2005	2006	2007
Inward remittance flows	13	12	12	12	12	13	3ª	3
of which								
Workers' remittances	..	..	..	..	..	..	..	..
Compensation of employees	13	12	12	12	12	13	3	..
Migrants' transfer	..	..	..	..	..	..	..	..
Outward remittance flows	16	16	16	15	15	16	6ᵇ	..
of which								
Workers' remittances	..	..	..	..	..	..	..	..
Compensation of employees	16	16	16	15	15	16	6	..
Migrants' transfer	..	..	..	..	..	..	..	..

a. 0.002% of GDP in 2006.
b. 0.004% of GDP in 2006.

China

LOWER MIDDLE INCOME

Population (millions, 2006)	1,312
Population growth (avg. annual %, 1997–2006)	0.7
Population density (people per sq. km, 2006)	141
Labor force (millions, 2006)	783
Urban population (% of pop., 2006)	41.3
Age dependency ratio	0.4
Surface area (1,000 sq. km, 2006)	9,598
GNI ($ billions, 2006)	2,695
GNI per capita, Atlas method ($, 2006)	2,010
GDP growth (avg. annual %, 2002–06)	10
Poverty headcount ratio at national poverty line (% of pop., 2004)	10.3

Migration

EMIGRATION, 2005
- Stock of emigrants: **7,258,333**
- Stock of emigrants as percentage of population: **0.6%**
- Top 10 destination countries: the United States, Singapore, Japan, Canada, Thailand, Malaysia, the Republic of Korea, Australia, Italy, Germany

SKILLED EMIGRATION, 2000
- Emigration rate of tertiary educated: **4.2%**
- Emigration of physicians: **2,407** or **0.1%** of physicians trained in the country

IMMIGRATION, 2005
- Stock of immigrants: **595,658**
- Stock of immigrants as percentage of population: **0.1%**
- Females as percentage of immigrants: **49.1%**
- Refugees as percentage of immigrants: **50.3%**

Remittances

US$ millions	2000	2001	2002	2003	2004	2005	2006	2007
Inward remittance flows	6,244	8,385	13,012	17,815	19,014	20,337	23,319[a]	25,703
of which								
Workers' remittances	556	912	1,679	3,343	4,627	5,495	6,830	..
Compensation of employees	202	297	674	1,283	2,014	3,337	4,319	..
Migrants' transfer	..	..	..	..	..	..	..	..
Outward remittance flows	790	990	1,223	1,645	2,067	2,602	3,025[b]	..
of which								
Workers' remittances	75	84	223	477	616	732	695	..
Compensation of employees	679	852	950	1,120	1,382	1,817	2,330	..
Migrants' transfer	35	54	50	48	69	53	..	..

a. 0.9% of GDP in 2006.
b. 0.1% of GDP in 2006.

Migration and Remittances Factbook 2008

Colombia

Population (millions, 2006)	46
Population growth (avg. annual %, 1997-2006)	1.6
Population density (people per sq. km, 2006)	41
Labor force (millions, 2006)	23
Urban population (% of pop., 2006)	73
Age dependency ratio	0.56
Surface area (1,000 sq. km, 2006)	1,142
GNI ($ billions, 2006)	130
GNI per capita, Atlas method ($, 2006)	2,740
GDP growth (avg. annual %, 2002-06)	4.4
Poverty headcount ratio at national poverty line (% of pop., 2004)	7.6

Migration

EMIGRATION, 2005
- Stock of emigrants: **1,969,282**
- Stock of emigrants as percentage of population: **4.3%**
- Top 10 destination countries: República Bolivariana de Venezuela, the United States, Spain, Ecuador, Panama, Canada, Italy, France, the United Kingdom, Germany

SKILLED EMIGRATION, 2000
- Emigration rate of tertiary educated: **11.0%**
- Emigration of physicians: **945** or **2.0%** of physicians trained in the country

IMMIGRATION, 2005
- Stock of immigrants: **122,713**
- Stock of immigrants as percentage of population: **0.3%**
- Females as percentage of immigrants: **49.9%**
- Refugees as percentage of immigrants: **0.1%**
- Top 10 source countries: República Bolivariana de Venezuela, the United States, Ecuador, Spain, Peru, Germany, Argentina, Italy, Panama, Lebanon

Remittances

US$ millions	2000	2001	2002	2003	2004	2005	2006	2007
Inward remittance flows	1,610	2,056	2,480	3,076	3,190	3,346	3,929[a]	4,600
of which								
Workers' remittances	1,578	2,021	2,454	3,060	3,170	3,314	3,890	..
Compensation of employees	32	35	26	16	20	32	39	..
Migrants' transfer	..	..	..	..	..	..	..	..
Outward remittance flows	219	204	158	65	50	56	66[b]	..
of which								
Workers' remittances	207	192	144	52	31	37	47	..
Compensation of employees	12	12	14	12	19	19	19	..
Migrants' transfer	..	..	..	..	..	..	..	..

a. 2.9% of GDP in 2006.
b. 0.05% of GDP in 2006.

Comoros

LOW INCOME

Population (thousands, 2006)	614
Population growth (avg. annual %, 1997–2006)	2.1
Population density (people per sq. km, 2006)	275
Labor force (thousands, 2006)	259
Urban population (% of pop., 2006)	37.7
Age dependency ratio	0.8
Surface area (1,000 sq. km, 2006)	2
GNI ($ millions, 2006)	401
GNI per capita, Atlas method ($, 2006)	660
GDP growth (avg. annual %, 2002–06)	2.2
Poverty headcount ratio at national poverty line (% of pop., 2004)	..

Migration

EMIGRATION, 2005
- Stock of emigrants: **38,433**
- Stock of emigrants as percentage of population: **4.8%**
- Top 10 destination countries: France, Madagascar, Tanzania, the United States, Germany, the United Kingdom, Canada, Bahrain, Belgium, Australia

SKILLED EMIGRATION, 2000
- Emigration rate of tertiary educated: **14.5%**
- Emigration of physicians:
  a) **1** or **3.4%** of physicians trained in the country *(Source: Docquier and Bhargava 2006)*
  b) **24** or **32.4%** of physicians trained in the country *(Source: Clemens and Pettersson 2006)*
- Emigration of nurses: **70** or **23.3%** of nurses trained in the country

IMMIGRATION, 2005
- Stock of immigrants: **67,185**
- Stock of immigrants as percentage of population: **8.4%**
- Females as percentage of immigrants: **52.6%**
- Refugees as percentage of immigrants: **0%**
- Top source countries: France, Madagascar, India

Remittances

US$ millions	2000	2001	2002	2003	2004	2005	2006	2007
Inward remittance flows	12	12	12	12	12	12	12[a]	12
of which								
Workers' remittances	..	..	..	..	..	..	..	..
Compensation of employees	..	..	..	..	..	..	..	..
Migrants' transfer	..	..	..	..	..	..	..	..
Outward remittance flows	..	..	..	..	..	..	..	..
of which								
Workers' remittances	..	..	..	..	..	..	..	..
Compensation of employees	..	..	..	..	..	..	..	..
Migrants' transfer	..	..	..	..	..	..	..	..

a. 3.0% of GDP in 2006.

Congo, The Democratic Republic of

LOW INCOME

Population (millions, 2006)	59
Population growth (avg. annual %, 1997–2006)	2.5
Population density (people per sq. km, 2006)	26
Labor force (millions, 2006)	24
Urban population (% of pop., 2006)	32.7
Age dependency ratio	1
Surface area (1,000 sq. km, 2006)	2,345
GNI ($ billions, 2006)	8.1
GNI per capita, Atlas method ($, 2006)	130
GDP growth (avg. annual %, 2002–06)	5.5
Poverty headcount ratio at national poverty line (% of pop., 2004)	..

Migration

EMIGRATION, 2005

- Stock of emigrants: **571,625**
- Stock of emigrants as percentage of population: **1.0%**
- Top 10 destination countries: the Republic of Congo, Rwanda, Uganda, Zambia, Belgium, France, Germany, the Central African Republic, Canada, the United Kingdom

SKILLED EMIGRATION, 2000

- Emigration rate of tertiary educated: **7.9%**
- Emigration of physicians:
  a) **212** or **5.9%** of physicians trained in the country *(Source: Docquier and Bhargava 2006)*
  b) **552** or **8.9%** of physicians trained in the country *(Source: Clemens and Pettersson 2006)*
- Emigration of nurses: **2,288** or **11.9%** of nurses trained in the country

IMMIGRATION, 2005

- Stock of immigrants: **538,838**
- Stock of immigrants as percentage of population: **0.9%**
- Females as percentage of immigrants: **46.2%**
- Refugees as percentage of immigrants: **34.1%**

Remittances

Remittance data are currently not available for this country.

Congo, The Republic of

LOWER MIDDLE INCOME

Population (millions, 2006)	4.1
Population growth (avg. annual %, 1997–2006)	3.1
Population density (people per sq. km, 2006)	12
Labor force (millions, 2006)	1.5
Urban population (% of pop., 2006)	60.6
Age dependency ratio	1.01
Surface area (1,000 sq. km, 2006)	342
GNI ($ billions, 2006)	4.5
GNI per capita, Atlas method ($, 2006)	950
GDP growth (avg. annual %, 2002–06)	4.8
Poverty headcount ratio at national poverty line (% of pop., 2004)	..

Migration

EMIGRATION, 2005
- Stock of emigrants: **194,079**
- Stock of emigrants as percentage of population: **4.9%**
- Top 10 destination countries: Tanzania, France, Belgium, Gabon, the United States, Zambia, the United Kingdom, the Netherlands, Spain, Germany

SKILLED EMIGRATION, 2000
- Emigration rate of tertiary educated: **19.1%**
- Emigration of physicians:
  a) **75** or **8.0%** of physicians trained in the country *(Source: Docquier and Bhargava 2006)*
  b) **747** or **52.7%** of physicians trained in the country *(Source: Clemens and Pettersson 2006)*
- Emigration of nurses: **660** or **11.8%** of nurses trained in the country

IMMIGRATION, 2005
- Stock of immigrants: **287,603**
- Stock of immigrants as percentage of population: **7.2%**
- Females as percentage of immigrants: **49.6%**
- Refugees as percentage of immigrants: **20.6%**
- Top 10 source countries: the Democratic Republic of Congo, France, Angola, the Central African Republic, Mali, Benin, Senegal, Chad, Cameroon, Mauritania

Remittances

US$ millions	2000	2001	2002	2003	2004	2005	2006	2007
Inward remittance flows	10	12	1	13	15	11	11[a]	11
of which								
Workers' remittances	1	2	1	5	6	..	..	..
Compensation of employees	9	10	..	8	9	11	..	..
Migrants' transfer	..	..	..	..	..	..	..	..
Outward remittance flows	37	32	35	40	50	45	45[b]	..
of which								
Workers' remittances	4	3	4	6	7	..	..	..
Compensation of employees	32	29	31	34	43	45	..	..
Migrants' transfer	..	..	..	..	..	..	..	..

a. 0.1% of GDP in 2006.
b. 0.6% of GDP in 2006.

Migration and Remittances Factbook 2008

Costa Rica

UPPER MIDDLE INCOME

Population (millions, 2006)	4.4
Population growth (avg. annual %, 1997–2006)	2.1
Population density (people per sq. km, 2006)	86
Labor force (millions, 2006)	2.0
Urban population (% of pop., 2006)	62.2
Age dependency ratio	0.51
Surface area (1,000 sq. km, 2006)	51
GNI ($ billions, 2006)	21
GNI per capita, Atlas method ($, 2006)	4,980
GDP growth (avg. annual %, 2002–06)	5.5
Poverty headcount ratio at national poverty line (% of pop., 2004)	1.8

Migration

EMIGRATION, 2005
- Stock of emigrants: **127,061**
- Stock of emigrants as percentage of population: **2.9%**
- Top 10 destination countries: the United States, Panama, Nicaragua, Spain, Mexico, Canada, Germany, República Bolivariana de Venezuela, the Dominican Republic, Guatemala

SKILLED EMIGRATION, 2000
- Emigration rate of tertiary educated: **6.6%**
- Emigration of physicians: **161** or **2.4%** of physicians trained in the country

IMMIGRATION, 2005
- Stock of immigrants: **440,957**
- Stock of immigrants as percentage of population: **10.2%**
- Females as percentage of immigrants: **49.8%**
- Refugees as percentage of immigrants: **2.1%**
- Top source countries: Nicaragua, Panama, El Salvador, Honduras, Guatemala, Belize

Remittances

US$ millions	2000	2001	2002	2003	2004	2005	2006	2007
Inward remittance flows	**136**	**198**	**250**	**321**	**319**	**421**	**513ª**	**590**
of which								
Workers' remittances	120	184	234	306	302	400	490	..
Compensation of employees	16	14	16	15	17	21	23	..
Migrants' transfer	..	..	..	..	..	..	..	..
Outward remittance flows	**142**	**140**	**148**	**192**	**192**	**209**	**246ᵇ**	..
of which								
Workers' remittances	108	107	112	156	155	196	233	..
Compensation of employees	34	34	35	36	37	13	13	..
Migrants' transfer	..	..	..	..	..	..	..	..

a. 2.3% of GDP in 2006.
b. 1.1% of GDP in 2006.

Côte d'Ivoire

Sub-Saharan Africa	LOW INCOME
Population (millions, 2006)	18
Population growth (avg. annual %, 1997–2006)	2.0
Population density (people per sq. km, 2006)	58
Labor force (millions, 2006)	6.9
Urban population (% of pop., 2006)	45.4
Age dependency ratio	0.81
Surface area (1,000 sq. km, 2006)	322
GNI ($ billions, 2006)	16
GNI per capita, Atlas method ($, 2006)	870
GDP growth (avg. annual %, 2002–06)	0.4
Poverty headcount ratio at national poverty line (% of pop., 2004)	18

Migration

EMIGRATION, 2005
- Stock of emigrants: **151,755**
- Stock of emigrants as percentage of population: **0.8%**
- Top 10 destination countries: France, Burkina Faso, Benin, Italy, the United States, Niger, Germany, Nigeria, the United Kingdom, Canada

SKILLED EMIGRATION, 2000
- Emigration rate of tertiary educated: **7.8**%
- Emigration of physicians:
  a) **11** or **0.8%** of physicians trained in the country *(Source: Docquier and Bhargava 2006)*
  b) **284** or **13.9%** of physicians trained in the country *(Source: Clemens and Pettersson 2006)*
- Emigration of nurses: **509** or **6.6%** of nurses trained in the country

IMMIGRATION, 2005
- Stock of immigrants: **2,371,277**
- Stock of immigrants as percentage of population: **13.1%**
- Females as percentage of immigrants: **45.1%**
- Refugees as percentage of immigrants: **3.0%**
- Top source countries: Burkina Faso, Mali, Ghana, Guinea, Niger, Benin, France, Lebanon, the United States

Remittances

US$ millions	2000	2001	2002	2003	2004	2005	2006	2007
Inward remittance flows	119	116	120	142	159	163	164[a]	176
of which								
Workers' remittances	..	..	0	..	1	2	..	..
Compensation of employees	119	116	120	142	158	161	164	..
Migrants' transfer	..	..	..	..	..	..	..	..
Outward remittance flows	390	380	574	628	591	597	597[b]	..
of which								
Workers' remittances	379	368	562	613	575	580	..	..
Compensation of employees	11	11	12	15	16	17	17	..
Migrants' transfer	..	..	..	..	..	..	..	..

a. 0.9% of GDP in 2006.
b. 3.4% of GDP in 2006.

Croatia

Population (millions, 2006)	4.4
Population growth (avg. annual %, 1997–2006)	-0.1
Population density (people per sq. km, 2006)	79
Labor force (millions, 2006)	1.9
Urban population (% of pop., 2006)	56.8
Age dependency ratio	0.48
Surface area (1,000 sq. km, 2006)	57
GNI ($ billions, 2006)	41
GNI per capita, Atlas method ($, 2006)	9,330
GDP growth (avg. annual %, 2002–06)	4.7
Poverty headcount ratio at national poverty line (% of pop., 2004)	0

Migration

EMIGRATION, 2005
- Stock of emigrants: **726,031**
- Stock of emigrants as percentage of population: **16.0%**
- Top 10 destination countries: Germany, Australia, Austria, the United States, Canada, France, Italy, Slovenia, Switzerland, Bosnia and Herzegovina

SKILLED EMIGRATION, 2000
- Emigration rate of tertiary educated: **29.4%**
- Emigration of physicians: **286** or **2.7%** of physicians trained in the country

IMMIGRATION, 2005
- Stock of immigrants: **661,417**
- Stock of immigrants as percentage of population: **14.5%**
- Females as percentage of immigrants: **52.9%**
- Refugees as percentage of immigrants: **0.5%**
- Top 10 source countries: Bosnia and Herzegovina, Serbia and Montenegro, Slovenia, FYR Macedonia, Germany, Italy, Austria, the United States, Australia, Switzerland

Remittances

US$ millions	2000	2001	2002	2003	2004	2005	2006	2007
Inward remittance flows	**641**	**747**	**885**	**1,085**	**1,221**	**1,222**	**1,233ª**	**1,788**
of which								
Workers' remittances	534	583	677	797	851	845	689	..
Compensation of employees	83	141	177	247	333	359	510	..
Migrants' transfer	24	23	31	41	37	18	34	..
Outward remittance flows	**44**	**46**	**51**	**67**	**69**	**62**	**274ᵇ**	..
of which								
Workers' remittances	27	29	26	17	17	21	27	..
Compensation of employees	13	13	19	38	43	36	39	..
Migrants' transfer	4	5	7	12	9	5	208	..

a. 2.9% of GDP in 2006.
b. 0.6% of GDP in 2006.

Cuba

Population (millions, 2006)	11
Population growth (avg. annual %, 1997–2006)	0.3
Population density (people per sq. km, 2006)	103
Labor force (millions, 2006)	5.4
Urban population (% of pop., 2006)	75.4
Age dependency ratio	0.42
Surface area (1,000 sq. km, 2006)	111
GNI ($ millions, 2006)	..
GNI per capita, Atlas method ($, 2006)	..
GDP growth (avg. annual %, 2002–06)	3.7
Poverty headcount ratio at national poverty line (% of pop., 2004)	..

Migration

EMIGRATION, 2005
- Stock of emigrants: **1,291,970**
- Stock of emigrants as percentage of population: **11.5%**
- Top 10 destination countries: the United States, Spain, Italy, Germany, República Bolivariana de Venezuela, Mexico, Canada, Haiti, Chile, the Dominican Republic

SKILLED EMIGRATION, 2000
- Emigration rate of tertiary educated: **28.9%**
- Emigration of physicians: **1,231** or **1.8%** of physicians trained in the country

IMMIGRATION, 2005
- Stock of immigrants: **73,938**
- Stock of immigrants as percentage of population: **0.7%**
- Females as percentage of immigrants: **26.7%**
- Refugees as percentage of immigrants: **1.0%**
- Top source countries: Haiti, Jamaica, Mexico, the Dominican Republic, República Bolivariana de Venezuela, Argentina, Colombia, Bolivia

Remittances

Remittance data are currently not available for this country.

Cyprus

Population (thousands, 2006)	765
Population growth (avg. annual %, 1997–2006)	1.5
Population density (people per sq. km, 2006)	83
Labor force (thousands, 2006)	381
Urban population (% of pop., 2006)	69.5
Age dependency ratio	0.46
Surface area (1,000 sq. km, 2006)	9
GNI ($ billions, 2006)	15
GNI per capita, Atlas method ($, 2006)	18,430
GDP growth (avg. annual %, 2002–06)	2.6
Poverty headcount ratio at national poverty line (% of pop., 2004)	..

Migration

IMMIGRATION, 2005

- Stock of immigrants: **116,137**
- Stock of immigrants as percentage of population: **13.9%**
- Females as percentage of immigrants: **58.7%**
- Refugees as percentage of immigrants: **0.6%**
- Top 10 source countries: the United Kingdom, Greece, Georgia, Russia, Sri Lanka, the Philippines, Bulgaria, Romania, Egypt, South Africa

EMIGRATION, 2005

- Stock of emigrants: **160,728**
- Stock of emigrants as percentage of population: **19.2%**
- Top 10 destination countries: the United Kingdom, Australia, Greece, the United States, Turkey, Canada, Germany, France, Sweden, Ireland

SKILLED EMIGRATION, 2000

- Emigration rate of tertiary educated: **17.9%**
- Emigration of physicians: **132** or **5.5%** of physicians trained in the country

Remittances

US$ millions	2000	2001	2002	2003	2004	2005	2006	2007
Inward remittance flows	64	105	61	83	245	190	172	172
of which								
Workers' remittances	..	..	5	6	44	51	71	..
Compensation of employees	45	78	15	25	33	54	35	..
Migrants' transfer	19	27	41	52	168	85	66	..
Outward remittance flows	63	100	117	202	255	273	283	..
of which								
Workers' remittances	..	..	26	47	54	55	56	..
Compensation of employees	48	79	81	137	159	185	187	..
Migrants' transfer	14	21	10	18	42	33	40	..

Czech Republic, The

Population (millions, 2006)	10
Population growth (avg. annual %, 1997–2006)	–0.1
Population density (people per sq. km, 2006)	132
Labor force (millions, 2006)	5.2
Urban population (% of pop., 2006)	73.5
Age dependency ratio	0.4
Surface area (1,000 sq. km, 2006)	79
GNI ($ billions, 2006)	134
GNI per capita, Atlas method ($, 2006)	12,680
GDP growth (avg. annual %, 2002–06)	4.4
Poverty headcount ratio at national poverty line (% of pop., 2004)	0

Migration

EMIGRATION, 2005

- Stock of emigrants: **418,175**
- Stock of emigrants as percentage of population: **4.1%**
- Top 10 destination countries: the Slovak Republic, Austria, the United States, Germany, Canada, Israel, the United Kingdom, Switzerland, France, Australia

SKILLED EMIGRATION, 2000

- Emigration rate of tertiary educated: **9.9%**
- Emigration of physicians: **1,112** or **3.1%** of physicians trained in the country

IMMIGRATION, 2005

- Stock of immigrants: **453,265**
- Stock of immigrants as percentage of population: **4.4%**
- Females as percentage of immigrants: **53.8%**
- Refugees as percentage of immigrants: **0.2%**
- Top 10 source countries: the Slovak Republic, Ukraine, Poland, Vietnam, Russia, Romania, Germany, Austria, Hungary, Serbia and Montenegro

Remittances

US$ millions	2000	2001	2002	2003	2004	2005	2006	2007
Inward remittance flows	297	257	335	499	814	1,018	1,186ª	1,300
of which								
Workers' remittances	..	..	..	..	..	92	128	..
Compensation of employees	294	256	333	494	805	917	1,050	..
Migrants' transfer	3	0	2	5	9	9	8	..
Outward remittance flows	605	718	898	1,103	1,431	2,030	2,831ᵇ	..
of which								
Workers' remittances	..	..	..	..		130	186	..
Compensation of employees	603	711	893	1,100	1,426	1,898	2,642	..
Migrants' transfer	2	7	5	3	5	2	3	..

a. 0.8% of GDP in 2006.
b. 2.0% of GDP in 2006.

Denmark

Population (millions, 2006)	5.4
Population growth (avg. annual %, 1997–2006)	0.3
Population density (people per sq. km, 2006)	128
Labor force (millions, 2006)	2.8
Urban population (% of pop., 2006)	85.7
Age dependency ratio	0.51
Surface area (1,000 sq. km, 2006)	43
GNI ($ billions, 2006)	276
GNI per capita, Atlas method ($, 2006)	51,700
GDP growth (avg. annual %, 2002–06)	1.9
Poverty headcount ratio at national poverty line (% of pop., 2004)	..

Migration

IMMIGRATION, 2005
- Stock of immigrants: **388,535**
- Stock of immigrants as percentage of population: **7.2%**
- Females as percentage of immigrants: **50.8%**
- Refugees as percentage of immigrants: **16.3%**
- Top 10 source countries: Turkey, Germany, Sweden, Iraq, Bosnia and Herzegovina, Norway, the United Kingdom, Lebanon, Somalia, Serbia and Montenegro

EMIGRATION, 2005
- Stock of emigrants: **234,008**
- Stock of emigrants as percentage of population: **4.3%**
- Top 10 destination countries: Sweden, the United States, Germany, the United Kingdom, Norway, Canada, Spain, Australia, France, Switzerland

SKILLED EMIGRATION, 2000
- Emigration rate of tertiary educated: **7.0%**
- Emigration of physicians: **927** or **4.9%** of physicians trained in the country

Remittances

US$ millions	2000	2001	2002	2003	2004	2005	2006	2007
Inward remittance flows	667	699	785	941	1,075	868	869[a]	869
of which								
Workers' remittances	..	..	..	..	..	..	..	..
Compensation of employees	667	699	785	941	1,075	868	869	..
Migrants' transfer	..	..	..	..	..	..	..	..
Outward remittance flows	662	745	860	1,029	1,226	1,480	1,792[b]	..
of which								
Workers' remittances	..	..	..	..	..	..	..	..
Compensation of employees	662	745	860	1,029	1,226	1,480	1,792	..
Migrants' transfer	..	..	..	..	..	..	..	..

a. 0.3% of GDP in 2006.
b. 0.7% of GDP in 2006.

Djibouti

Population (thousands, 2006)	806
Population growth (avg. annual %, 1997–2006)	2.5
Population density (people per sq. km, 2006)	35
Labor force (thousands, 2006)	322
Urban population (% of pop., 2006)	86.5
Age dependency ratio	0.79
Surface area (1,000 sq. km, 2006)	23
GNI ($ millions, 2006)	838
GNI per capita, Atlas method ($, 2006)	1,060
GDP growth (avg. annual %, 2002-06)	3.4
Poverty headcount ratio at national poverty line (% of pop., 2004)	..

Migration

EMIGRATION, 2005
- Stock of emigrants: **13,021**
- Stock of emigrants as percentage of population: **1.6%**
- Top 10 destination countries: France, Ethiopia, Canada, the United States, the United Kingdom, the Netherlands, Germany, Sudan, Australia, Sweden

SKILLED EMIGRATION, 2000
- Emigration rate of tertiary educated: **17.8%**
- Emigration of physicians:
  - a) **2** or **2.6%** of physicians trained in the country *(Source: Docquier and Bhargava 2006)*
  - b) **26** or **23.2%** of physicians trained in the country *(Source: Clemens and Pettersson 2006)*
- Emigration of nurses: **9** or **2.1%** of nurses trained in the country

IMMIGRATION, 2005
- Stock of immigrants: **20,272**
- Stock of immigrants as percentage of population: **2.6%**
- Females as percentage of immigrants: **46.5%**
- Refugees as percentage of immigrants: **72.7%**

Remittances

US$ millions	2000	2001	2002	2003	2004	2005	2006	2007
Inward remittance flows	12	12	15	25	25	26	28[a]	28
of which								
Workers' remittances	1	1	1	3	3	3	4	..
Compensation of employees	12	11	14	22	22	23	25	..
Migrants' transfer	..	..	..	..	..	..	..	..
Outward remittance flows	2	2	2	5	5	5	5[b]	..
of which								
Workers' remittances	2	2	2	5	5	5	5	..
Compensation of employees	..	..	..	..	..	..	..	..
Migrants' transfer	..	..	..	..	..	..	..	..

a. 3.8% of GDP in 2006.
b. 0.6% of GDP in 2006.

Dominica

Population (thousands, 2006)	72
Population growth (avg. annual %, 1997-2006)	0
Population density (people per sq. km, 2006)	97
Labor force (millions, 2006)	..
Urban population (% of pop., 2006)	73.2
Age dependency ratio	..
Surface area (sq. km, 2006)	750
GNI ($ millions, 2006)	278
GNI per capita, Atlas method ($, 2006)	3,960
GDP growth (avg. annual %, 2002-06)	2.4
Poverty headcount ratio at national poverty line (% of pop., 2004)	..

Migration

EMIGRATION, 2005
- Stock of emigrants: **42,723**
- Stock of emigrants as percentage of population: **54.1%**
- Top 10 destination countries: the United States, the United Kingdom, Virgin Islands (U.S.), Antigua and Barbuda, Canada, Spain, France, Barbados, Greece, Italy

SKILLED EMIGRATION, 2000
- Emigration rate of tertiary educated: **58.9%**
- Emigration of physicians: **1,214** or **97.2%** of physicians trained in the country

IMMIGRATION, 2005
- Stock of immigrants: **4,526**
- Stock of immigrants as percentage of population: **5.7%**
- Females as percentage of immigrants: **46.2%**
- Refugees as percentage of immigrants: **0.0%**
- Top 10 source countries: the United Kingdom, the United States, Antigua and Barbuda, Guadeloupe, Martinique, Canada, Barbados, Trinidad and Tobago, Grenada, Guyana

Remittances

US$ millions	2000	2001	2002	2003	2004	2005	2006	2007
Inward remittance flows	3	4	4	4	4	4	4[a]	4
of which								
Workers' remittances	..	..	..	..	..	..	..	..
Compensation of employees	1	1	1	1	2	1	..	..
Migrants' transfer	3	3	3	3	3	3	..	..
Outward remittance flows	0	0	0	0	0	0	0[b]	..
of which								
Workers' remittances	..	..	..	..	..	..	..	..
Compensation of employees	0	..	..	..	..	..	..	..
Migrants' transfer	0	0	0	0	0	0	..	..

a. 1.3% of GDP in 2006.
b. 0.03% of GDP in 2006.

Dominican Republic, The

Latin America and the Caribbean   **LOWER MIDDLE INCOME**

Population (millions, 2006)	9.6
Population growth (avg. annual %, 1997–2006)	1.7
Population density (people per sq. km, 2006)	199
Labor force (millions, 2006)	4.2
Urban population (% of pop., 2006)	67.5
Age dependency ratio	0.58
Surface area (1,000 sq. km, 2006)	49
GNI ($ billions, 2006)	29
GNI per capita, Atlas method ($, 2006)	2,850
GDP growth (avg. annual %, 2002–06)	4.9
Poverty headcount ratio at national poverty line (% of pop., 2004)	2.8

Migration

EMIGRATION, 2005
- Stock of emigrants: **1,068,919**
- Stock of emigrants as percentage of population: **12.0%**
- Top 10 destination countries: the United States, Spain, Italy, República Bolivariana de Venezuela, Netherlands Antilles, Haiti, Germany, Panama, the Netherlands, Guadeloupe

SKILLED EMIGRATION, 2000
- Emigration rate of tertiary educated: **21.7%**
- Emigration of physicians: **3,573** or **18.5%** of physicians trained in the country

IMMIGRATION, 2005
- Stock of immigrants: **156,493**
- Stock of immigrants as percentage of population: **1.8%**
- Females as percentage of immigrants: **38.9%**
- Refugees as percentage of immigrants: **0.0%**
- Top 10 source countries: Haiti, República Bolivariana de Venezuela, the United States, Puerto Rico, Spain, Italy, Cuba, Germany, Colombia, Canada

Remittances

US$ millions	2000	2001	2002	2003	2004	2005	2006	2007
Inward remittance flows	1,839	1,982	2,195	2,326	2,501	2,719	3,044[a]	3,200
of which								
Workers' remittances	1,689	1,808	1,960	2,061	2,230	2,430	2,748	..
Compensation of employees	150	174	235	265	271	289	296	..
Migrants' transfer	..	..	..	..	..	..	..	..
Outward remittance flows	19	22	23	23	24	25	27[b]	..
of which								
Workers' remittances	..	..	..	..	..	..	..	..
Compensation of employees	19	22	23	23	24	25	27	..
Migrants' transfer	..	..	..	..	..	..	..	..

a. 10.0% of GDP in 2006.
b. 0.1% of GDP in 2006.

Ecuador

Latin America and the Caribbean   LOWER MIDDLE INCOME

Population (millions, 2006)	13
Population growth (avg. annual %, 1997–2006)	1.5
Population density (people per sq. km, 2006)	48
Labor force (millions, 2006)	6.5
Urban population (% of pop., 2006)	63.3
Age dependency ratio	0.61
Surface area (1,000 sq. km, 2006)	284
GNI ($ billions, 2006)	39
GNI per capita, Atlas method ($, 2006)	2,840
GDP growth (avg. annual %, 2002–06)	5.0
Poverty headcount ratio at national poverty line (% of pop., 2004)	14.7

Migration

EMIGRATION, 2005
- Stock of emigrants: **1,016,037**
- Stock of emigrants as percentage of population: **7.7%**
- Top 10 destination countries: Spain, the United States, República Bolivariana de Venezuela, Italy, Canada, Chile, Colombia, Germany, the United Kingdom, Panama

SKILLED EMIGRATION, 2000
- Emigration rate of tertiary educated: **10.9%**
- Emigration of physicians: **234** or **1.3%** of physicians trained in the country

IMMIGRATION, 2005
- Stock of immigrants: **114,370**
- Stock of immigrants as percentage of population: **0.9%**
- Females as percentage of immigrants: **49.6%**
- Refugees as percentage of immigrants: **8.5%**
- Top 10 source countries: Colombia, the United States, Peru, Chile, República Bolivariana de Venezuela, Spain, Argentina, Germany, Italy, Cuba

Remittances

US$ millions	2000	2001	2002	2003	2004	2005	2006	2007
Inward remittance flows	1,322	1,421	1,438	1,633	1,838	2,461	2,922ª	3,178
of which								
Workers' remittances	1,317	1,415	1,432	1,627	1,832	2,454	2,916	..
Compensation of employees	6	6	6	6	6	7	6	..
Migrants' transfer	..	..	..	..	..	..	..	..
Outward remittance flows	6	7	7	7	7	54	62ᵇ	..
of which								
Workers' remittances	..	..	..	..	..	48	57	..
Compensation of employees	6	7	7	7	7	6	5	..
Migrants' transfer	..	..	..	..	..	..	..	..

a. 7.2% of GDP in 2006.
b. 0.2% of GDP in 2006.

Egypt, The Arab Republic of

Middle East and North Africa	LOWER MIDDLE INCOME
Population (millions, 2006)	75
Population growth (avg. annual %, 1997–2006)	1.9
Population density (people per sq. km, 2006)	76
Labor force (millions, 2006)	23
Urban population (% of pop., 2006)	43
Age dependency ratio	0.62
Surface area (1,000 sq. km, 2006)	1,001
GNI ($ billions, 2006)	108
GNI per capita, Atlas method ($, 2006)	1,350
GDP growth (avg. annual %, 2002–06)	4.4
Poverty headcount ratio at national poverty line (% of pop., 2004)	2.3

Migration

EMIGRATION, 2005
- Stock of emigrants: **2,399,251**
- Stock of emigrants as percentage of population: **3.2%**
- Top 10 destination countries: Saudi Arabia, Libya, the United States, West Bank and Gaza, Italy, Canada, Oman, Australia, Israel, Greece

SKILLED EMIGRATION, 2000
- Emigration rate of tertiary educated: **4.2%**
- Emigration of physicians:
  a) **2,968** or **2.1%** of physicians trained in the country *(Source: Docquier and Bhargava 2006)*
  b) **7,119** or **4.7%** of physicians trained in the country *(Source: Clemens and Pettersson 2006)*
- Emigration of nurses: **992** or **0.5%** of nurses trained in the country

IMMIGRATION, 2005
- Stock of immigrants: **166,047**
- Stock of immigrants as percentage of population: **0.2%**
- Females as percentage of immigrants: **46.7%**
- Refugees as percentage of immigrants: **54.9%**

Remittances

US$ millions	2000	2001	2002	2003	2004	2005	2006	2007
Inward remittance flows	2,852	2,911	2,893	2,961	3,341	5,017	5,330[a]	5,865
of which								
Workers' remittances	2,852	2,911	2,893	2,961	3,341	5,017	5,330	..
Compensation of employees	..	..	..	..	..	..	..	..
Migrants' transfer	..	..	..	..	..	..	..	..
Outward remittance flows	32	35	14	79	13	57	135[b]	..
of which								
Workers' remittances	32	35	14	79	13	57	135	..
Compensation of employees	..	..	..	..	..	..	..	..
Migrants' transfer	..	..	..	..	..	..	..	..

a. 5.0% of GDP in 2006.
b. 0.1% of GDP in 2006.

El Salvador

Latin America and the Caribbean	LOWER MIDDLE INCOME
Population (millions, 2006)	7.0
Population growth (avg. annual %, 1997–2006)	1.9
Population density (people per sq. km, 2006)	337
Labor force (millions, 2006)	2.8
Urban population (% of pop., 2006)	60.1
Age dependency ratio	0.64
Surface area (1,000 sq. km, 2006)	21
GNI ($ billions, 2006)	18
GNI per capita, Atlas method ($, 2006)	2,540
GDP growth (avg. annual %, 2002–06)	2.6
Poverty headcount ratio at national poverty line (% of pop., 2004)	20.4

Migration

EMIGRATION, 2005
- Stock of emigrants: **1,128,701**
- Stock of emigrants as percentage of population: **16.4%**
- Top 10 destination countries: the United States, Canada, Guatemala, Costa Rica, Australia, Belize, Mexico, Spain, Honduras, Panama

SKILLED EMIGRATION, 2000
- Emigration rate of tertiary educated: **31.5%**
- Emigration of physicians: **159** or **2.1%** of physicians trained in the country

IMMIGRATION, 2005
- Stock of immigrants: **23,504**
- Stock of immigrants as percentage of population: **0.3%**
- Females as percentage of immigrants: **54.9%**
- Refugees as percentage of immigrants: **1.0%**
- Top 10 source countries: Honduras, the United States, Nicaragua, Mexico, Costa Rica, Spain, Panama, Canada, Italy, Colombia

Remittances

US$ millions	2000	2001	2002	2003	2004	2005	2006	2007
Inward remittance flows	1,765	1,926	1,953	2,122	2,564	2,842	3,330ᵃ	3,600
of which								
Workers' remittances	1,751	1,911	1,935	2,105	2,548	2,830	3,316	..
Compensation of employees	14	14	17	16	15	11	12	..
Migrants' transfer	1	2	1	1	1	1	2	..
Outward remittance flows	20	26	22	25	33	24	29ᵇ	..
of which								
Workers' remittances	..	..	..	..	..	..	..	..
Compensation of employees	19	26	22	24	32	24	28	..
Migrants' transfer	0	0	1	1	1	0	1	..

a. **18.2% of GDP in 2006.**
b. **0.2% of GDP in 2006.**

Equatorial Guinea

UPPER MIDDLE INCOME

Population (thousands, 2006)	515
Population growth (avg. annual %, 1997–2006)	2.3
Population density (people per sq. km, 2006)	18
Labor force (thousands, 2006)	201
Urban population (% of pop., 2006)	39.1
Age dependency ratio	0.94
Surface area (1,000 sq. km, 2006)	28
GNI ($ billions, 2006)	5.3
GNI per capita, Atlas method ($, 2006)	8,250
GDP growth (avg. annual %, 2002-06)	12.8
Poverty headcount ratio at national poverty line (% of pop., 2004)	..

Migration

EMIGRATION, 2005
- Stock of emigrants: **92,893**
- Stock of emigrants as percentage of population: **18.4%**
- Top 10 destination countries: Gabon, Spain, Nigeria, the Republic of Congo, São Tomé and Principe, the United States, Germany, France, the Central African Republic, Portugal

SKILLED EMIGRATION, 2000
- Emigration rate of tertiary educated: **34.1%**
- Emigration of physicians:
  a) **2** or **1.5%** of physicians trained in the country *(Source: Docquier and Bhargava 2006)*
  b) **81** or **63.3%** of physicians trained in the country *(Source: Clemens and Pettersson 2006)*
- Emigration of nurses: **98** or **37.7%** of nurses trained in the country

IMMIGRATION, 2005
- Stock of immigrants: **5,800**
- Stock of immigrants as percentage of population: **1.2%**
- Females as percentage of immigrants: **47.0%**
- Refugees as percentage of immigrants: **0.0%**
- Top source countries: Cameroon, Nigeria, Spain, France

Remittances
Remittance data are currently not available for this country.

Eritrea

Population (millions, 2006)	4.5
Population growth (avg. annual %, 1997–2006)	3.7
Population density (people per sq. km, 2006)	45
Labor force (millions, 2006)	1.8
Urban population (% of pop., 2006)	19.8
Age dependency ratio	0.89
Surface area (1,000 sq. km, 2006)	118
GNI ($ billions, 2006)	1.1
GNI per capita, Atlas method ($, 2006)	200
GDP growth (avg. annual %, 2002–06)	1.6
Poverty headcount ratio at national poverty line (% of pop., 2004)	..

Migration

EMIGRATION, 2005
- Stock of emigrants: **848,815**
- Stock of emigrants as percentage of population: **19.3%**
- Top 10 destination countries: Sudan, Ethiopia, Saudi Arabia, the United States, Italy, the United Kingdom, Germany, Canada, Sweden, Australia

SKILLED EMIGRATION, 2000
- Emigration rate of tertiary educated: **45.8%**
- Emigration of physicians:
  a) **12** or **8.6%** of physicians trained in the country *(Source: Docquier and Bhargava 2006)*
  b) **98** or **36.2%** of physicians trained in the country *(Source: Clemens and Pettersson 2006)*
- Emigration of nurses: **497** or **38.0%** of nurses trained in the country

IMMIGRATION, 2005
- Stock of immigrants: **14,612**
- Stock of immigrants as percentage of population: **0.3%**
- Females as percentage of immigrants: **46.5%**
- Refugees as percentage of immigrants: **30.3%**

Remittances

US$ millions	2000	2001	2002	2003	2004	2005	2006	2007
Inward remittance flows	3	..	..	..	..	..	..	..
of which								
Workers' remittances	..	..	..	..	..	..	..	..
Compensation of employees	3	..	..	..	..	..	..	..
Migrants' transfer	..	..	..	..	..	..	..	..
Outward remittance flows	1	..	..	..	..	..	..	..
of which								
Workers' remittances	..	..	..	..	..	..	..	..
Compensation of employees	1	..	..	..	..	..	..	..
Migrants' transfer	..	..	..	..	..	..	..	..

Estonia

Population (millions, 2006)	1.3
Population growth (avg. annual %, 1997–2006)	-0.5
Population density (people per sq. km, 2006)	32
Labor force (thousands, 2006)	664
Urban population (% of pop., 2006)	69.1
Age dependency ratio	0.46
Surface area (1,000 sq. km, 2006)	45
GNI ($ billions, 2006)	16
GNI per capita, Atlas method ($, 2006)	11,410
GDP growth (avg. annual %, 2002–06)	9.0
Poverty headcount ratio at national poverty line (% of pop., 2004)	1

Migration

EMIGRATION, 2005
- Stock of emigrants: **182,726**
- Stock of emigrants as percentage of population: **13.7%**
- Top 10 destination countries: Russia, Finland, Sweden, the United States, Canada, Israel, Germany, Latvia, Australia, the United Kingdom

SKILLED EMIGRATION, 2000
- Emigration rate of tertiary educated: **13.9%**
- Emigration of physicians: **123** or **2.7%** of physicians trained in the country

IMMIGRATION, 2005
- Stock of immigrants: **201,743**
- Stock of immigrants as percentage of population: **15.2%**
- Females as percentage of immigrants: **59.6%**
- Refugees as percentage of immigrants: **0.0%**
- Top source countries: Russia, Ukraine, Belarus, Latvia, Lithuania, Finland

Remittances

US$ millions	2000	2001	2002	2003	2004	2005	2006	2007
Inward remittance flows	3	9	19	51	167	265	402ª	442
of which								
Workers' remittances	0	3	5	9	12	10	10	..
Compensation of employees	4	8	14	42	155	255	392	..
Migrants' transfer	..	..	..	..	..	..	..	..
Outward remittance flows	3	2	5	18	26	50	76ᵇ	..
of which								
Workers' remittances	1	1	3	2	1	1	2	..
Compensation of employees	2	1	2	16	25	49	74	..
Migrants' transfer	..	..	..	..	..	..	..	..

a. 2.4% of GDP in 2006.
b. 0.5% of GDP in 2006.

Migration and Remittances Factbook 2008

Ethiopia

Population (millions, 2006)	73
Population growth (avg. annual %, 1997-2006)	2.2
Population density (people per sq. km, 2006)	73
Labor force (millions, 2006)	32
Urban population (% of pop., 2006)	16.3
Age dependency ratio	0.89
Surface area (1,000 sq. km, 2006)	1,104
GNI ($ billions, 2006)	13
GNI per capita, Atlas method ($, 2006)	180
GDP growth (avg. annual %, 2002-06)	6.0
Poverty headcount ratio at national poverty line (% of pop., 2004)	12.5

Migration

EMIGRATION, 2005
- Stock of emigrants: **445,926**
- Stock of emigrants as percentage of population: **0.6%**
- Top 10 destination countries: Sudan, the United States, Israel, Saudi Arabia, Germany, Canada, Sweden, Italy, the United Kingdom, the Netherlands

SKILLED EMIGRATION, 2000
- Emigration rate of tertiary educated: **17.0%**
- Emigration of physicians:
  a) **459** or **25.6%** of physicians trained in the country *(Source: Docquier and Bhargava 2006)*
  b) **553** or **29.7%** of physicians trained in the country *(Source: Clemens and Pettersson 2006)*
- Emigration of nurses: **1,077** or **16.8%** of nurses trained in the country

IMMIGRATION, 2005
- Stock of immigrants: **555,054**
- Stock of immigrants as percentage of population: **0.7%**
- Females as percentage of immigrants: **46.5%**
- Refugees as percentage of immigrants: **19.7%**
- Top source countries: Eritrea, Somalia, Sudan, Djibouti, Kenya

Remittances

US$ millions	2000	2001	2002	2003	2004	2005	2006	2007
Inward remittance flows	53	18	33	47	134	174	172[a]	172
of which								
Workers' remittances	53	18	33	46	134	174	169	..
Compensation of employees	..	..	..	..	..	..	3	..
Migrants' transfer	..	..	..	..	..	..	..	..
Outward remittance flows	13	14	17	17	9	16	14[b]	..
of which								
Workers' remittances	13	14	17	17	9	16	14	..
Compensation of employees	..	..	..	1	..	..	..	..
Migrants' transfer	..	..	..	..	..	..	..	..

a. 1.3% of GDP in 2006.
b. 0.1% of GDP in 2006.

Faeroe Islands

Population (thousands, 2006)	48
Population growth (avg. annual %, 1997–2006)	..
Population density (people per sq. km, 2006)	35
Labor force (millions, 2006)	..
Urban population (% of pop., 2006)	39
Age dependency ratio	..
Surface area (1,000 sq. km, 2006)	1
GNI ($ millions, 2006)	..
GNI per capita, Atlas method ($, 2006)	..
GDP growth (avg. annual %, 2002–06)	..
Poverty headcount ratio at national poverty line (% of pop., 2004)	..

Migration

IMMIGRATION, 2005
- Stock of immigrants: **5,345**
- Stock of immigrants as percentage of population: **11.4%**
- Females as percentage of immigrants: **43.8%**
- Refugees as percentage of immigrants: **0.0%**

EMIGRATION, 2005
- Stock of emigrants: **467**
- Stock of emigrants as percentage of population: **1.0%**
- Top 10 destination countries: Iceland, Australia, Panama, New Zealand, Ecuador, the Netherlands, Mexico, Uruguay

SKILLED EMIGRATION, 2000
Skilled emigration data are currently not available for this country.

Remittances

US$ millions	2000	2001	2002	2003	2004	2005	2006	2007
Inward remittance flows	43	39	40	44	44	44	44	44
of which								
Workers' remittances	..	..	..	..	..	..	..	..
Compensation of employees	43	39	40	44	..	..	..	..
Migrants' transfer	..	..	..	..	..	..	..	..
Outward remittance flows	6	13	10	5	5	5	5	..
of which								
Workers' remittances	..	..	..	..	..	..	..	..
Compensation of employees	6	13	10	5	..	..	..	..
Migrants' transfer	..	..	..	..	..	..	..	..

Fiji

East Asia and Pacific	LOWER MIDDLE INCOME
Population (thousands, 2006)	853
Population growth (avg. annual %, 1997–2006)	0.9
Population density (people per sq. km, 2006)	47
Labor force (thousands, 2006)	393
Urban population (% of pop., 2006)	51.3
Age dependency ratio	0.55
Surface area (1,000 sq. km, 2006)	18
GNI ($ billions, 2006)	2.7
GNI per capita, Atlas method ($, 2006)	3,300
GDP growth (avg. annual %, 2002-06)	2.7
Poverty headcount ratio at national poverty line (% of pop., 2004)	..

Migration

EMIGRATION, 2005
- Stock of emigrants: **148,355**
- Stock of emigrants as percentage of population: **17.5%**
- Top 10 destination countries: Australia, the United States, Canada, New Zealand, the United Kingdom, New Caledonia, Samoa, India, the Solomon Islands, Japan

SKILLED EMIGRATION, 2000
- Emigration rate of tertiary educated: **58.7%**
- Emigration of physicians: **257** or **48.4%** of physicians trained in the country

IMMIGRATION, 2005
- Stock of immigrants: **17,176**
- Stock of immigrants as percentage of population: **2.0%**
- Females as percentage of immigrants: **47.9%**
- Refugees as percentage of immigrants: **0.0%**
- Top 10 source countries: India, Australia, New Zealand, the United Kingdom, Papua New Guinea, French Polynesia, Samoa, Guam, Pakistan, Bangladesh

Remittances

US$ millions	2000	2001	2002	2003	2004	2005	2006	2007
Inward remittance flows	**44**	**82**	**97**	**123**	**172**	**184**	**165**[a]	**165**
of which								
Workers' remittances	26	37	46	53	55	135	127	..
Compensation of employees	17	40	51	69	116	47	37	..
Migrants' transfer	1	6	0	1	1	2	1	..
Outward remittance flows	**26**	**24**	**20**	**26**	**41**	**33**	**31**[b]	..
of which								
Workers' remittances	2	2	2	2	13	5	5	..
Compensation of employees	0	2	2	2	2	2	3	..
Migrants' transfer	23	20	16	22	26	26	23	..

a. 5.8% of GDP in 2006.
b. 1.1% of GDP in 2006.

Finland

Population (millions, 2006)	5.3
Population growth (avg. annual %, 1997–2006)	0.3
Population density (people per sq. km, 2006)	17
Labor force (millions, 2006)	2.7
Urban population (% of pop., 2006)	61.2
Age dependency ratio	0.5
Surface area (1,000 sq. km, 2006)	338
GNI ($ billions, 2006)	209
GNI per capita, Atlas method ($, 2006)	40,650
GDP growth (avg. annual %, 2002-06)	3.2
Poverty headcount ratio at national poverty line (% of pop., 2004)	..

Migration

IMMIGRATION, 2005
- Stock of immigrants: **156,179**
- Stock of immigrants as percentage of population: **3.0%**
- Females as percentage of immigrants: **51.0%**
- Refugees as percentage of immigrants: **7.4%**
- Top 10 source countries: Estonia, Sweden, Russia, Somalia, Germany, Iraq, the United States, Vietnam, the United Kingdom, Turkey

EMIGRATION, 2005
- Stock of emigrants: **333,155**
- Stock of emigrants as percentage of population: **6.3%**
- Top 10 destination countries: Sweden, the United States, Germany, Canada, the United Kingdom, Spain, Australia, Norway, Switzerland, France

SKILLED EMIGRATION, 2000
- Emigration rate of tertiary educated: **8.4%**
- Emigration of physicians: **941** or **5.6%** of physicians trained in the country

Remittances

US$ millions	2000	2001	2002	2003	2004	2005	2006	2007
Inward remittance flows	**473**	**491**	**477**	**526**	**666**	**695**	**698**[a]	**698**
of which								
Workers' remittances	..	..	..	..	..	..	..	..
Compensation of employees	473	491	477	526	666	695	698	..
Migrants' transfer	..	..	..	..	..	..	..	..
Outward remittance flows	**100**	**97**	**113**	**149**	**225**	**249**	**251**[b]	..
of which								
Workers' remittances	..	..	..	..	..	..	..	..
Compensation of employees	100	97	113	149	225	249	251	..
Migrants' transfer	..	..	..	..	..	..	..	..

a. 0.3% of GDP in 2006.
b. 0.1% of GDP in 2006.

France

Population (millions, 2006)	61
Population growth (avg. annual %, 1997-2006)	0.5
Population density (people per sq. km, 2006)	111
Labor force (millions, 2006)	27
Urban population (% of pop., 2006)	76.9
Age dependency ratio	0.53
Surface area (1,000 sq. km, 2006)	552
GNI ($ billions, 2006)	2,253
GNI per capita, Atlas method ($, 2006)	36,550
GDP growth (avg. annual %, 2002-06)	1.5
Poverty headcount ratio at national poverty line (% of pop., 2004)	..

Migration

IMMIGRATION, 2005
- Stock of immigrants: **6,471,029**
- Stock of immigrants as percentage of population: **10.7%**
- Females as percentage of immigrants: **51.6%**
- Refugees as percentage of immigrants: **2.2%**
- Top 10 source countries: Algeria, Morocco, Portugal, Italy, Spain, Tunisia, Germany, Turkey, Belgium, Vietnam

EMIGRATION, 2005
- Stock of emigrants: **1,889,164**
- Stock of emigrants as percentage of population: **3.1%**
- Top 10 destination countries: Spain, the United States, Germany, Portugal, the United Kingdom, Switzerland, Belgium, Canada, Italy, Israel

SKILLED EMIGRATION, 2000
- Emigration rate of tertiary educated: **3.9%**
- Emigration of physicians: **4,195** or **2.1%** of physicians trained in the country

Remittances

US$ millions	2000	2001	2002	2003	2004	2005	2006	2007
Inward remittance flows	8,631	9,194	10,353	11,311	12,277	12,306	12,479[a]	12,500
of which								
Workers' remittances	680	751	768	451	460	512	477	..
Compensation of employees	7,930	8,442	9,596	10,860	11,817	11,794	12,002	..
Migrants' transfer	..	..	..	..	..	..	..	..
Outward remittance flows	3,791	3,960	3,804	4,388	4,262	4,306	4,330[b]	..
of which								
Workers' remittances	2,681	2,844	2,534	2,851	3,093	3,110	3,077	..
Compensation of employees	1,089	1,109	1,280	1,537	1,169	1,196	1,253	..
Migrants' transfer	..	..	..	..	..	..	..	..

a. 0.6% of GDP in 2006.
b. 0.2% of GDP in 2006.

Gabon

UPPER MIDDLE INCOME

Population (millions, 2006)	1.4
Population growth (avg. annual %, 1997–2006)	2.0
Population density (people per sq. km, 2006)	5
Labor force (thousands, 2006)	610
Urban population (% of pop., 2006)	84.1
Age dependency ratio	0.78
Surface area (1,000 sq. km, 2006)	268
GNI ($ billions, 2006)	7.5
GNI per capita, Atlas method ($, 2006)	5,000
GDP growth (avg. annual %, 2002–06)	1.6
Poverty headcount ratio at national poverty line (% of pop., 2004)	..

Migration

EMIGRATION, 2005
- Stock of emigrants: **27,330**
- Stock of emigrants as percentage of population: **2.0%**
- Top 10 destination countries: France, Sierra Leone, Cameroon, the Republic of Congo, São Tomé and Principe, the United States, Canada, Germany, Chad, Spain

SKILLED EMIGRATION, 2000
- Emigration rate of tertiary educated: **19.3%**
- Emigration of physicians:
  a) **4** or **1.1%** of physicians trained in the country *(Source: Docquier and Bhargava 2006)*
  b) **65** or **15.0%** of physicians trained in the country *(Source: Clemens and Pettersson 2006)*
- Emigration of nurses: **107** or **6.4%** of nurses trained in the country

IMMIGRATION, 2005
- Stock of immigrants: **244,550**
- Stock of immigrants as percentage of population: **17.7%**
- Females as percentage of immigrants: **43.0%**
- Refugees as percentage of immigrants: **5.6%**
- Top 10 source countries: Equatorial Guinea, Mali, Benin, Cameroon, Senegal, Nigeria, Togo, France, the Republic of Congo, Lebanon

Remittances

US$ millions	2000	2001	2002	2003	2004	2005	2006	2007
Inward remittance flows	6	5	3	6	6	6	6[a]	6
of which								
Workers' remittances	2	1	1	4	1	..	..	..
Compensation of employees	4	4	2	2	5	..	..	..
Migrants' transfer	..	..	..	..	..	..	..	..
Outward remittance flows	78	96	96	115	110	110	110[b]	..
of which								
Workers' remittances	42	82	79	109	91	..	..	..
Compensation of employees	36	14	17	6	19	..	..	..
Migrants' transfer	..	..	..	..	..	..	..	..

a. **0.1% of GDP in 2006.**
b. **1.2% of GDP in 2006.**

Gambia, The

Population (millions, 2006)	1.6
Population growth (avg. annual %, 1997–2006)	3.0
Population density (people per sq. km, 2006)	155
Labor force (thousands, 2006)	675
Urban population (% of pop., 2006)	54.7
Age dependency ratio	0.78
Surface area (1,000 sq. km, 2006)	11
GNI ($ millions, 2006)	499
GNI per capita, Atlas method ($, 2006)	310
GDP growth (avg. annual %, 2002–06)	3.7
Poverty headcount ratio at national poverty line (% of pop., 2004)	23.3

Migration

EMIGRATION, 2005
- Stock of emigrants: **56,762**
- Stock of emigrants as percentage of population: **3.7%**
- Top 10 destination countries: Spain, Senegal, the United States, Nigeria, the United Kingdom, Germany, Sweden, France, Norway, Guinea-Bissau

SKILLED EMIGRATION, 2000
- Emigration rate of tertiary educated: **64.7%**
- Emigration of physicians:
  a) **8** or **14.1%** of physicians trained in the country *(Source: Docquier and Bhargava 2006)*
  b) **46** or **53.5%** of physicians trained in the country *(Source: Clemens and Pettersson 2006)*
- Emigration of Nurses: **282** or **66.2%** of nurses trained in the country

IMMIGRATION, 2005
- Stock of immigrants: **231,739**
- Stock of immigrants as percentage of population: **15.3%**
- Females as percentage of immigrants: **48.7%**
- Refugees as percentage of immigrants: **3.1%**
- Top source countries: Senegal, Guinea, Guinea-Bissau, Mali, Mauritania, Sierra Leone

Remittances

US$ millions	2000	2001	2002	2003	2004	2005	2006	2007
Inward remittance flows	14	7	7	65	62	58	64[a]	64
of which								
Workers' remittances	..	..	..	64	61	57	63	..
Compensation of employees	..	..	..	1	1	1	1	..
Migrants' transfer	..	..	..	..	..	..	..	..
Outward remittance flows	..	..	..	1	1	1	1[b]	..
of which								
Workers' remittances	..	..	..	..	..	..	..	..
Compensation of employees	..	..	..	1	1	1	1	..
Migrants' transfer	..	..	..	..	..	..	..	..

a. 12.5% of GDP in 2006.
b. 0.2% of GDP in 2006.

Georgia

LOWER MIDDLE INCOME

Population (millions, 2006)	4
Population growth (avg. annual %, 1997-2006)	-1.1
Population density (people per sq. km, 2006)	64
Labor force (millions, 2006)	2
Urban population (% of pop., 2006)	52.3
Age dependency ratio	0.49
Surface area (1,000 sq. km, 2006)	70
GNI ($ billions, 2006)	7
GNI per capita, Atlas method ($, 2006)	1,560
GDP growth (avg. annual %, 2002-06)	8.2
Poverty headcount ratio at national poverty line (% of pop., 2004)	6.4

Migration

EMIGRATION, 2005
- Stock of emigrants: **1,024,598**
- Stock of emigrants as percentage of population: **22.9%**
- Top 10 destination countries: Russia, Ukraine, Greece, Armenia, Israel, Germany, the United States, Cyprus, Turkey, Latvia

SKILLED EMIGRATION, 2000
- Emigration rate of tertiary educated: **2.6%**
- Emigration of physicians: **13** or **0.1%** of physicians trained in the country

IMMIGRATION, 2005
- Stock of immigrants: **191,220**
- Stock of immigrants as percentage of population: **4.3%**
- Females as percentage of immigrants: **37.4%**
- Refugees as percentage of immigrants: **1.1%**
- Top 10 source countries: Russia, Armenia, Azerbaijan, Ukraine, Turkey, Germany, Pakistan, the United States, Greece, Bulgaria

Remittances

US$ millions	2000	2001	2002	2003	2004	2005	2006	2007
Inward remittance flows	274	181	231	235	303	346	485ᵃ	533
of which								
Workers' remittances	95	87	75	64	64	94	153	..
Compensation of employees	179	94	152	168	236	247	315	..
Migrants' transfer	..	..	4	3	3	5	17	..
Outward remittance flows	39	26	26	30	25	29	24ᵇ	..
of which								
Workers' remittances	19	13	2	6	7	8	4	..
Compensation of employees	15	7	15	16	15	18	19	..
Migrants' transfer	5	5	9	8	3	3	1	..

a. 6.4% of GDP in 2006.
b. 0.3% of GDP in 2006.

Germany

Population (millions, 2006)	82
Population growth (avg. annual %, 1997–2006)	0.1
Population density (people per sq. km, 2006)	236
Labor force (millions, 2006)	41
Urban population (% of pop., 2006)	75.3
Age dependency ratio	0.5
Surface area (1,000 sq. km, 2006)	357
GNI ($ billions, 2006)	2,914
GNI per capita, Atlas method ($, 2006)	36,620
GDP growth (avg. annual %, 2002–06)	1.1
Poverty headcount ratio at national poverty line (% of pop., 2004)	..

Migration

IMMIGRATION, 2005
- Stock of immigrants: **10,143,626**
- Stock of immigrants as percentage of population: **12.3%**
- Females as percentage of immigrants: **48.3%**
- Refugees as percentage of immigrants: **8.3%**
- Top 10 source countries: Turkey, Serbia and Montenegro, Italy, Greece, Poland, Croatia, Austria, Bosnia and Herzegovina, Russia, Portugal

EMIGRATION, 2005
- Stock of emigrants: **4,095,015**
- Stock of emigrants as percentage of population: **5.0%**
- Top 10 destination countries: the United States, Spain, the United Kingdom, Turkey, France, Canada, Switzerland, Austria, Kazakhstan, the Netherlands

SKILLED EMIGRATION, 2000
- Emigration rate of tertiary educated: **8.8%**
- Emigration of physicians: **8,822** or **3.1%** of physicians trained in the country

Remittances

US$ millions	2000	2001	2002	2003	2004	2005	2006	2007
Inward remittance flows	3,644	3,933	4,685	5,784	6,560	6,363	6,667[a]	7,000
of which								
Workers' remittances	..	..	..	..	..	..	..	..
Compensation of employees	3,604	3,882	4,649	5,744	6,489	6,297	6,581	..
Migrants' transfer	40	51	36	40	71	66	86	..
Outward remittance flows	7,761	7,609	9,572	11,190	11,977	12,282	12,345[b]	..
of which								
Workers' remittances	3,191	3,151	3,277	3,766	3,951	3,646	3,676	..
Compensation of employees	5,165	5,496	6,009	7,098	7,623	8,198	8,287	..
Migrants' transfer	379	265	283	326	403	438	382	..

a. 0.2% of GDP in 2006.
b. 0.4% of GDP in 2006.

Ghana

| **LOW INCOME**

Population (millions, 2006)	23
Population growth (avg. annual %, 1997–2006)	2.2
Population density (people per sq. km, 2006)	99
Labor force (millions, 2006)	10
Urban population (% of pop., 2006)	48.5
Age dependency ratio	0.73
Surface area (1,000 sq. km, 2006)	239
GNI ($ billions, 2006)	13
GNI per capita, Atlas method ($, 2006)	520
GDP growth (avg. annual %, 2002-06)	5.5
Poverty headcount ratio at national poverty line (% of pop., 2004)	16.6

Migration

EMIGRATION, 2005
- Stock of emigrants: **906,698**
- Stock of emigrants as percentage of population: **4.1%**
- Top 10 destination countries: Côte d'Ivoire, Nigeria, the United States, Burkina Faso, the United Kingdom, Togo, Germany, Canada, Benin, the Netherlands

SKILLED EMIGRATION, 2000
- Emigration rate of tertiary educated: **42.9%**
- Emigration of physicians:
  a) **450** or **22.3%** of physicians trained in the country *(Source: Docquier and Bhargava 2006)*
  b) **1,639** or **55.9%** of physicians trained in the country *(Source: Clemens and Pettersson 2006)*
- Emigration of nurses: **4,766** or **24.1%** of nurses trained in the country

IMMIGRATION, 2005
- Stock of immigrants: **1,669,267**
- Stock of immigrants as percentage of population: **7.6%**
- Females as percentage of immigrants: **55.6%**
- Refugees as percentage of immigrants: **2.5%**

Remittances

US$ millions	2000	2001	2002	2003	2004	2005	2006	2007
Inward remittance flows	32	46	44	65	82	99	105[a]	105
of which								
Workers' remittances	32	46	44	65	82	99	105	..
Compensation of employees	..	..	..	..	..	..	..	..
Migrants' transfer	..	..	..	..	..	..	..	..
Outward remittance flows	6	6	6	6	6	6	6[b]	..
of which								
Workers' remittances	6	6	..	..	..	..	..	..
Compensation of employees	..	..	..	..	..	..	..	..
Migrants' transfer	..	..	..	..	..	..	..	..

a. 0.8% of GDP in 2006.
b. 0.05% of GDP in 2006.

Greece

Population (millions, 2006)	11
Population growth (avg. annual %, 1997–2006)	0.4
Population density (people per sq. km, 2006)	86
Labor force (millions, 2006)	5.2
Urban population (% of pop., 2006)	59.1
Age dependency ratio	0.48
Surface area (1,000 sq. km, 2006)	132
GNI ($ billions, 2006)	240
GNI per capita, Atlas method ($, 2006)	21,690
GDP growth (avg. annual %, 2002–06)	4.2
Poverty headcount ratio at national poverty line (% of pop., 2004)	..

Migration

IMMIGRATION, 2005
- Stock of immigrants: **973,677**
- Stock of immigrants as percentage of population: **8.8%**
- Females as percentage of immigrants: **55.6%**
- Refugees as percentage of immigrants: **0.2%**
- Top 10 source countries: Albania, Germany, Turkey, Russia, Georgia, Bulgaria, Egypt, Romania, Kazakhstan, the United States

EMIGRATION, 2005
- Stock of emigrants: **1,218,233**
- Stock of emigrants as percentage of population: **11.0%**
- Top 10 destination countries: Germany, the United States, Australia, Canada, Albania, Turkey, the United Kingdom, Italy, Israel, Cyprus

SKILLED EMIGRATION, 2000
- Emigration rate of tertiary educated: **14.0%**
- Emigration of physicians: **2,819** or **5.6%** of physicians trained in the country

Remittances

US$ millions	2000	2001	2002	2003	2004	2005	2006	2007
Inward remittance flows	**2,194**	**2,014**	**1,659**	**1,564**	**1,242**	**1,220**	**1,543**[a]	**1,543**
of which								
Workers' remittances	1,613	1,471	1,181	1,183	894	863	1,143	..
Compensation of employees	581	543	478	381	348	357	400	..
Migrants' transfer	..	..	..	..	..	..	..	..
Outward remittance flows	**545**	**536**	**412**	**380**	**497**	**903**	**982**[b]	..
of which								
Workers' remittances	295	285	186	187	262	630	629	..
Compensation of employees	251	251	226	193	235	273	353	..
Migrants' transfer	..	..	..	..	..	..	..	..

a. 0.6% of GDP in 2006.
b. 0.4% of GDP in 2006.

Greenland

Population (thousands, 2006)	57
Population growth (avg. annual %, 1997–2006)	0.2
Population density (people per sq. km, 2006)	-
Labor force (millions, 2006)	..
Urban population (% of pop., 2006)	83.2
Age dependency ratio	..
Surface area (1,000 sq. km, 2006)	410
GNI ($ millions, 2006)	..
GNI per capita, Atlas method ($, 2006)	..
GDP growth (avg. annual %, 2002–06)	..
Poverty headcount ratio at national poverty line (% of pop., 2004)	..

Migration

IMMIGRATION, 2005
- Stock of immigrants: **12,210**
- Stock of immigrants as percentage of population: **21.5%**
- Females as percentage of immigrants: **26.9%**
- Refugees as percentage of immigrants: **0.0%**

EMIGRATION, 2005
- Stock of emigrants: **4,084**
- Stock of emigrants as percentage of population: **7.2%**
- Top destination countries: Norway, Guatemala, Iceland, Australia, the Netherlands, Panama, Mexico, New Zealand

SKILLED EMIGRATION, 2000
Skilled emigration data are currently not available for this country.

Remittances
Remittance data are currently not available for this country.

Grenada

Population (thousands, 2006)	108
Population growth (avg. annual %, 1997–2006)	0.9
Population density (people per sq. km, 2006)	318
Labor force (millions, 2006)	..
Urban population (% of pop., 2006)	30.7
Age dependency ratio	..
Surface area (sq. km, 2006)	340
GNI ($ millions, 2006)	475
GNI per capita, Atlas method ($, 2006)	4,420
GDP growth (avg. annual %, 2002–06)	2.6
Poverty headcount ratio at national poverty line (% of pop., 2004)	..

Migration

EMIGRATION, 2005
- Stock of emigrants: **71,396**
- Stock of emigrants as percentage of population: **69.4%**
- Top 10 destination countries: the United States, the United Kingdom, Trinidad and Tobago, Canada, Barbados, Mexico, Antigua and Barbuda, Australia, República Bolivariana de Venezuela, Dominica

SKILLED EMIGRATION, 2000
- Emigration rate of tertiary educated: **66.7%**
- Emigration of physicians: **1,926** or **97.5%** of physicians trained in the country

IMMIGRATION, 2005
- Stock of immigrants: **10,843**
- Stock of immigrants as percentage of population: **10.5%**
- Females as percentage of immigrants: **53.3%**
- Refugees as percentage of immigrants: **0.0%**

Remittances

US$ millions	2000	2001	2002	2003	2004	2005	2006	2007
Inward remittance flows	22	22	23	23	24	25	25[a]	25
of which								
Workers' remittances	..	..	..	..	..	..	..	..
Compensation of employees	0	0	0	0	0	0	..	..
Migrants' transfer	22	22	23	23	24	25	..	..
Outward remittance flows	2	2	2	2	2	2	2[b]	..
of which								
Workers' remittances	..	..	..	..	..	..	..	..
Compensation of employees	..	..	..	..	..	..	..	..
Migrants' transfer	2	2	2	2	2	2	..	..

a. 4.8% of GDP in 2006.
b. 0.4% of GDP in 2006.

Guatemala

LOWER MIDDLE INCOME

Population (millions, 2006)	13
Population growth (avg. annual %, 1997-2006)	2.4
Population density (people per sq. km, 2006)	119
Labor force (millions, 2006)	4.2
Urban population (% of pop., 2006)	47.7
Age dependency ratio	0.9
Surface area (1,000 sq. km, 2006)	109
GNI ($ billions, 2006)	35
GNI per capita, Atlas method ($, 2006)	2,640
GDP growth (avg. annual %, 2002-06)	3.0
Poverty headcount ratio at national poverty line (% of pop., 2004)	13.1

Migration

EMIGRATION, 2005

- Stock of emigrants: **685,713**
- Stock of emigrants as percentage of population: **5.4%**
- Top 10 destination countries: the United States, Mexico, Belize, Canada, Spain, Honduras, Costa Rica, France, Germany, Nicaragua

SKILLED EMIGRATION, 2000

- Emigration rate of tertiary educated: **21.5%**
- Emigration of physicians: **168** or **1.6%** of physicians trained in the country

IMMIGRATION, 2005

- Stock of immigrants: **52,967**
- Stock of immigrants as percentage of population: **0.4%**
- Females as percentage of immigrants: **58.1%**
- Refugees as percentage of immigrants: **1.2%**
- Top 10 source countries: El Salvador, Mexico, Nicaragua, Honduras, the United States, the Republic of Korea, Spain, Costa Rica, Colombia, Belize

Remittances

US$ millions	2000	2001	2002	2003	2004	2005	2006	2007
Inward remittance flows	596	634	1,600	2,147	2,592	3,033	3,626[a]	4,100
of which								
Workers' remittances	563	592	1,579	2,107	2,551	2,993	3,610	..
Compensation of employees	33	41	21	40	41	40	16	..
Migrants' transfer	..	..	..	..	..	..	..	..
Outward remittance flows	56	32	82	86	35	33	34[b]	..
of which								
Workers' remittances	39	21	76	80	32	33	34	..
Compensation of employees	17	11	6	6	3	0	0	..
Migrants' transfer	..	..	..	..	..	..	..	..

a. 10.3% of GDP in 2006.
b. 0.1% of GDP in 2006.

Guinea

Population (millions, 2006)	9.2
Population growth (avg. annual %, 1997–2006)	2.0
Population density (people per sq. km, 2006)	37
Labor force (millions, 2006)	4.3
Urban population (% of pop., 2006)	33.5
Age dependency ratio	0.89
Surface area (1,000 sq. km, 2006)	246
GNI ($ billions, 2006)	3.3
GNI per capita, Atlas method ($, 2006)	410
GDP growth (avg. annual %, 2002–06)	2.9
Poverty headcount ratio at national poverty line (% of pop., 2004)	..

Migration

EMIGRATION, 2005
- Stock of emigrants: **520,835**
- Stock of emigrants as percentage of population: **5.5%**
- Top 10 destination countries: Côte d'Ivoire, Senegal, Sierra Leone, the Gambia, Liberia, Spain, France, the United States, Nigeria, Guinea-Bissau

SKILLED EMIGRATION, 2000
- Emigration rate of tertiary educated: **11.1%**
- Emigration of physicians:
  a) **80** or **10.3%** of physicians trained in the country *(Source: Docquier and Bhargava 2006)*
  b) **115** or **11.4%** of physicians trained in the country *(Source: Clemens and Pettersson 2006)*
- Emigration of nurses: **267** or **6.5%** of nurses trained in the country

IMMIGRATION, 2005
- Stock of immigrants: **405,772**
- Stock of immigrants as percentage of population: **4.3%**
- Females as percentage of immigrants: **52.7%**
- Refugees as percentage of immigrants: **29.8%**

Remittances

US$ millions	2000	2001	2002	2003	2004	2005	2006	2007
Inward remittance flows	1	9	15	111	42	42	42[a]	42
of which								
Workers' remittances	1	9	15	111	42	..	..	..
Compensation of employees	..	..	0	..	..	..	..	..
Migrants' transfer	..	..	..	..	..	..	..	..
Outward remittance flows	27	37	18	46	48	48	48[b]	..
of which								
Workers' remittances	26	33	15	42	46	..	..	..
Compensation of employees	1	4	3	4	2	..	..	..
Migrants' transfer	..	..	..	..	..	..	..	..

a. 1.3% of GDP in 2006.
b. 1.4% of GDP in 2006.

Guinea-Bissau

LOW INCOME

Population (millions, 2006)	1.6
Population growth (avg. annual %, 1997-2006)	2.9
Population density (people per sq. km, 2006)	58
Labor force (thousands, 2006)	654
Urban population (% of pop., 2006)	29.7
Age dependency ratio	1.03
Surface area (1,000 sq. km, 2006)	36
GNI ($ millions, 2006)	295
GNI per capita, Atlas method ($, 2006)	190
GDP growth (avg. annual %, 2002-06)	0.7
Poverty headcount ratio at national poverty line (% of pop., 2004)	..

Migration

EMIGRATI ON, 2005
- Stock of emigrants: **116,124**
- Stock of emigrants as percentage of population: **7.3%**
- Top 10 destination countries: Senegal, Portugal, the Gambia, France, Spain, Nigeria, Mauritania, Cape Verde, Germany, the United States

SKILLED EMIGRATION, 2000
- Emigration rate of tertiary educated: **29.4%**
- Emigration of physicians:
  a) **2** or **0.9%** of physicians trained in the country *(Source: Docquier and Bhargava 2006)*
  b) **251** or **70.9%** of physicians trained in the country *(Source: Clemens and Pettersson 2006)*
  Emigration of nurses: **262** or **24.7%** of nurses trained in the country

IMMIGRATION, 2005
- Stock of immigrants: **19,171**
- Stock of immigrants as percentage of population: **1.2%**
- Females as percentage of immigrants: **50.0%**
- Refugees as percentage of immigrants: **39.3%**
- Top source countries: Senegal, Guinea, the Gambia, Portugal, Mauritania, Cape Verde, France

Remittances

US$ millions	2000	2001	2002	2003	2004	2005	2006	2007
Inward remittance flows	2	10	18	23	28	28	28[a]	29
of which								
Workers' remittances	..	10	17	21	27	..	..	..
Compensation of employees	..	0	0	2	1	..	..	..
Migrants' transfer	..	..	..	..	..	..	..	..
Outward remittance flows	..	..	5	6	5	5	5[b]	..
of which								
Workers' remittances	..	-	5	6	5	..	..	..
Compensation of employees	..	-	0	0	0	..	..	..
Migrants' transfer	..	..	..	..	..	..	..	..

a. 9.2% of GDP in 2006.
b. 1.6% of GDP in 2006.

Migration and Remittances Factbook 2008

Guyana

Latin America and the Caribbean	LOWER MIDDLE INCOME
Population (thousands, 2006)	751
Population growth (avg. annual %, 1997-2006)	0.2
Population density (people per sq. km, 2006)	4
Labor force (thousands, 2006)	332
Urban population (% of pop., 2006)	28.3
Age dependency ratio	0.52
Surface area (1,000 sq. km, 2006)	215
GNI ($ millions, 2006)	862
GNI per capita, Atlas method ($, 2006)	1,130
GDP growth (avg. annual %, 2002-06)	1.2
Poverty headcount ratio at national poverty line (% of pop., 2004)	2

Migration

EMIGRATION, 2005

- Stock of emigrants: **417,469**
- Stock of emigrants as percentage of population: **55.6%**
- Top 10 destination countries: the United States, Canada, the United Kingdom, República Bolivariana de Venezuela, Trinidad and Tobago, Antigua and Barbuda, French Guiana, Barbados, the Netherlands, Brazil

SKILLED EMIGRATION, 2000

- Emigration rate of tertiary educated: **85.9%**
- Emigration of physicians: **6** or **1.6%** of physicians trained in the country

IMMIGRATION, 2005

- Stock of immigrants: **1,114**
- Stock of immigrants as percentage of population: **0.2%**
- Females as percentage of immigrants: **47.6%**
- Refugees as percentage of immigrants: **0.0%**
- Top source countries: Suriname, Brazil, República Bolivariana de Venezuela, the United States, China, Trinidad and Tobago, the United Kingdom, Barbados, Canada

Remittances

US$ millions	2000	2001	2002	2003	2004	2005	2006	2007
Inward remittance flows	27	22	51	99	153	201	218[a]	218
of which								
Workers' remittances	27	22	51	99	153	201	218	..
Compensation of employees	..	..	..	..	..	..	..	..
Migrants' transfer	..	..	..	..	..	..	..	..
Outward remittance flows	27	25	54	51	81	55	48[b]	..
of which								
Workers' remittances	23	19	48	45	75	49	42	..
Compensation of employees	4	6	6	6	6	6	6	..
Migrants' transfer	..	..	..	..	..	..	..	..

a. 24.3% of GDP in 2006.
b. 5.4% of GDP in 2006. This table reports officially recorded remittances.

Haiti

Population (millions, 2006)	8.6
Population growth (avg. annual %, 1997–2006)	1.4
Population density (people per sq. km, 2006)	314
Labor force (millions, 2006)	3.8
Urban population (% of pop., 2006)	39.5
Age dependency ratio	0.7
Surface area (1,000 sq. km, 2006)	28
GNI ($ billions, 2006)	4.3
GNI per capita, Atlas method ($, 2006)	480
GDP growth (avg. annual %, 2002–06)	0.1
Poverty headcount ratio at national poverty line (% of pop., 2004)	50.7

Migration

EMIGRATION, 2005
- Stock of emigrants: **834,364**
- Stock of emigrants as percentage of population: **9.8%**
- Top 10 destination countries: the United States, the Dominican Republic, Canada, Guadeloupe, France, French Guiana, the Bahamas, Cuba, Martinique, Netherlands Antilles

SKILLED EMIGRATION, 2000
- Emigration rate of tertiary educated: **81.6%**
- Emigration of physicians: **557** or **21.9%** of physicians trained in the country

IMMIGRATION, 2005
- Stock of immigrants: **30,054**
- Stock of immigrants as percentage of population: **0.4%**
- Females as percentage of immigrants: **61.7%**
- Refugees as percentage of immigrants: **0.0%**
- Top 10 source countries: the Dominican Republic, the United States, Cuba, Jamaica, Colombia, Mexico, Chile, Brazil, Peru, Argentina

Remittances

US$ millions	2000	2001	2002	2003	2004	2005	2006	2007
Inward remittance flows	**578**	**624**	**676**	**811**	**932**	**985**	**1,070**[a]	**1,184**
of which								
Workers' remittances	578	624	676	811	932	985	1,070	..
Compensation of employees	..	..	..	..	..	..	..	..
Migrants' transfer	..	..	..	..	..	..	..	..
Outward remittance flows	**11**	**19**	**22**	**31**	**39**	**59**	**68**[b]	..
of which								
Workers' remittances	11	19	22	31	39	59	68	..
Compensation of employees	..	..	..	..	..	..	..	..
M igrants' transfer	..	..	..	..	..	..	..	..

a. 21.6% of GDP in 2006.
b. 1.4% of GDP in 2006.

Honduras

Population (millions, 2006)	7.4
Population growth (avg. annual %, 1997–2006)	2.4
Population density (people per sq. km, 2006)	66
Labor force (millions, 2006)	3.3
Urban population (% of pop., 2006)	47
Age dependency ratio	0.74
Surface area (1,000 sq. km, 2006)	112
GNI ($ billions, 2006)	8.9
GNI per capita, Atlas method ($, 2006)	1,200
GDP growth (avg. annual %, 2002–06)	4.3
Poverty headcount ratio at national poverty line (% of pop., 2004)	14.1

Migration

EMIGRATION, 2005
- Stock of emigrants: **414,955**
- Stock of emigrants as percentage of population: **5.8%**
- Top 10 destination countries: the United States, Nicaragua, El Salvador, Spain, Belize, Guatemala, Canada, Mexico, Costa Rica, Cayman Islands

EMIGRATION, 2000
- Emigration rate of tertiary educated: **21.8%**
- Emigration of physicians: **62** or **1.1%** of physicians trained in the country

IMMIGRATION, 2005
- Stock of immigrants: **26,333**
- Stock of immigrants as percentage of population: **0.4%**
- Females as percentage of immigrants: **48.6%**
- Refugees as percentage of immigrants: **0.1%**
- Top 10 source countries: El Salvador, the United States, Guatemala, Mexico, Colombia, Costa Rica, Cuba, China, Spain, Ecuador

Remittances

US$ millions	2000	2001	2002	2003	2004	2005	2006	2007
Inward remittance flows	416	540	718	867	1,151	1,796	2,367[a]	2,600
of which								
Workers' remittances	410	534	711	860	1,144	1,788	2,359	..
Compensation of employees	6	7	7	7	7	8	8	..
Migrants' transfer	..	..	..	..	..	..	..	..
Outward remittance flows	1	1	1	1	1	1	1[b]	..
of which								
Workers' remittances	1	1	1	1	1	1	1	..
Compensation of employees	..	..	..	..	..	..	..	..
Migrants' transfer	..	..	..	..	..	..	..	..

a. 25.6% of GDP in 2006.
b. 0.01% of GDP in 2006.

Hong Kong, China

Population (millions, 2006)	7.0
Population growth (avg. annual %, 1997–2006)	0.9
Population density (people per sq. km, 2006)	6,728
Labor force (millions, 2006)	3.7
Urban population (% of pop., 2006)	100
Age dependency ratio	0.35
Surface area (1,000 sq. km, 2006)	1
GNI ($ billions, 2006)	190
GNI per capita, Atlas method ($, 2006)	28,460
GDP growth (avg. annual %, 2002–06)	5.6
Poverty headcount ratio at national poverty line (% of pop., 2004)	..

Migration

IMMIGRATION, 2005
- Stock of immigrants: **2,998,686**
- Stock of immigrants as percentage of population: **42.6%**
- Females as percentage of immigrants: **54.0%**
- Refugees as percentage of immigrants: **0.0%**
- Top source country: China

EMIGRATION, 2005
- Stock of emigrants: **716,246**
- Stock of emigrants as percentage of population: **10.2%**
- Top 10 destination countries: Canada, the United States, the United Kingdom, Australia, the Netherlands, New Zealand, Ireland, Singapore, France, Belgium

SKILLED EMIGRATION, 2000
- Emigration rate of tertiary educated: **28.7%**
- Emigration of physicians: **1,293** or **12.8%** of physicians trained in the country

Remittances

US$ millions	2000	2001	2002	2003	2004	2005	2006	2007
Inward remittance flows	136	153	121	120	240	297	297ª	297
of which								
Workers' remittances	..	..	..	..	..	..	..	..
Compensation of employees	136	153	121	120	240	297	297	..
Migrants' transfer	..	..	..	..	..	..	..	..
Outward remittance flows	225	309	299	317	321	348	365ᵇ	..
of which								
Workers' remittances	..	..	..	..	..	..	..	..
Compensation of employees	225	309	299	317	321	348	365	..
Migrants' transfer	..	..	..	..	..	..	..	..

a. 0.2% of GDP in 2006.
b. 0.2% of GDP in 2006.

Hungary

Population (millions, 2006)	10
Population growth (avg. annual %, 1997–2006)	-0.3
Population density (people per sq. km, 2006)	112
Labor force (millions, 2006)	4.2
Urban population (% of pop., 2006)	66.7
Age dependency ratio	0.45
Surface area (1,000 sq. km, 2006)	93
GNI ($ billions, 2006)	105
GNI per capita, Atlas method ($, 2006)	10,950
GDP growth (avg. annual %, 2002–06)	4.3
Poverty headcount ratio at national poverty line (% of pop., 2004)	0

Migration

EMIGRATION, 2005
- Stock of emigrants: **471,298**
- Stock of emigrants as percentage of population: **4.7%**
- Top 10 destination countries: the United States, Germany, Canada, Austria, Australia, the Slovak Republic, Israel, the United Kingdom, Sweden, Switzerland

SKILLED EMIGRATION, 2000
- Emigration rate of tertiary educated: **12.1%**
- Emigration of physicians: **1,782** or **5.6%** of physicians trained in the country

IMMIGRATION, 2005
- Stock of immigrants: **316,209**
- Stock of immigrants as percentage of population: **3.1%**
- Females as percentage of immigrants: **52.4%**
- Refugees as percentage of immigrants: **2.6%**
- Top 10 source countries: Romania, the Slovak Republic, Serbia and Montenegro, Ukraine, Germany, Russia, Croatia, China, Austria, Poland

Remittances

US$ millions	2000	2001	2002	2003	2004	2005	2006	2007
Inward remittance flows	281	296	279	295	307	300	363[a]	363
of which								
Workers' remittances	53	51	39	39	26	20	40	..
Compensation of employees	221	242	232	249	265	262	317	..
Migrants' transfer	7	3	8	7	16	18	6	..
Outward remittance flows	86	101	107	114	128	155	190[b]	..
of which								
Workers' remittances	14	16	15	20	17	16	15	..
Compensation of employees	70	84	90	91	108	136	170	..
Migrants' transfer	3	1	1	3	3	3	5	..

a. 0.3% of GDP in 2006.
b. 0.2% of GDP in 2006.

Iceland

Population (thousands, 2006)	299
Population growth (avg. annual %, 1997-2006)	1.0
Population density (people per sq. km, 2006)	3
Labor force (thousands, 2006)	179
Urban population (% of pop., 2006)	92.9
Age dependency ratio	0.5
Surface area (1,000 sq. km, 2006)	103
GNI ($ billions, 2006)	15
GNI per capita, Atlas method ($, 2006)	50,580
GDP growth (avg. annual %, 2002-06)	3.7
Poverty headcount ratio at national poverty line (% of pop., 2004)	..

Migration

IMMIGRATION, 2005
- Stock of immigrants: **23,097**
- Stock of immigrants as percentage of population: **7.8%**
- Females as percentage of immigrants: **53.8%**
- Refugees as percentage of immigrants: **1.0%**
- Top 10 source countries: Denmark, Poland, Sweden, the United States, Germany, Norway, the Philippines, the United Kingdom, Russia, Thailand

EMIGRATION, 2005
- Stock of emigrants: **33,362**
- Stock of emigrants as percentage of population: **11.3%**
- Top 10 destination countries: the United States, Denmark, Norway, Sweden, Germany, the United Kingdom, Spain, Canada, Australia, the Netherlands

SKILLED EMIGRATION, 2000
- Emigration rate of tertiary educated: **16.3%**
- Emigration of physicians: **343** or **26.2%** of physicians trained in the country

Remittances

US$ millions	2000	2001	2002	2003	2004	2005	2006	2007
Inward remittance flows	88	74	74	96	112	88	87[a]	87
of which								
Workers' remittances	..	..	..	..	..	..	..	..
Compensation of employees	70	59	60	81	80	74	72	..
Migrants' transfer	17	15	14	15	32	14	15	..
Outward remittance flows	31	17	23	26	47	65	80[b]	..
of which								
Workers' remittances	..	..	..	..	..	..	..	..
Compensation of employees	10	5	8	6	12	24	39	..
Migrants' transfer	21	12	15	20	35	41	41	..

a. 0.5% of GDP in 2006.
b. 0.5% of GDP in 2006.

India

South Asia	LOW INCOME
Population (millions, 2006)	1,110
Population growth (avg. annual %, 1997-2006)	1.6
Population density (people per sq. km, 2006)	373
Labor force (millions, 2006)	443
Urban population (% of pop., 2006)	29
Age dependency ratio	0.59
Surface area (1,000 sq. km, 2006)	3,287
GNI ($ billions, 2006)	901
GNI per capita, Atlas method ($, 2006)	820
GDP growth (avg. annual %, 2002-06)	7.8
Poverty headcount ratio at national poverty line (% of pop., 2004)	34.3

Migration

EMIGRATION, 2005
- Stock of emigrants: **9,987,129**
- Stock of emigrants as percentage of population: **0.9%**
- Top 10 destination countries: the United Arab Emirates, Saudi Arabia, the United States, Bangladesh, Nepal, the United Kingdom, Sri Lanka, Canada, Kuwait, Oman

SKILLED EMIGRATION, 2000
- Emigration rate of tertiary educated: **4.2%**
- Emigration of physicians: **20,315** or **3.8%** of physicians trained in the country

IMMIGRATION, 2005
- Stock of immigrants: **5,700,147**
- Stock of immigrants as percentage of population: **0.5%**
- Females as percentage of immigrants: **47.4%**
- Refugees as percentage of immigrants: **2.8%**
- Top 10 source countries: Bangladesh, Pakistan, Nepal, Sri Lanka, Myanmar, China, Malaysia, the United Arab Emirates, Afghanistan, Bhutan

Remittances

US$ millions	2000	2001	2002	2003	2004	2005	2006	2007
Inward remittance flows	12,890	14,273	15,736	20,999	18,750	21,293	25,426[a]	27,000
of which								
Workers' remittances	12,745	14,144	15,629	20,884	18,397	21,030	25,109	..
Compensation of employees	145	129	107	115	353	263	317	..
Migrants' transfer	..	..	..	..	..	..	..	..
Outward remittance flows	486	751	1,187	1,265	1,653	1,341	1,580[b]	..
of which								
Workers' remittances	102	289	638	487	453	361	713	..
Compensation of employees	384	462	549	778	1,200	980	867	..
Migrants' transfer	..	..	..	..	..	..	..	..

a. 2.8% of GDP in 2006.
b. 0.2% of GDP in 2006.

Indonesia

Population (millions, 2006)	223
Population growth (avg. annual %, 1997-2006)	1.3
Population density (people per sq. km, 2006)	123
Labor force (millions, 2006)	109
Urban population (% of pop., 2006)	49.2
Age dependency ratio	0.51
Surface area (1,000 sq. km, 2006)	1,905
GNI ($ billions, 2006)	349
GNI per capita, Atlas method ($, 2006)	1,420
GDP growth (avg. annual %, 2002-06)	5.1
Poverty headcount ratio at national poverty line (% of pop., 2004)	5.4

Migration

EMIGRATION, 2005
- Stock of emigrants: **1,736,717**
- Stock of emigrants as percentage of population: **0.8%**
- Top 10 destination countries: Malaysia, Saudi Arabia, the Netherlands, Singapore, the United States, Australia, the Republic of Korea, Japan, Germany, Canada

SKILLED EMIGRATION, 2000
- Emigration rate of tertiary educated: **2.0%**
- Emigration of physicians: **434** or **1.3%** of physicians trained in the country

IMMIGRATION, 2005
- Stock of immigrants: **159,731**
- Stock of immigrants as percentage of population: **0.1%**
- Females as percentage of immigrants: **46.0%**
- Refugees as percentage of immigrants: **0.0%**

Remittances

US$ millions	2000	2001	2002	2003	2004	2005	2006	2007
Inward remittance flows	**1,190**	**1,046**	**1,259**	**1,489**	**1,866**	**5,419**	**5,722**[a]	**6,000**
of which								
Workers' remittances	1,190	1,046	1,259	1,489	1,700	5,296	5,560	..
Compensation of employees	..	..	..	..	166	123	162	..
Migrants' transfer	..	..	..	..	..	..	..	..
Outward remittance flows	..	..	..	..	**913**	**1,178**	**1,359**[b]	..
of which								
Workers' remittances	..	..	..	..	775	834	1,060	..
Compensation of employees	..	..	..	-	138	344	299	..
Migrants' transfer	..	..	..	..	..	..	..	..

a. 1.6% of GDP in 2006.
b. 0.4% of GDP in 2006.

Iran, The Islamic Republic of

Population (millions, 2006)	69
Population growth (avg. annual %, 1997–2006)	1.4
Population density (people per sq. km, 2006)	42
Labor force (millions, 2006)	29
Urban population (% of pop., 2006)	67.4
Age dependency ratio	0.47
Surface area (1,000 sq. km, 2006)	1,648
GNI ($ billions, 2006)	221
GNI per capita, Atlas method ($, 2006)	3,000
GDP growth (avg. annual %, 2002–06)	6.0
Poverty headcount ratio at national poverty line (% of pop., 2004)	0.1

Migration

EMIGRATION, 2005
- Stock of emigrants: **969,920**
- Stock of emigrants as percentage of population: **1.4%**
- Top 10 destination countries: the United States, Germany, Canada, Israel, Sweden, the United Kingdom, the Netherlands, France, Australia, Austria

SKILLED EMIGRATION, 2000
- Emigration rate of tertiary educated: **13.1%**
- Emigration of physicians: **4,354** or **6.1%** of physicians trained in the country

IMMIGRATION, 2005
- Stock of immigrants: **1,958,703**
- Stock of immigrants as percentage of population: **2.8%**
- Females as percentage of immigrants: **39.7%**
- Refugees as percentage of immigrants: **55.0%**
- Top source countries: Afghanistan, Iraq, Pakistan, Azerbaijan, Turkey, Armenia, Turkmenistan

Remittances

US$ millions	2000	2001	2002	2003	2004	2005	2006	2007
Inward remittance flows	536	682	851	1,178	1,032	1,032	1,032[a]	1,115
of which								
Workers' remittances	..	..	..	..	..	..	..	..
Compensation of employees	..	..	..	..	..	..	..	..
Migrants' transfer	..	..	..	..	..	..	..	..
Outward remittance flows	..	..	..	..	..	..	..	..
of which								
Workers' remittances	..	..	..	..	..	..	..	..
Compensation of employees	..	..	..	..	..	..	..	..
Migrants' transfer	..	..	..	..	..	..	..	..

a. 0.5% of GDP in 2006.

Iraq

LOWER MIDDLE INCOME

Population (millions, 2006)	..
Population growth (avg. annual %, 1997–2006)	3.0
Population density (people per sq. km, 2006)	..
Labor force (millions, 2006)	..
Urban population (% of pop., 2006)	66.8
Age dependency ratio	.:
Surface area (1,000 sq. km, 2006)	438
GNI ($ millions, 2006)	..
GNI per capita, Atlas method ($, 2006)	..
GDP growth (avg. annual %, 2002-06)	-0.9
Poverty headcount ratio at national poverty line (% of pop., 2004)	..

Migration

EMIGRATION, 2005
- Stock of emigrants: **1,024,070**
- Stock of emigrants as percentage of population: **3.6%**
- Top 10 destination countries: the Islamic Republic of Iran, Germany, the United States, Israel, Sweden, the United Kingdom, the Netherlands, Canada, Australia, Denmark

SKILLED EMIGRATION, 2000
- Emigration rate of tertiary educated: **9.1%**
- Emigration of physicians: **1,527** or **10.7%** of physicians trained in the country

IMMIGRATION, 2005
- Stock of immigrants: **28,372**
- Stock of immigrants as percentage of population: **0.1%**
- Females as percentage of immigrants: **31.2%**
- Refugees as percentage of immigrants: **95.1%**

Remittances

Remittance data are currently not available for this country.

Ireland

Population (millions, 2006)	4.2
Population growth (avg. annual %, 1997–2006)	1.5
Population density (people per sq. km, 2006)	61
Labor force (millions, 2006)	2.1
Urban population (% of pop., 2006)	60.8
Age dependency ratio	0.45
Surface area (1,000 sq. km, 2006)	70
GNI ($ billions, 2006)	191
GNI per capita, Atlas method ($, 2006)	45,580
GDP growth (avg. annual %, 2002–06)	5.3
Poverty headcount ratio at national poverty line (% of pop., 2004)	..

Migration

IMMIGRATION, 2005
- Stock of immigrants: **585,429**
- Stock of immigrants as percentage of population: **14.1%**
- Females as percentage of immigrants: **50.0%**
- Refugees as percentage of immigrants: **1.4%**
- Top 10 source countries: the United Kingdom, the United States, Nigeria, Germany, France, South Africa, Australia, Romania, China, Spain

EMIGRATION, 2005
- Stock of emigrants: **927,904**
- Stock of emigrants as percentage of population: **22.4%**
- Top 10 destination countries: the United Kingdom, the United States, Australia, Canada, Germany, Spain, New Zealand, France, Italy, the Netherlands

SKILLED EMIGRATION, 2000
- Emigration rate of tertiary educated: **34.4%**
- Emigration of physicians: **2,742** or **24.6%** of physicians trained in the country

Remittances

US$ millions	2000	2001	2002	2003	2004	2005	2006	2007
Inward remittance flows	252	244	316	337	414	513	532[a]	532
of which								
Workers' remittances	55	54	42	33	25	25	19	..
Compensation of employees	197	190	274	304	389	488	513	..
Migrants' transfer	..	..	..	..	..	..	..	..
Outward remittance flows	181	274	588	788	997	1,536	1,947[b]	..
of which								
Workers' remittances	4	4	97	154	169	378	575	..
Compensation of employees	107	202	419	548	734	1,063	1,277	..
Migrants' transfer	70	68	72	86	94	95	95	..

a. 0.2% of GDP in 2006.
b. 0.9% of GDP in 2006.

Israel

Population (millions, 2006)	7.0
Population growth (avg. annual %, 1997–2006)	2.1
Population density (people per sq. km, 2006)	325
Labor force (millions, 2006)	2.8
Urban population (% of pop., 2006)	91.6
Age dependency ratio	0.61
Surface area (1,000 sq. km, 2006)	22
GNI ($ billions, 2006)	122
GNI per capita, Atlas method ($, 2006)	18,580
GDP growth (avg. annual %, 2002–06)	2.5
Poverty headcount ratio at national poverty line (% of pop., 2004)	..

Migration

IMMIGRATION, 2005
- Stock of immigrants: **2,660,881**
- Stock of immigrants as percentage of population: **39.6%**
- Females as percentage of immigrants: **55.9%**
- Refugees as percentage of immigrants: **0.0%**
- Top 10 source countries: Russia, Ukraine, Morocco, Romania, Poland, Iraq, Uzbekistan, Ethiopia, Kazakhstan, the Islamic Republic of Iran

EMIGRATION, 2005
- Stock of emigrants: **808,078**
- Stock of emigrants as percentage of population: **12.0%**
- Top 10 destination countries: West Bank and Gaza, the United States, Canada, Germany, the United Kingdom, France, Australia, the Netherlands, Italy, Turkey

SKILLED EMIGRATION, 2000
- Emigration rate of tertiary educated: **6.5%**
- Emigration of physicians: **1,274** or **5.1%** of physicians trained in the country

Remittances

US$ millions	2000	2001	2002	2003	2004	2005	2006	2007
Inward remittance flows	401	499	410	424	715	851	1,063ᵃ	1,063
of which								
Workers' remittances	..	..	..	..	..	..	..	..
Compensation of employees	183	196	167	171	298	377	463	..
Migrants' transfer	218	303	243	252	417	473	600	..
Outward remittance flows	3,255	3,039	2,781	2,502	2,247	2,235	2,428ᵇ	..
of which								
Workers' remittances	..	..	..	..	..	..	..	..
Compensation of employees	3,255	3,039	2,781	2,502	2,247	2,235	2,428	..
Migrants' transfer	..	..	..	..	..	..	..	..

a. 0.9% of GDP in 2006.
b. 2.0% of GDP in 2006.

Italy

Population (millions, 2006)	59
Population growth (avg. annual %, 1997–2006)	0.3
Population density (people per sq. km, 2006)	199
Labor force (millions, 2006)	24
Urban population (% of pop., 2006)	67.8
Age dependency ratio	0.52
Surface area (1,000 sq. km, 2006)	301
GNI ($ billions, 2006)	1,839
GNI per capita, Atlas method ($, 2006)	32,020
GDP growth (avg. annual %, 2002–06)	0.7
Poverty headcount ratio at national poverty line (% of pop., 2004)	..

Migration

IMMIGRATION, 2005
- Stock of immigrants: **2,519,040**
- Stock of immigrants as percentage of population: **4.3%**
- Females as percentage of immigrants: **55.8%**
- Refugees as percentage of immigrants: **0.7%**
- Top 10 source countries: Morocco, Albania, Romania, the Philippines, China, the United States, Serbia and Montenegro, Senegal, Germany, Sri Lanka

EMIGRATION, 2005
- Stock of emigrants: **3,459,027**
- Stock of emigrants as percentage of population: **6.0%**
- Top 10 destination countries: Germany, the United States, France, Canada, Switzerland, Australia, Argentina, the United Kingdom, Belgium, Spain

SKILLED EMIGRATION, 2000
- Emigration rate of tertiary educated: **7.0%**
- Emigration of physicians: **5,842** or **1.7%** of physicians trained in the country

Remittances

US$ millions	2000	2001	2002	2003	2004	2005	2006	2007
Inward remittance flows	**1,937**	**2,266**	**2,263**	**2,140**	**2,173**	**2,394**	**2,626ª**	**2,626**
of which								
Workers' remittances	359	322	296	288	284	289	312	..
Compensation of employees	1,511	1,845	1,881	1,726	1,807	2,026	2,246	..
Migrants' transfer	67	99	86	126	82	79	68	..
Outward remittance flows	**2,582**	**2,710**	**3,579**	**4,369**	**5,512**	**7,621**	**8,217ᵇ**	..
of which								
Workers' remittances	541	670	752	1,328	3,370	4,827	5,483	..
Compensation of employees	1,960	1,905	2,757	2,984	2,069	2,717	2,645	..
Migrants' transfer	81	135	70	57	73	77	89	..

a. 0.1% of GDP in 2006.
b. 0.4% of GDP in 2006.

Jamaica

Latin America and the Caribbean	LOWER MIDDLE INCOME
Population (millions, 2006)	2.7
Population growth (avg. annual %, 1997–2006)	0.6
Population density (people per sq. km, 2006)	246
Labor force (millions, 2006)	1.2
Urban population (% of pop., 2006)	53.4
Age dependency ratio	0.62
Surface area (1,000 sq. km, 2006)	11
GNI ($ billions, 2006)	9.4
GNI per capita, Atlas method ($, 2006)	3,480
GDP growth (avg. annual %, 2002–06)	2.0
Poverty headcount ratio at national poverty line (% of pop., 2004)	0.5

Migration

EMIGRATION, 2005
- Stock of emigrants: **1,037,599**
- Stock of emigrants as percentage of population: **39.1%**
- Top 10 destination countries: the United States, the United Kingdom, Canada, Cayman Islands, Cuba, the Bahamas, Antigua and Barbuda, Germany, Netherlands Antilles, the Netherlands

SKILLED EMIGRATION, 2000
- Emigration rate of tertiary educated: **82.5%**
- Emigration of physicians: **569** or **16.7%** of physicians trained in the country

IMMIGRATION, 2005
- Stock of immigrants: **17,645**
- Stock of immigrants as percentage of population: **0.7%**
- Females as percentage of immigrants: **52.5%**
- Refugees as percentage of immigrants: **0.0%**
- Top 10 source countries: the United Kingdom, Cuba, China, the United States, India, Canada, Trinidad and Tobago, Barbados, Guyana, Cayman Islands

Remittances

US$ millions	2000	2001	2002	2003	2004	2005	2006	2007
Inward remittance flows	892	1,058	1,261	1,399	1,623	1,783	1,946[a]	2,021
of which								
Workers' remittances	790	940	1,131	1,270	1,466	1,621	1,769	..
Compensation of employees	88	107	111	110	135	140	154	..
Migrants' transfer	14	12	19	19	22	22	23	..
Outward remittance flows	179	217	278	341	425	394	385[b]	..
of which								
Workers' remittances	131	147	213	283	340	317	300	..
Compensation of employees	21	32	29	39	51	52	58	..
Migrants' transfer	27	38	36	19	34	25	27	..

a. 18.5% of GDP in 2006.
b. 3.7% of GDP in 2006.

Japan

Population (millions, 2006)	128
Population growth (avg. annual %, 1997–2006)	0.1
Population density (people per sq. km, 2006)	350
Labor force (millions, 2006)	66
Urban population (% of pop., 2006)	66
Age dependency ratio	0.52
Surface area (1,000 sq. km, 2006)	378
GNI ($ billions, 2006)	4,443
GNI per capita, Atlas method ($, 2006)	38,410
GDP growth (avg. annual %, 2002-06)	1.8
Poverty headcount ratio at national poverty line (% of pop., 2004)	..

Migration

IMMIGRATION, 2005
- Stock of immigrants: **2,048,487**
- Stock of immigrants as percentage of population: **1.6%**
- Females as percentage of immigrants: **53.8%**
- Refugees as percentage of immigrants: **0.1%**
- Top 10 source countries: the Republic of Korea, China, Brazil, the Democratic People's Republic of Korea, the Philippines, the United States, Peru, Thailand, Indonesia, Vietnam

EMIGRATION, 2005
- Stock of emigrants: **940,028**
- Stock of emigrants as percentage of population: **0.7%**
- Top 10 destination countries: the United States, Brazil, the Republic of Korea, Germany, the United Kingdom, Canada, Australia, Thailand, France, Italy

SKILLED EMIGRATION, 2000
- Emigration rate of tertiary educated: **1.5%**
- Emigration of physicians: **461** or **0.2%** of physicians trained in the country

Remittances

US$ millions	2000	2001	2002	2003	2004	2005	2006	2007
Inward remittance flows	1,374	1,984	1,821	1,079	930	1,080	1,380ª	1,578
of which								
Workers' remittances	505	1,037	947	657	600	733	1,026	..
Compensation of employees	269	212	180	155	173	172	151	..
Migrants' transfer	600	734	694	267	157	175	203	..
Outward remittance flows	3,167	2,946	3,349	1,774	1,410	1,281	3,476ᵇ	..
of which								
Workers' remittances	2,259	2,092	2,414	1,231	926	851	3,152	..
Compensation of employees	272	253	265	274	286	299	180	..
Migrants' transfer	637	601	670	269	198	131	144	..

a. 0.03% of GDP in 2006.
b. 0.1% of GDP in 2006.

Jordan

LOWER MIDDLE INCOME

Population (millions, 2006)	5.6
Population growth (avg. annual %, 1997–2006)	2.6
Population density (people per sq. km, 2006)	63
Labor force (millions, 2006)	1.9
Urban population (% of pop., 2006)	82.6
Age dependency ratio	0.67
Surface area (1,000 sq. km, 2006)	89
GNI ($ billions, 2006)	15
GNI per capita, Atlas method ($, 2006)	2,660
GDP growth (avg. annual %, 2002–06)	6.4
Poverty headcount ratio at national poverty line (% of pop., 2004)	0.1

Migration

EMIGRATION, 2005
- Stock of emigrants: **641,154**
- Stock of emigrants as percentage of population: **11.2%**
- Top 10 destination countries: West Bank and Gaza, Saudi Arabia, the United States, Germany, Oman, Canada, the United Kingdom, Australia, Spain, Sweden '

SKILLED EMIGRATION, 2000
- Emigration rate of tertiary educated: **6.4%**
- Emigration of physicians: **672** or **6.4%** of physicians trained in the country

IMMIGRATION, 2005
- Stock of immigrants: **2,224,890**
- Stock of immigrants as percentage of population: **39.0%**
- Females as percentage of immigrants: **49.1%**
- Refugees as percentage of immigrants: **81.0%**

Remittances

US$ millions	2000	2001	2002	2003	2004	2005	2006	2007
Inward remittance flows	**1,845**	**2,011**	**2,135**	**2,201**	**2,331**	**2,500**	**2,883**[a]	**2,934**
of which								
Workers' remittances	1,661	1,810	1,921	1,981	2,059	2,179	2,514	..
Compensation of employees	185	201	222	220	272	321	369	..
Migrants' transfer	..	..	..	..	..	..	..	..
Outward remittance flows	**197**	**193**	**194**	**227**	**272**	**349**	**401**[b]	..
of which								
Workers' remittances	174	170	171	200	240	308	354	..
Compensation of employees	23	23	23	27	32	41	47	..
Migrants' transfer	..	..	..	..	..	..	..	..

a. 20.3% of GDP in 2006.
b. 2.8% of GDP in 2006.

Kazakhstan

Population (millions, 2006)	15
Population growth (avg. annual %, 1997–2006)	-0.2
Population density (people per sq. km, 2006)	6
Labor force (millions, 2006)	8.3
Urban population (% of pop., 2006)	57.6
Age dependency ratio	0.45
Surface area (1,000 sq. km, 2006)	2,725
GNI ($ billions, 2006)	68
GNI per capita, Atlas method ($, 2006)	3,790
GDP growth (avg. annual %, 2002–06)	9.8
Poverty headcount ratio at national poverty line (% of pop., 2004)	0.9

Migration

EMIGRATION, 2005
- Stock of emigrants: **3,710,351**
- Stock of emigrants as percentage of population: **25.0%**
- Top 10 destination countries: Russia, Ukraine, Uzbekistan, Israel, Germany, Greece, Turkmenistan, Latvia, the United States, the Kyrgyz Republic

SKILLED EMIGRATION, 2000
- Emigration rate of tertiary educated: **1.1%**
- Emigration of physicians: **117** or **0.2%** of physicians trained in the country

IMMIGRATION, 2005
- Stock of immigrants: **2,501,779**
- Stock of immigrants as percentage of population: **16.9%**
- Females as percentage of immigrants: **57.8%**
- Refugees as percentage of immigrants: **0.6%**
- Top 10 source countries: Russia, Ukraine, Uzbekistan, Germany, Belarus, Azerbaijan, Turkey, Poland, Tajikistan, Moldova

Remittances

US$ millions	2000	2001	2002	2003	2004	2005	2006	2007
Inward remittance flows	**122**	**171**	**205**	**147**	**165**	**178**	**188**[a]	**188**
of which								
Workers' remittances	64	81	107	38	53	56	73	..
Compensation of employees	4	4	4	4	4	6	11	..
Migrants' transfer	54	86	94	105	108	116	104	..
Outward remittance flows	**440**	**487**	**594**	**802**	**1,354**	**2,000**	**3,037**[b]	..
of which								
Workers' remittances	74	143	286	421	806	1,158	2,000	..
Compensation of employees	47	60	79	230	414	735	962	..
Migrants' transfer	319	284	230	151	134	107	75	..

a. 0.2% of GDP in 2006.
b. 3.9% of GDP in 2006. *

Kenya

LOW INCOME

Population (millions, 2006)	35
Population growth (avg. annual %, 1997–2006)	2.3
Population density (people per sq. km, 2006)	62
Labor force (millions, 2006)	16
Urban population (% of pop., 2006)	21
Age dependency ratio	0.84
Surface area (1,000 sq. km, 2006)	580
GNI ($ billions, 2006)	21
GNI per capita, Atlas method ($, 2006)	580
GDP growth (avg. annual %, 2002–06)	4.0
Poverty headcount ratio at national poverty line (% of pop., 2004)	12.1

Migration

EMIGRATION, 2005
- Stock of emigrants: **427,324**
- Stock of emigrants as percentage of population: **1.2%**
- Top 10 destination countries: the United Kingdom, Tanzania, the United States, Uganda, Canada, Germany, Australia, India, the Netherlands, Switzerland

SKILLED EMIGRATION, 2000
- Emigration rate of tertiary educated: **26.3%**
- Emigration of physicians:
  a) **204** or **4.9%** of physicians trained in the country (Source: Docquier and Bhargava 2006)
  b) **3,975** or **50.8%** of physicians trained in the country (Source: Clemens and Pettersson 2006)
- Emigration of nurses: **2,372** or **8.3%** of nurses trained in the country

IMMIGRATION, 2005
- Stock of immigrants: **344,857**
- Stock of immigrants as percentage of population: **1.0%**
- Females as percentage of immigrants: **47.9%**
- Refugees as percentage of immigrants: **69.9%**

Remittances

US$ millions	2000	2001	2002	2003	2004	2005	2006	2007
Inward remittance flows	538	550	433	538	620	805	1,128[a]	1,300
of which								
Workers' remittances	-	51	57	66	376	425	570	..
Compensation of employees	..	..	..	..	..	..	..	..
Migrants' transfer	..	..	..	..	..	..	..	..
Outward remittance flows	34	5	6	7	34	56	25[b]	..
of which								
Workers' remittances	-	5	6	7	34	56	25	..
Compensation of employees	..	..	..	..	..	..	..	..
Migrants' transfer	..	..	..	..	..	..	..	..

a. 5.3% of GDP in 2006.
b. 0.1% of GDP in 2006.

Migration and Remittances Factbook 2008

Kiribati

LOWER MIDDLE INCOME

Population (thousands, 2006)	101
Population growth (avg. annual %, 1997–2006)	2.1
Population density (people per sq. km, 2006)	138
Labor force (millions, 2006)	..
Urban population (% of pop., 2006)	48.2
Age dependency ratio	..
Surface area (sq. km, 2006)	730
GNI ($ millions, 2006)	120
GNI per capita, Atlas method ($, 2006)	1,230
GDP growth (avg. annual %, 2002–06)	2.0
Poverty headcount ratio at national poverty line (% of pop., 2004)	..

Migration

EMIGRATION, 2005
- Stock of emigrants: **4,837**
- Stock of emigrants as percentage of population: **4.9%**
- Top 10 destination countries: the United States, Germany, the Solomon Islands, New Zealand, Australia, Fiji, the United Kingdom, Canada, Samoa, Japan

SKILLED EMIGRATION, 2000
- Emigration rate of tertiary educated: **24.9%**
- Emigration of physicians: **0** or **0.0%** of physicians trained in the country

IMMIGRATION, 2005
- Stock of immigrants: **2,574**
- Stock of immigrants as percentage of population: **2.6%**
- Females as percentage of immigrants: **48.8%**
- Refugees as percentage of immigrants: **0.0%**
- Top source countries: French Polynesia, Samoa, Tonga, American Samoa

Remittances

US$ millions	2000	2001	2002	2003	2004	2005	2006	2007
Inward remittance flows	7	7	7	7	7	7	7[a]	7
of which								
Workers' remittances	..	..	..	..	..	..	..	..
Compensation of employees	..	..	..	..	..	..	..	..
Migrants' transfer	..	..	..	..	..	..	..	..
Outward remittance flows	..	..	..	..	..	..	..	..
of which								
Workers' remittances	..	..	..	..	..	..	..	..
Compensation of employees	..	..	..	..	..	..	..	..
Migrants' transfer	..	..	..	..	..	..	..	..

a. 9.9% of GDP in 2006.

Korea, The Democratic People's Republic of

LOW INCOME

Population (millions, 2006)	23
Population growth (avg. annual %, 1997–2006)	0.7
Population density (people per sq. km, 2006)	187
Labor force (millions, 2006)	11
Urban population (% of pop., 2006)	62
Age dependency ratio	0.46
Surface area (1,000 sq. km, 2006)	121
GNI ($ millions, 2006)	..
GNI per capita, Atlas method ($, 2006)	..
GDP growth (avg. annual %, 2002–06)	..
Poverty headcount ratio at national poverty line (% of pop., 2004)	..

Migration

EMIGRATION, 2005
- Stock of emigrants: **580,623**
- Stock of emigrants as percentage of population: **2.6%**
- Top 10 destination countries: Japan, the United States, Germany, Brazil, Paraguay, Denmark, Ireland, Ecuador, Cambodia, Mexico

SKILLED EMIGRATION, 2000
- Emigration rate of tertiary educated: **5.3%**
- Emigration of physicians: **0,000** or **0.0%** of physicians trained in the country

IMMIGRATION, 2005
- Stock of immigrants: **36,765**
- Stock of immigrants as percentage of population: **0.2%**
- Females as percentage of immigrants: **54.0%**
- Refugees as percentage of immigrants: **5.0%**

Remittances

Remittance data are currently not available for this country.

Korea, The Republic of

Population (millions, 2006)	48
Population growth (avg. annual %, 1997-2006)	0.6
Population density (people per sq. km, 2006)	490
Labor force (millions, 2006)	25
Urban population (% of pop., 2006)	81
Age dependency ratio	0.39
Surface area (1,000 sq. km, 2006)	99
GNI ($ billions, 2006)	888
GNI per capita, Atlas method ($, 2006)	17,690
GDP growth (avg. annual %, 2002-06)	4.8
Poverty headcount ratio at national poverty line (% of pop., 2004)	..

Migration

IMMIGRATION, 2005
- Stock of immigrants: **551,193**
- Stock of immigrants as percentage of population: **1.2%**
- Females as percentage of immigrants: **53.5%**
- Refugees as percentage of immigrants: **0.0%**
- Top 10 source countries: China, Japan, the Philippines, the United States, Indonesia, Vietnam, Bangladesh, Thailand, Pakistan, Canada

EMIGRATION, 2005
- Stock of emigrants: **1,609,206**
- Stock of emigrants as percentage of population: **3.4%**
- Top 10 destination countries: the United States, Japan, Canada, Australia, Germany, France, New Zealand, the United Kingdom, Sweden, Denmark

SKILLED EMIGRATION, 2000
- Emigration rate of tertiary educated: **7.9%**
- Emigration of physicians: **1,686** or **1.9%** of physicians trained in the country

Remittances

US$ millions	2000	2001	2002	2003	2004	2005	2006	2007
Inward remittance flows	735	652	662	827	799	847	918[a]	985
of which								
Workers' remittances	63	48	34	42	30	64	136	..
Compensation of employees	582	566	590	732	713	745	606	..
Migrants' transfer	90	38	38	53	56	38	176	..
Outward remittance flows	972	1,014	1,474	1,852	2,497	3,336	4,244[b]	..
of which								
Workers' remittances	227	239	297	359	559	839	961	..
Compensation of employees	51	69	64	97	126	119	140	..
Migrants' transfer	694	706	1,113	1,396	1,812	2,378	3,143	..

a. 0.1% of GDP in 2006.
b. 0.5% of GDP in 2006.

Kuwait

Population (millions, 2006)	2.6
Population growth (avg. annual %, 1997–2006)	3.2
Population density (people per sq. km, 2006)	148
Labor force (millions, 2006)	1.4
Urban population (% of pop., 2006)	98.3
Age dependency ratio	0.35
Surface area (1,000 sq. km, 2006)	18
GNI ($ billions, 2006)	90
GNI per capita, Atlas method ($, 2006)	30,630
GDP growth (avg. annual %, 2002–06)	8.3
Poverty headcount ratio at national poverty line (% of pop., 2004)	..

Migration

IMMIGRATION, 2005

- Stock of immigrants: **1,668,991**
- Stock of immigrants as percentage of population: **62.1%**
- Females as percentage of immigrants: **31.0%**
- Refugees as percentage of immigrants: **0.1%**
- Top source country: India

EMIGRATION, 2005

- Stock of emigrants: **185,802**
- Stock of emigrants as percentage of population: **6.9%**
- Top 10 destination countries: Saudi Arabia, the United States, Canada, India, the United Kingdom, Australia, the Netherlands, Denmark, Sweden, France

SKILLED EMIGRATION, 2000

- Emigration rate of tertiary educated: **10.0%**
- Emigration of physicians: **57** or **1.6%** of physicians trained in the country

Remittances

US$ millions	2000	2001	2002	2003	2004	2005	2006	2007
Inward remittance flows	..	..	..	..	..	..	..	..
of which								
Workers' remittances	..	..	..	..	..	..	..	..
Compensation of employees	..	..	..	..	..	..	..	..
Migrants' transfer	..	..	..	..	..	..	..	..
Outward remittance flows	1,734	1,784	1,925	2,144	2,403	2,648	3,021[a]	..
of which								
Workers' remittances	1,734	1,785	1,926	2,144	2,403	2,648	3,021	..
Compensation of employees	..	..	..	..	..	..	..	..
Migrants' transfer	..	..	..	..	..	..	..	..

a. 3.7% of GDP in 2006.

Kyrgyz Republic, The

Population (millions, 2006)	5.2
Population growth (avg. annual %, 1997-2006)	1.1
Population density (people per sq. km, 2006)	27
Labor force (millions, 2006)	2.3
Urban population (% of pop., 2006)	36
Age dependency ratio	0.58
Surface area (1,000 sq. km, 2006)	200
GNI ($ billions, 2006)	2.6
GNI per capita, Atlas method ($, 2006)	490
GDP growth (avg. annual %, 2002-06)	3.3
Poverty headcount ratio at national poverty line (% of pop., 2004)	0.4

Migration

EMIGRATION, 2005
- Stock of emigrants: **615,290**
- Stock of emigrants as percentage of population: **11.7%**
- Top 10 destination countries: Russia, Ukraine, Israel, Germany, Tajikistan, Kazakhstan, Latvia, the United States, Turkey, Canada

SKILLED EMIGRATION, 2000
- Emigration rate of tertiary educated: **0.7%**
- Emigration of physicians: **0** or **0.0%** of physicians trained in the country

IMMIGRATION, 2005
- Stock of immigrants: **287,791**
- Stock of immigrants as percentage of population: **5.5%**
- Females as percentage of immigrants: **58.2%**
- Refugees as percentage of immigrants: **1.1%**
- Top source countries: Uzbekistan, Russia, Ukraine, Kazakhstan, Tajikistan, Turkey, Germany

Remittances

US$ millions	2000	2001	2002	2003	2004	2005	2006	2007
Inward remittance flows	9	11	37	78	189	322	739[a]	739
of which								
Workers' remittances	2	5	30	70	179	313	731	..
Compensation of employees	..	..	..	..	..	..	..	..
Migrants' transfer	7	7	6	8	10	9	8	..
Outward remittance flows	45	54	57	55	82	122	145[b]	..
of which								
Workers' remittances	1	3	2	5	15	33	44	..
Compensation of employees	10	10	12	13	14	17	19	..
Migrants' transfer	34	41	43	37	53	72	82	..

a. 27.4% of GDP in 2006.
b. 5.4% of GDP in 2006.

Lao, The People's Democratic Republic

Population (millions, 2006)	5.8
Population growth (avg. annual %, 1997–2006)	1.8
Population density (people per sq. km, 2006)	25
Labor force (millions, 2006)	2.3
Urban population (% of pop., 2006)	21
Age dependency ratio	0.79
Surface area (1,000 sq. km, 2006)	237
GNI ($ billions, 2006)	3.0
GNI per capita, Atlas method ($, 2006)	500
GDP growth (avg. annual %, 2002–06)	6.6
Poverty headcount ratio at national poverty line (% of pop., 2004)	20.6

Migration

EMIGRATION, 2005

- Stock of emigrants: **413,379**
- Stock of emigrants as percentage of population: **7.0%**
- Top 10 destination countries: the United States, Thailand, France, Canada, Australia, Japan, Germany, Cambodia, New Zealand, Switzerland

SKILLED EMIGRATION, 2000

- Emigration rate of tertiary educated: **13.8%**
- Emigration of physicians: **33** or **1.0%** of physicians trained in the country

IMMIGRATION, 2005

- Stock of immigrants: **24,646**
- Stock of immigrants as percentage of population: **0.4%**
- Females as percentage of immigrants: **48.2%**
- Refugees as percentage of immigrants: **0.0%**
- Top source countries: Vietnam, China, Thailand, Cambodia, Myanmar, Australia

Remittances

US$ millions	2000	2001	2002	2003	2004	2005	2006	2007
Inward remittance flows	1	1	1	1	1	1	1[a]	1
of which								
Workers' remittances	..	..	..	..	..	..	..	..
Compensation of employees	1	1	..	..	..	..	..	..
Migrants' transfer	..	..	..	..	..	..	..	..
Outward remittance flows	0	1	1	1	1	1	1[b]	..
of which								
Workers' remittances	..	..	..	..	..	..	..	..
Compensation of employees	0	0	..	..	..	..	..	..
Migrants' transfer	..	..	..	..	..	..	..	..

a. 0.03% of GDP in 2006.
b. 0.01% of GDP in 2006.

Latvia

Population (millions, 2006)	2.3
Population growth (avg. annual %, 1997–2006)	-0.9
Population density (people per sq. km, 2006)	37
Labor force (millions, 2006)	1.1
Urban population (% of pop., 2006)	67.9
Age dependency ratio	0.46
Surface area (1,000 sq. km, 2006)	65
GNI ($ billions, 2006)	19
GNI per capita, Atlas method ($, 2006)	8,100
GDP growth (avg. annual %, 2002–06)	9.0
Poverty headcount ratio at national poverty line (% of pop., 2004)	0.5

Migration

EMIGRATION, 2005
- Stock of emigrants: **232,865**
- Stock of emigrants as percentage of population: **10.1%**
- Top 10 destination countries: Russia, the United States, Germany, Israel, Canada, Lithuania, Australia, the United Kingdom, Estonia, Ireland

SKILLED EMIGRATION, 2000
- Emigration rate of tertiary educated: **10.2%**
- Emigration of physicians: **101** or **1.3%** of physicians trained in the country

IMMIGRATION, 2005
- Stock of immigrants: **449,215**
- Stock of immigrants as percentage of population: **19.5%**
- Females as percentage of immigrants: **57.8%**
- Refugees as percentage of immigrants: **0.0%**
- Top 10 source countries: Russia, Ukraine, Uzbekistan, Belarus, Kazakhstan, Lithuania, Azerbaijan, Georgia, Estonia, Tajikistan

Remittances

US$ millions	2000	2001	2002	2003	2004	2005	2006	2007
Inward remittance flows	72	112	138	173	230	381	483[a]	500
of which								
Workers' remittances	3	2	2	2	2	2	2	..
Compensation of employees	70	110	136	172	228	379	481	..
Migrants' transfer	..	..	..	..	..	..	..	..
Outward remittance flows	7	8	7	8	14	20	29[b]	..
of which								
Workers' remittances	3	3	3	3	4	4	4	..
Compensation of employees	4	5	5	5	10	16	25	..
Migrants' transfer	..	..	..	..	..	..	..	..

a. 2.4% of GDP in 2006.
b. 0.1% of GDP in 2006.

Lebanon

Population (millions, 2006)	4.1
Population growth (avg. annual %, 1997–2006)	1.3
Population density (people per sq. km, 2006)	396
Labor force (millions, 2006)	1.6
Urban population (% of pop., 2006)	86.7
Age dependency ratio	0.55
Surface area (1,000 sq. km, 2006)	10
GNI ($ billions, 2006)	22
GNI per capita, Atlas method ($, 2006)	5,490
GDP growth (avg. annual %, 2002–06)	3.2
Poverty headcount ratio at national poverty line (% of pop., 2004)	..

Migration

EMIGRATION, 2005
- Stock of emigrants: **621,903**
- Stock of emigrants as percentage of population: **17.4%**
- Top 10 destination countries: the United States, Canada, Australia, Germany, Saudi Arabia, France, Sweden, Brazil, West Bank and Gaza, Denmark

SKILLED EMIGRATION, 2000
- Emigration rate of tertiary educated: **29.7%**
- Emigration of physicians: **1,327** or **9.3%** of physicians trained in the country

IMMIGRATION, 2005
- Stock of immigrants: **656,727**
- Stock of immigrants as percentage of population: **18.4%**
- Females as percentage of immigrants: **57.5%**
- Refugees as percentage of immigrants: **61.4%**

Remittances

US$ millions	2000	2001	2002	2003	2004	2005	2006	2007
Inward remittance flows	1,582	2,307	2,544	4,743	5,592	4,924	5,183ᵃ	5,500
of which								
Workers' remittances	..	..	2,544	3,964	5,183	4,257	4,603	..
Compensation of employees	..	..	0	779	409	667	580	..
Migrants' transfer	..	..	..	..	..	..	..	..
Outward remittance flows	..	..	2,521	4,081	4,233	4,012	4,132ᵇ	..
of which								
Workers' remittances	..	..	2,510	3,694	3,573	3,281	3,471	..
Compensation of employees	..	..	11	387	660	731	661	..
Migrants' transfer	..	..	..	..	..	..	..	..

a. 22.8% of GDP in 2006.
b. 18.2% of GDP in 2006.

Lesotho

Population (millions, 2006)	1.8
Population growth (avg. annual %, 1997–2006)	0.4
Population density (people per sq. km, 2006)	59
Labor force (thousands, 2006)	632
Urban population (% of pop., 2006)	19
Age dependency ratio	0.77
Surface area (1,000 sq. km, 2006)	30
GNI ($ billions, 2006)	1.8
GNI per capita, Atlas method ($, 2006)	1,030
GDP growth (avg. annual %, 2002–06)	3.1
Poverty headcount ratio at national poverty line (% of pop., 2004)	44.4

Migration

EMIGRATION, 2005
- Stock of emigrants: **258,589**
- Stock of emigrants as percentage of population: **14.4%**
- Top 10 destination countries: South Africa, Mozambique, Tanzania, the United Kingdom, the United States, Canada, Germany, Switzerland, the Netherlands, Ireland

SKILLED EMIGRATION, 2000
- Emigration rate of tertiary educated: **2.4%**
- Emigration of physicians:
  a) **0** or **0.0%** of physicians trained in the country *(Source: Docquier and Bhargava 2006)*
  b) **57** or **33.3%** of physicians trained in the country *(Source: Clemens and Pettersson 2006)*
- Emigration of nurses: **36** or **2.8%** of nurses trained in the country

IMMIGRATION, 2005
- Stock of immigrants: **5,886**
- Stock of immigrants as percentage of population: **0.3%**
- Females as percentage of immigrants: **50.3%**
- Refugees as percentage of immigrants: **0.0%**
- Top 10 source countries: South Africa, Zimbabwe, Tanzania, Botswana, Zambia, Swaziland, Malawi, Mozambique, Namibia, Angola

Remittances

US$ millions	2000	2001	2002	2003	2004	2005	2006	2007
Inward remittance flows	252	209	194	287	355	327	361[a]	371
of which								
Workers' remittances	0	1	10	11	14	7	4	..
Compensation of employees	252	208	184	276	341	320	357	..
Migrants' transfer	..	..	..	..	..	..	..	..
Outward remittance flows	28	25	21	27	29	17	11[b]	..
of which								
Workers' remittances	-	..	..	..	..	..	..	..
Compensation of employees	28	25	21	27	29	17	11	..
Migrants' transfer	..	..	..	..	..	..	..	..

a. 24.5% of GDP in 2006.
b. 0.7% of GDP in 2006.

Liberia

Population (millions, 2006)	3.4
Population growth (avg. annual %, 1997-2006)	3.9
Population density (people per sq. km, 2006)	35
Labor force (millions, 2006)	1.2
Urban population (% of pop., 2006)	58.8
Age dependency ratio	0.98
Surface area (1,000 sq. km, 2006)	111
GNI ($ millions, 2006)	494
GNI per capita, Atlas method ($, 2006)	140
GDP growth (avg. annual %, 2002-06)	-2.4
Poverty headcount ratio at national poverty line (% of pop., 2004)	. .

Migration

EMIGRATION, 2005
- Stock of emigrants: **89,075**
- Stock of emigrants as percentage of population: **2.7%**
- Top 10 destination countries: the United States, Nigeria, Sierra Leone, Germany, Spain, the Netherlands, the United Kingdom, France, Canada, Sweden

SKILLED EMIGRATION, 2000
- Emigration rate of tertiary educated: **37.4%**
- Emigration of physicians:
  a) **37** or **33.9%** of physicians trained in the country *(Source: Docquier and Bhargava 2006)*
  b) **126** or **63.3%** of physicians trained in the country *(Source: Clemens and Pettersson 2006)*
- Emigration of nurses: **807** or **81.4%** of nurses trained in the country

IMMIGRATION, 2005
- Stock of immigrants: **50,172**
- Stock of immigrants as percentage of population: **1.5%**
- Females as percentage of immigrants: **45.1%**
- Refugees as percentage of immigrants: **20.2%**
- Top 10 source countries: Guinea, Ghana, Sierra Leone, Lebanon, the United States, Nigeria, Côte d'Ivoire, Mali, the United Kingdom, Sweden

Remittances
Remittance data are currently not available for this country.

Libya

Population (millions, 2006)	6.0
Population growth (avg. annual %, 1997-2006)	2.0
Population density (people per sq. km, 2006)	3
Labor force (millions, 2006)	2.4
Urban population (% of pop., 2006)	85.1
Age dependency ratio	0.52
Surface area (1,000 sq. km, 2006)	1,760
GNI ($ billions, 2006)	50
GNI per capita, Atlas method ($, 2006)	7,380
GDP growth (avg. annual %, 2002-06)	3.5
Poverty headcount ratio at national poverty line (% of pop., 2004)	..

Migration

EMIGRATION, 2005
- Stock of emigrants: **90,138**
- Stock of emigrants as percentage of population: **1.5%**
- Top 10 destination countries: Israel, Chad, the United Kingdom, the United States, Germany, Turkey, Canada, France, Australia, Italy

SKILLED EMIGRATION, 2000
- Emigration rate of tertiary educated: **3.8%**
- Emigration of physicians:
  a) **521** or **7.2%** of physicians trained in the country (Source: Docquier and Bhargava 2006)
  b) **585** or **8.4%** of physicians trained in the country (Source: Clemens and Pettersson 2006)
- Emigration of nurses: **391** or **2.2%** of nurses trained in the country

IMMIGRATION, 2005
- Stock of immigrants: **617,536**
- Stock of immigrants as percentage of population: **10.6%**
- Females as percentage of immigrants: **35.5%**
- Refugees as percentage of immigrants: **2.0%**
- Top source countries: Egypt, Tunisia, West Bank and Gaza, Syria

Remittances

US$ millions	2000	2001	2002	2003	2004	2005	2006	2007
Inward remittance flows	9	10	7	8	10	15	16[a]	16
of which								
Workers' remittances	6	5	3	3	5	7	6	..
Compensation of employees	3	5	4	5	5	8	10	..
Migrants' transfer	..	..	..	..	..	..	..	..
Outward remittance flows	463	683	694	676	790	914	945[b]	..
of which								
Workers' remittances	454	675	776	644	940	854	880	..
Compensation of employees	9	8	10	32	35	60	65	..
Migrants' transfer	..	..	..	..	..	..	..	..

a. 0.03% of GDP in 2006.
b. 1.9% of GDP in 2006.

Lithuania

Population (millions, 2006)	3.4
Population growth (avg. annual %, 1997–2006)	-0.6
Population density (people per sq. km, 2006)	54
Labor force (millions, 2006)	1.6
Urban population (% of pop., 2006)	66.6
Age dependency ratio	0.47
Surface area (1,000 sq. km, 2006)	65
GNI ($ billions, 2006)	27
GNI per capita, Atlas method ($, 2006)	7,870
GDP growth (avg. annual %, 2002–06)	7.9
Poverty headcount ratio at national poverty line (% of pop., 2004)	0.6

Migration

EMIGRATION, 2005
- Stock of emigrants: **320,473**
- Stock of emigrants as percentage of population: **9.3%**
- Top 10 destination countries: Russia, Poland, the United States, Germany, Israel, Latvia, Spain, Canada, the United Kingdom, Belarus

SKILLED EMIGRATION, 2000
- Emigration rate of tertiary educated: **11.8%**
- Emigration of physicians: **137** or **1.0%** of physicians trained in the country

IMMIGRATION, 2005
- Stock of immigrants: **165,197**
- Stock of immigrants as percentage of population: **4.8%**
- Females as percentage of immigrants: **56.6%**
- Refugees as percentage of immigrants: **0.2%**
- Top 10 source countries: Russia, Belarus, Ukraine, Latvia, Kazakhstan, Poland, Uzbekistan, Germany, Azerbaijan, Estonia

Remittances

US$ millions	2000	2001	2002	2003	2004	2005	2006	2007
Inward remittance flows	**50**	**79**	**109**	**115**	**325**	**534**	**622**[a]	**650**
of which								
Workers' remittances	2	3	35	33	162	310	374	..
Compensation of employees	48	76	74	82	163	224	248	..
Migrants' transfer	..	..	..	..	..	..	..	..
Outward remittance flows	**38**	**29**	**31**	**42**	**28**	**47**	**54**[b]	..
of which								
Workers' remittances	1	1	1	6	2	2	3	..
Compensation of employees	37	28	30	36	26	45	51	..
Migrants' transfer	..	..	..	..	..	..	..	..

a. 2.1% of GDP in 2006.
b. 0.2% of GDP in 2006.

Luxembourg

Population (thousands, 2006)	462
Population growth (avg. annual %, 1997–2006)	1.1
Population density (people per sq. km, 2006)	178
Labor force (thousands, 2006)	205
Urban population (% of pop., 2006)	82.7
Age dependency ratio	0.48
Surface area (1,000 sq. km, 2006)	3
GNI ($ billions, 2006)	36
GNI per capita, Atlas method ($, 2006)	76,040
GDP growth (avg. annual %, 2002–06)	4.0
Poverty headcount ratio at national poverty line (% of pop., 2004)	..

Migration

IMMIGRATION, 2005
- Stock of immigrants: **173,645**
- Stock of immigrants as percentage of population: **37.4%**
- Females as percentage of immigrants: **50.1%**
- Refugees as percentage of immigrants: **3.0%**
- Top 10 source countries: Portugal, France, Belgium, Germany, Italy, Serbia and Montenegro, the Netherlands, the United Kingdom, Cape Verde, Spain

EMIGRATION, 2005
- Stock of emigrants: **42,361**
- Stock of emigrants as percentage of population: **9.1%**
- Top 10 destination countries: France, Germany, Belgium, Portugal, the United States, Spain, Switzerland, the United Kingdom, the Netherlands, Austria

SKILLED EMIGRATION, 2000
- Emigration rate of tertiary educated: **7.6%**
- Emigration of physicians: **286** or **20.7%** of physicians trained in the country

Remittances

US$ millions	2000	2001	2002	2003	2004	2005	2006	2007
Inward remittance flows	**579**	**577**	**826**	**1,034**	**1,169**	**1,201**	**1,289**[a]	**1,480**
of which								
Workers' remittances	..	..	1	1	4	4	6	..
Compensation of employees	579	576	801	1,005	1,154	1,192	1,271	..
Migrants' transfer	..	..	24	28	11	5	12	..
Outward remittance flows	**2,720**	**3,138**	**4,011**	**5,077**	**6,012**	**6,689**	**7,534**[b]	..
of which								
Workers' remittances	..	..	44	53	65	68	81	..
Compensation of employees	2,720	3,138	3,949	4,997	5,940	6,604	7,423	..
Migrants' transfer	..	..	18	27	7	17	30	..

a. 3.1% of GDP in 2006.
b. 18.2% of GDP in 2006.

Macedonia, The Former Yugoslav Republic of

LOWER MIDDLE INCOME

Population (millions, 2006)	2.0
Population growth (avg. annual %, 1997–2006)	0.3
Population density (people per sq. km, 2006)	80
Labor force (thousands, 2006)	869
Urban population (% of pop., 2006)	69.6
Age dependency ratio	0.44
Surface area (1,000 sq. km, 2006)	26
GNI ($ billions, 2006)	6.2
GNI per capita, Atlas method ($, 2006)	3,060
GDP growth (avg. annual %, 2002–06)	2.9
Poverty headcount ratio at national poverty line (% of pop., 2004)	0.2

Migration

EMIGRATION, 2005
- Stock of emigrants: **370,826**
- Stock of emigrants as percentage of population: **18.2%**
- Top 10 destination countries: Germany, Switzerland, Australia, Italy, Turkey, the United States, Austria, Slovenia, Croatia, France

SKILLED EMIGRATION, 2000
- Emigration rate of tertiary educated: **20.9%**
- Emigration of physicians: **62** or **1.4%** of physicians trained in the country

IMMIGRATION, 2005
- Stock of immigrants: **121,291**
- Stock of immigrants as percentage of population: **6.0%**
- Females as percentage of immigrants: **58.3%**
- Refugees as percentage of immigrants: **1.9%**
- Top 10 source countries: Albania, Turkey, Serbia and Montenegro, Bosnia and Herzegovina, Egypt, Croatia, Bulgaria, Slovenia, Greece, Russia

Remittances

US$ millions	2000	2001	2002	2003	2004	2005	2006	2007
Inward remittance flows	81	73	106	174	213	226	267[a]	267
of which								
Workers' remittances	80	68	92	146	161	169	198	..
Compensation of employees	0	5	14	28	52	57	69	..
Migrants' transfer	..	..	..	..	..	..	..	..
Outward remittance flows	14	21	23	16	16	16	18[b]	..
of which								
Workers' remittances	14	21	23	15	15	14	16	..
Compensation of employees	..	..	1	1	1	2	2	..
Migrants' transfer	..	..	..	..	..	..	..	..

a. 4.3% of GDP in 2006.
b. 0.3% of GDP in 2006.

Madagascar

Population (millions, 2006)	19
Population growth (avg. annual %, 1997–2006)	2.8
Population density (people per sq. km, 2006)	33
Labor force (millions, 2006)	8.9
Urban population (% of pop., 2006)	27.1
Age dependency ratio	0.88
Surface area (1,000 sq. km, 2006)	587
GNI ($ billions, 2006)	5.4
GNI per capita, Atlas method ($, 2006)	280
GDP growth (avg. annual %, 2002–06)	2.4
Poverty headcount ratio at national poverty line (% of pop., 2004)	62.8

Migration

EMIGRATION, 2005
- Stock of emigrants: **151,364**
- Stock of emigrants as percentage of population: **0.8%**
- Top 10 destination countries: France, Comoros, Canada, Italy, the United States, Switzerland, Germany, the United Kingdom, Belgium, Mauritius

SKILLED EMIGRATION, 2000
- Emigration rate of tertiary educated: **36.0%**
- Emigration of physicians:
  a) **34** or **2.1%** of physicians trained in the country *(Source: Docquier and Bhargava 2006)*
  b) **920** or **39.2%** of physicians trained in the country *(Source: Clemens and Pettersson 2006)*
- Emigration of nurses: **1,171** or **27.5%** of nurses trained in the country

IMMIGRATION, 2005
- Stock of immigrants: **62,787**
- Stock of immigrants as percentage of population: **0.3%**
- Females as percentage of immigrants: **38.2%**
- Refugees as percentage of immigrants: **0.0%**
- Top 10 source countries: France, Comoros, India, Algeria, China, Pakistan, Mauritius, Germany, Italy, the United States

Remittances

US$ millions	2000	2001	2002	2003	2004	2005	2006	2007
Inward remittance flows	11	11	17	16	11	11	11[a]	11
of which								
Workers' remittances	..	..	..	8	4	1	..	..
Compensation of employees	11	11	29	8	7	10	..	..
Migrants' transfer	..	..	..	..	..	..	..	..
Outward remittance flows	12	11	3	18	9	21	21[b]	..
of which								
Workers' remittances	10	..	..	13	3	8	..	..
Compensation of employees	1	11	5	5	6	13	..	..
Migrants' transfer	..	..	..	..	..	..	..	..

a. 0.2% of GDP in 2006.
b. 0.4% of GDP in 2006.

Malawi

Population (millions, 2006)	13
Population growth (avg. annual %, 1997–2006)	2.4
Population density (people per sq. km, 2006)	140
Labor force (millions, 2006)	6.1
Urban population (% of pop., 2006)	17.7
Age dependency ratio	1.01
Surface area (1,000 sq. km, 2006)	118
GNI ($ billions, 2006)	2.2
GNI per capita, Atlas method ($, 2006)	170
GDP growth (avg. annual %, 2002–06)	5.5
Poverty headcount ratio at national poverty line (% of pop., 2004)	20.8

Migration

EMIGRATION, 2005

- Stock of emigrants: **93,223**
- Stock of emigrants as percentage of population: **0.7%**
- Top 10 destination countries: Tanzania, Zambia, the United Kingdom, South Africa, Mozambique, the United States, Australia, Canada, the Netherlands, Portugal

SKILLED EMIGRATION, 2000

- Emigration rate of tertiary educated: **9.4%**
- Emigration of physicians:
  a) **44** or **13.3%** of physicians trained in the country *(Source: Docquier and Bhargava 2006)*
  b) **293** or **59.4%** of physicians trained in the country *(Source: Clemens and Pettersson 2006)*
- Emigration of nurses: **377** or **16.8%** of nurses trained in the country

IMMIGRATION, 2005

- Stock of immigrants: **278,793**
- Stock of immigrants as percentage of population: **2.2%**
- Females as percentage of immigrants: **51.6%**
- Refugees as percentage of immigrants: **1.4%**
- Top source countries: Mozambique, Zambia, Zimbabwe, Tanzania, India, South Africa

Remittances

US$ millions	2000	2001	2002	2003	2004	2005	2006	2007
Inward remittance flows	1	1	1	1	1	1	1[a]	1
of which								
Workers' remittances	1	1	1	..	..	..	..	..
Compensation of employees	..	..	..	..	..	..	..	..
Migrants' transfer	..	..	..	..	..	..	..	..
Outward remittance flows	1	1	1	1	1	1	1[b]	..
of which								
Workers' remittances	0	1	0	..	..	..	..	..
Compensation of employees	..	..	..	..	..	..	..	..
Migrants' transfer	..	..	..	..	..	..	..	..

a. 0.04% of GDP in 2006.
b. 0.04% of GDP in 2006.

Malaysia

Population (millions, 2006)	26
Population growth (avg. annual %, 1997–2006)	2.1
Population density (people per sq. km, 2006)	78
Labor force (millions, 2006)	11
Urban population (% of pop., 2006)	68.2
Age dependency ratio	0.58
Surface area (1,000 sq. km, 2006)	330
GNI ($ billions, 2006)	144
GNI per capita, Atlas method ($, 2006)	5,490
GDP growth (avg. annual %, 2002–06)	5.6
Poverty headcount ratio at national poverty line (% of pop., 2004)	0

Migration

EMIGRATION, 2005
- Stock of emigrants: **1,458,944**
- Stock of emigrants as percentage of population: **5.8%**
- Top 10 destination countries: Singapore, Australia, Brunei, the United States, the United Kingdom, Canada, India, New Zealand, Japan, Germany

SKILLED EMIGRATION, 2000
- Emigration rate of tertiary educated: **10.4%**
- Emigration of physicians: **2,211** or **11.9%** of physicians trained in the country

IMMIGRATION, 2005
- Stock of immigrants: **1,639,138**
- Stock of immigrants as percentage of population: **6.5%**
- Females as percentage of immigrants: **41.6%**
- Refugees as percentage of immigrants: **2.8%**
- Top source countries: Indonesia, the Philippines, China, India, Singapore, Thailand, Pakistan, Bangladesh, Sri Lanka

Remittances

US$ millions	2000	2001	2002	2003	2004	2005	2006	2007
Inward remittance flows	981	792	959	987	1,128	1,281	1,535ª	1,700
of which								
Workers' remittances	..	..	..	..	..	..	..	..
Compensation of employees	342	367	435	571	802	1,117	1,364	..
Migrants' transfer	..	..	..	..	..	..	..	..
Outward remittance flows	599	634	3,826	3,464	4,991	5,679	5,560ᵇ	..
of which								
Workers' remittances	..	..	3,081	2,643	4,001	4,435	4,118	..
Compensation of employees	599	634	745	821	1,064	1,244	1,442	..
Migrants' transfer	..	..	..	..	..	..	..	..

a. 1.0% of GDP in 2006.
b. 3.7% of GDP in 2006.

Maldives

Population (thousands, 2006)	337
Population growth (avg. annual %, 1997–2006)	2.6
Population density (people per sq. km, 2006)	1,123
Labor force (thousands, 2006)	123
Urban population (% of pop., 2006)	30.1
Age dependency ratio	0.77
Surface area (sq. km, 2006)	300
GNI ($ millions, 2006)	878
GNI per capita, Atlas method ($, 2006)	2,680
GDP growth (avg. annual %, 2002–06)	8.3
Poverty headcount ratio at national poverty line (% of pop., 2004)	..

Migration

EMIGRATION, 2005
- Stock of emigrants: **1,618**
- Stock of emigrants as percentage of population: **0.5%**
- Top 10 destination countries: Nepal, the United Kingdom, India, Australia, Germany, the United States, Switzerland, New Zealand, Japan, Italy

SKILLED EMIGRATION, 2000
- Emigration rate of tertiary educated: **2.2%**
- Emigration of physicians: **3** or **1.2%** of physicians trained in the country

IMMIGRATION, 2005
- Stock of immigrants: **3,370**
- Stock of immigrants as percentage of population: **1.0%**
- Females as percentage of immigrants: **44.8%**
- Refugees as percentage of immigrants: **0.0%**

Remittances

US$ millions	2000	2001	2002	2003	2004	2005	2006	2007
Inward remittance flows	2	2	2	2	3	2	2[a]	2
of which								
Workers' remittances	..	..	..	..	..	..	..	..
Compensation of employees	2	2	2	2	3	2	2	..
Migrants' transfer	..	..	..	..	..	..	..	..
Outward remittance flows	46	50	51	55	61	70	83[b]	..
of which								
Workers' remittances	46	50	50	55	61	70	83	..
Compensation of employees	0	0	0	0	0	0	0	..
Migrants' transfer	..	..	..	..	..	..	..	..

a. 0.2% of GDP in 2006.
b. 9.1% of GDP in 2006.

Mali

Sub-Saharan Africa **LOW INCOME**

Population (millions, 2006)	14
Population growth (avg. annual %, 1997–2006)	2.9
Population density (people per sq. km, 2006)	11
Labor force (millions, 2006)	5.6
Urban population (% of pop., 2006)	31.1
Age dependency ratio	1.03
Surface area (1,000 sq. km, 2006)	1,240
GNI ($ billions, 2006)	6.1
GNI per capita, Atlas method ($, 2006)	440
GDP growth (avg. annual %, 2002–06)	5.1
Poverty headcount ratio at national poverty line (% of pop., 2004)	38.9

Migration

EMIGRATION, 2005
- Stock of emigrants: **1,213,042**
- Stock of emigrants as percentage of population: **9.0%**
- Top 10 destination countries: Côte d'Ivoire, Burkina Faso, Nigeria, France, Niger, Gabon, Senegal, the Gambia, the Republic of Congo, Mauritania

SKILLED EMIGRATION, 2000
- Emigration rate of tertiary educated: **11.5%**
- Emigration of physicians:
  a) **18** or **3.6%** of physicians trained in the country (*Source: Docquier and Bhargava 2006*)
  b) **157** or **22.9%** of physicians trained in the country (*Source: Clemens and Pettersson 2006*)
- Emigration of nurses: **265** or **15.0%** of nurses trained in the country

IMMIGRATION, 2005
- Stock of immigrants: **46,318**
- Stock of immigrants as percentage of population: **0.3%**
- Females as percentage of immigrants: **48.2%**
- Refugees as percentage of immigrants: **25.8%**

Remittances

US$ millions	2000	2001	2002	2003	2004	2005	2006	2007
Inward remittance flows	73	88	137	154	155	177	177[a]	192
of which								
Workers' remittances	69	82	126	139	138	153	..	..
Compensation of employees	4	6	11	15	17	24	..	..
Migrants' transfer	..	..	..	..	..	..	..	..
Outward remittance flows	26	23	30	58	64	70	70[b]	..
of which								
Workers' remittances	24	20	24	48	52	51	..	..
Compensation of employees	2	3	6	10	12	19	..	..
Migrants' nsfer	..	..	..	..	..	..	..	.

a. 3.0% of GDP in 2006.
b. 1.2% of GDP in 2006.

Malta

Population (thousands, 2006)	405
Population growth (avg. annual %, 1997–2006)	0.7
Population density (people per sq. km, 2006)	1,266
Labor force (thousands, 2006)	172
Urban population (% of pop., 2006)	95.5
Age dependency ratio	0.45
Surface area (sq. km, 2006)	320
GNI ($ billions, 2006)	5.4
GNI per capita, Atlas method ($, 2006)	13,610
GDP growth (avg. annual %, 2002–06)	0
Poverty headcount ratio at national poverty line (% of pop., 2004)	..

Migration

IMMIGRATION, 2005

- Stock of immigrants: **10,676**
- Stock of immigrants as percentage of population: **2.7%**
- Females as percentage of immigrants: **56.2%**
- Refugees as percentage of immigrants: **19.2%**
- Top source countries: the United Kingdom, Australia, Canada, the United States, Italy, Libya, Germany, France

EMIGRATION, 2005

- Stock of emigrants: **106,350**
- Stock of emigrants as percentage of population: **26.5%**
- Top 10 destination countries: Australia, the United Kingdom, Canada, the United States, Italy, France, Germany, Ireland, New Zealand, Spain

SKILLED EMIGRATION, 2000

- Emigration rate of tertiary educated: **55.2%**
- Emigration of physicians: **80** or **7.2%** of physicians trained in the country

Remittances

US$ millions	2000	2001	2002	2003	2004	2005	2006	2007
Inward remittance flows	14	14	23	27	33	34	34[a]	34
of which								
Workers' remittances	1	1	0	1	0	0	0	..
Compensation of employees	16	12	21	25	33	34	34	..
Migrants' transfer	2	1	2	1	0	0	0	..
Outward remittance flows	14	11	11	12	22	33	32[b]	..
of which								
Workers' remittances	1	2	1	1	3	7	4	..
Compensation of employees	7	7	8	10	16	22	25	..
Migrants' transfer	5	3	2	1	3	4	3	..

a. 0.6% of GDP in 2006.
b. 0.6% of GDP in 2006.

Marshall Islands, The

Population (thousands, 2006)	65
Population growth (avg. annual %, 1997–2006)	2.4
Population density (people per sq. km, 2006)	363
Labor force (millions, 2006)	..
Urban population (% of pop., 2006)	66.9
Age dependency ratio	..
Surface area (sq. km, 2006)	180
GNI ($ millions, 2006)	193
GNI per capita, Atlas method ($, 2006)	3,000
GDP growth (avg. annual %, 2002–06)	2.7
Poverty headcount ratio at national poverty line (% of pop., 2004)	..

Migration

EMIGRATION, 2005
- Stock of emigrants: **10,183**
- Stock of emigrants as percentage of population: **16.4%**
- Top 10 destination countries: the United States, the Philippines, Guam, Fiji, Canada, Australia, Northern Mariana Islands, New Zealand, Japan, the Netherlands

SKILLED EMIGRATION, 2000
- Emigration rate of tertiary educated: **41.0%**
- Emigration of physicians: **0** or **0.0%** of physicians trained in the country

IMMIGRATION, 2005
- Stock of immigrants: **1,667**
- Stock of immigrants as percentage of population: **2.7%**
- Females as percentage of immigrants: **41.0%**
- Refugees as percentage of immigrants: **0.0%**
- Top source countries: Australia, Japan, China, the Philippines, the United States, New Zealand

Remittances

Remittance data are currently not available for this country.

Mauritania

LOW INCOME

Population (millions, 2006)	3.2
Population growth (avg. annual %, 1997–2006)	2.9
Population density (people per sq. km, 2006)	3
Labor force (millions, 2006)	1.2
Urban population (% of pop., 2006)	40.6
Age dependency ratio	0.87
Surface area (1,000 sq. km, 2006)	1,026
GNI ($ billions, 2006)	2.8
GNI per capita, Atlas method ($, 2006)	740
GDP growth (avg. annual %, 2002–06)	5.8
Poverty headcount ratio at national poverty line (% of pop., 2004)	17.7

Migration

EMIGRATION, 2005
- Stock of emigrants: **105,315**
- Stock of emigrants as percentage of population: **3.4%**
- Top 10 destination countries: Senegal, Nigeria, France, Spain, the Gambia, the United States, the Republic of Congo, Italy, Germany, Guinea-Bissau

SKILLED EMIGRATION, 2000
- Emigration rate of tertiary educated: **23.1%**
- Emigration of physicians:
  a) **2** or **0.5%** of physicians trained in the country *(Source: Docquier and Bhargava 2006)*
  b) **43** or **11.4%** of physicians trained in the country *(Source: Clemens and Pettersson 2006)*
- Emigration of nurses: **117** or **6.9%** of nurses trained in the country

IMMIGRATION, 2005
- Stock of immigrants: **65,889**
- Stock of immigrants as percentage of population: **2.2%**
- Females as percentage of immigrants: **42.1%**
- Refugees as percentage of immigrants: **0.7%**
- Top 10 source countries: Senegal, Mali, Guinea, Algeria, France, Guinea-Bissau, Benin, Cameroon, Morocco, Saudi Arabia

Remittances

US$ millions	2000	2001	2002	2003	2004	2005	2006	2007
Inward remittance flows	2	2	2	2	2	2	2[a]	2
of which								
Workers' remittances	..	..	..	..	..	..	..	..
Compensation of employees	..	..	..	..	..	..	..	..
Migrants' transfer	..	..	..	..	..	..	..	..
Outward remittance flows	..	..	..	..	..	..	..	..
of which								
Workers' remittances	..	..	..	..	..	..	..	..
Compensation of employees	..	..	..	..	..	..	..	..
Migrants' transfer	..	..	..	..	..	..	..	..

a. 0.1% of GDP in 2006.

Mauritius

Population (millions, 2006)	1.3
Population growth (avg. annual %, 1997–2006)	1.0
Population density (people per sq. km, 2006)	617
Labor force (thousands, 2006)	575
Urban population (% of pop., 2006)	42.5
Age dependency ratio	0.45
Surface area (1,000 sq. km, 2006)	2
GNI ($ billions, 2006)	6.5
GNI per capita, Atlas method ($, 2006)	5,450
GDP growth (avg. annual %, 2002–06)	3.7
Poverty headcount ratio at national poverty line (% of pop., 2004)	..

Migration

EMIGRATION, 2005

- Stock of emigrants: **119,424**
- Stock of emigrants as percentage of population: **9.6%**
- Top 10 destination countries: France, the United Kingdom, Australia, Italy, Canada, Switzerland, Belgium, the United States, Germany, Tanzania

SKILLED EMIGRATION, 2000

- Emigration rate of tertiary educated: **48.0%**
- Emigration of physicians:
  a) **83** or **7.6%** of physicians trained in the country *(Source: Docquier and Bhargava 2006)*
  b) **822** or **46.1%** of physicians trained in the country *(Source: Clemens and Pettersson 2006)*
- Emigration of nurses: **4,531** or **63.3%** of nurses trained in the country

IMMIGRATION, 2005

- Stock of immigrants: **20,725**
- Stock of immigrants as percentage of population: **1.7%**
- Females as percentage of immigrants: **63.3%**
- Refugees as percentage of immigrants: **0.0%**
- Top 10 source countries: China, India, France, the United Kingdom, South Africa, Germany, Madagascar, Italy, Australia, the United States

Remittances

US$ millions	2000	2001	2002	2003	2004	2005	2006	2007
Inward remittance flows	**177**	**215**	**215**	**215**	**215**	**215**	**215**[a]	**215**
of which								
Workers' remittances	..	..	..	..	..	..	..	..
Compensation of employees	..	1	1	1	1	1	1	..
Migrants' transfer	..	..	..	..	..	..	..	..
Outward remittance flows	**1**	**8**	**10**	**10**	**11**	**11**	**13**[b]	..
of which								
Workers' remittances	..	..	..	..	..	..	..	..
Compensation of employees	..	6	8	9	9	9	10	..
Migrants' transfer	1	2	2	1	2	2	3	..

a. 3.3% of GDP in 2006.
b. 0.2% of GDP in 2006.

Mexico

UPPER MIDDLE INCOME

Population (millions, 2006)	104
Population growth (avg. annual %, 1997–2006)	1.2
Population density (people per sq. km, 2006)	55
Labor force (millions, 2006)	43
Urban population (% of pop., 2006)	76.3
Age dependency ratio	0.56
Surface area (1,000 sq. km, 2006)	1,958
GNI ($ billions, 2006)	831
GNI per capita, Atlas method ($, 2006)	7,870
GDP growth (avg. annual %, 2002–06)	2.8
Poverty headcount ratio at national poverty line (% of pop., 2004)	1.9

Migration

EMIGRATION, 2005
- Stock of emigrants: **11,502,616**
- Stock of emigrants as percentage of population: **10.7%**
- Top 10 destination countries: the United States, Canada, Spain, Bolivia, Guatemala, Germany, Italy, France, the United Kingdom, Switzerland

SKILLED EMIGRATION, 2000
- Emigration rate of tertiary educated: **14.3%**
- Emigration of physicians: **5,579** or **4.1%** of physicians trained in the country

IMMIGRATION, 2005
- Stock of immigrants: **644,361**
- Stock of immigrants as percentage of population: **0.6%**
- Females as percentage of immigrants: **48.2%**
- Refugees as percentage of immigrants: **0.6%**
- Top 10 source countries: the United States, Guatemala, Spain, Cuba, Argentina, Colombia, Canada, France, Germany, El Salvador

Remittances

US$ millions	2000	2001	2002	2003	2004	2005	2006	2007
Inward remittance flows	7,525	10,146	11,029	14,911	18,143	21,917	24,732[a]	25,000
of which								
Workers' remittances	6,573	8,895	9,814	13,396	16,613	20,035	23,054	..
Compensation of employees	952	1,251	1,215	1,515	1,530	1,882	1,678	..
Migrants' transfer	..	..	..	..	..	..	..	..
Outward remittance flows	..	..	..	..	..	..	..	..
of which								
Workers' remittances	..	..	..	..	..	..	..	..
Compensation of employees	..	..	..	..	..	..	..	..
Migrants' transfer	..	..	..	..	..	..	..	..

a. 2.9% of GDP in 2006.

Migration and Remittances Factbook 2008

Micronesia, The Federated States of

Population (thousands, 2006)	111
Population growth (avg. annual %, 1997–2006)	0.3
Population density (people per sq. km, 2006)	159
Labor force (millions, 2006)	..
Urban population (% of pop., 2006)	22.4
Age dependency ratio	0.73
Surface area (sq. km, 2006)	700
GNI ($ millions, 2006)	262
GNI per capita, Atlas method ($, 2006)	2,380
GDP growth (avg. annual %, 2002–06)	0.2
Poverty headcount ratio at national poverty line (% of pop., 2004)	..

Migration

EMIGRATION, 2005
- Stock of emigrants: **23,019**
- Stock of emigrants as percentage of population: **20.8%**
- Top 10 destination countries: Guam, the United States, the Philippines, Fiji, Northern Mariana Islands, Spain, Palau, Japan, New Zealand, Canada

SKILLED EMIGRATION, 2000
- Emigration rate of tertiary educated: **36.4%**
- Emigration of physicians: **0** or **0.0%** of physicians trained in the country

IMMIGRATION, 2005
- Stock of immigrants: **3,562**
- Stock of immigrants as percentage of population: **3.2%**
- Females as percentage of immigrants: **35.0%**
- Refugees as percentage of immigrants: **0.0%**
- Top source country: the United States

Remittances
Remittance data are currently not available for this country.

Moldova

Population (millions, 2006)	3.8
Population growth (avg. annual %, 1997–2006)	-1.2
Population density (people per sq. km, 2006)	117
Labor force (millions, 2006)	2.0
Urban population (% of pop., 2006)	47
Age dependency ratio	0.38
Surface area (1,000 sq. km, 2006)	34
GNI ($ billions, 2006)	3.8
GNI per capita, Atlas method ($, 2006)	1,100
GDP growth (avg. annual %, 2002-06)	6.7
Poverty headcount ratio at national poverty line (% of pop., 2004)	1.1

Migration

EMIGRATION, 2005
- Stock of emigrants: **705,533**
- Stock of emigrants as percentage of population: **16.8%**
- Top 10 destination countries: Russia, Ukraine, Romania, the United States, Israel, Germany, Kazakhstan, Italy, Greece, Spain

SKILLED EMIGRATION, 2000
- Emigration rate of tertiary educated: **4.2%**
- Emigration of physicians: **7** or **0.1%** of physicians trained in the country

IMMIGRATION, 2005
- Stock of immigrants: **440,121**
- Stock of immigrants as percentage of population: **10.5%**
- Females as percentage of immigrants: **57.8%**
- Refugees as percentage of immigrants: **0.0%**
- Top source countries: Ukraine, Russia, Bulgaria, Belarus

Remittances

US$ millions	2000	2001	2002	2003	2004	2005	2006	2007
Inward remittance flows	**179**	**243**	**324**	**487**	**705**	**920**	**1,182**[a]	**1,200**
of which								
Workers' remittances	53	80	102	152	221	395	603	..
Compensation of employees	125	162	221	332	480	520	573	..
Migrants' transfer	1	1	1	3	4	5	6	..
Outward remittance flows	**46**	**59**	**56**	**68**	**67**	**68**	**85**[b]	..
of which								
Workers' remittances	0	0	1	1	1	3	6	..
Compensation of employees	29	39	35	43	41	43	50	..
Migrants' transfer	17	19	20	24	25	22	29	..

a. 36.2% of GDP in 2006.
b. 2.6% of GDP in 2006.

Mongolia

Population (millions, 2006)	2.6
Population growth (avg. annual %, 1997–2006)	1.1
Population density (people per sq. km, 2006)	2
Labor force (millions, 2006)	1.2
Urban population (% of pop., 2006)	56.9
Age dependency ratio	0.51
Surface area (1,000 sq. km, 2006)	1,567
GNI ($ billions, 2006)	2.6
GNI per capita, Atlas method ($, 2006)	880
GDP growth (avg. annual %, 2002–06)	7.3
Poverty headcount ratio at national poverty line (% of pop., 2004)	7.5

Migration

EMIGRATION, 2005
- Stock of emigrants: **15,140**
- Stock of emigrants as percentage of population: **0.6%**
- Top 10 destination countries: Germany, the United States, Japan, Hungary, the Czech Republic, the United Kingdom, France, Turkey, Switzerland, Poland

EMIGRATION, 2000
- Emigration rate of tertiary educated: **7.8%**
- Emigration of physicians: **28** or **0.5%** of physicians trained in the country

IMMIGRATION, 2005
- Stock of immigrants: **9,069**
- Stock of immigrants as percentage of population: **0.3%**
- Females as percentage of immigrants: **54.0%**
- Refugees as percentage of immigrants: **0.0%**
- Top source countries: Russia, China, Kazakhstan, the Republic of Korea

Remittances

US$ millions	2000	2001	2002	2003	2004	2005	2006	2007
Inward remittance flows	12	25	56	129	202	181	182[a]	194
of which								
Workers' remittances	12	25	56	129	195	178	180	..
Compensation of employees	..	..	..	..	7	3	2	..
Migrants' transfer	..	..	..	..	..	..	..	..
Outward remittance flows	3	3	14	54	49	40	77[b]	..
of which								
Workers' remittances	3	-	14	54	49	40	77	..
Compensation of employees	..	..	..	..	..	..	..	..
Migrants' transfer	..	..	..	..	..	..	..	..

a. 6.8% of GDP in 2006.
b. 2.9% of GDP in 2006.

Morocco

Population (millions, 2006)	30
Population growth (avg. annual %, 1997–2006)	1.3
Population density (people per sq. km, 2006)	68
Labor force (millions, 2006)	11
Urban population (% of pop., 2006)	59.3
Age dependency ratio	0.55
Surface area (1,000 sq. km, 2006)	447
GNI ($ billions, 2006)	57
GNI per capita, Atlas method ($, 2006)	1,900
GDP growth (avg. annual %, 2002–06)	4.4
Poverty headcount ratio at national poverty line (% of pop., 2004)	0.3

Migration

EMIGRATION, 2005
- Stock of emigrants: **2,718,665**
- Stock of emigrants as percentage of population: **8.6%**
- Top 10 destination countries: France, Spain, Italy, Israel, the Netherlands, Germany, Belgium, the United States, Canada, Saudi Arabia

SKILLED EMIGRATION, 2000
- Emigration rate of tertiary educated: **10.3%**
- Emigration of physicians:
  a) **953** or **6.7%** of physicians trained in the country *(Source: Docquier and Bhargava 2006)*
  b) **6,506** or **31.3%** of physicians trained in the country *(Source: Clemens and Pettersson 2006)*
- Emigration of nurses: **5,176** or **14.9** of nurses trained in the country

IMMIGRATION, 2005
- Stock of immigrants: **131,654**
- Stock of immigrants as percentage of population: **0.4%**
- Females as percentage of immigrants: **50.7%**
- Refugees as percentage of immigrants: **1.6%**

Remittances

US$ millions	2000	2001	2002	2003	2004	2005	2006	2007
Inward remittance flows	2,161	3,261	2,877	3,614	4,221	4,589	5,454[a]	5,700
of which								
Workers' remittances	2,161	3,261	2,877	3,614	4,221	4,589	5,454	..
Compensation of employees	..	..	..	..	..	..	..	..
Migrants' transfer	0	-	-	-	-	0	-	..
Outward remittance flows	29	36	36	44	42	40	41[b]	..
of which								
Workers' remittances	23	27	30	34	34	35	38	..
Compensation of employees	..	..	..	..	..	..	..	..
Migrants' transfer	6	9	6	10	8	5	3	..

a. 9.5% of GDP in 2006.
b. 0.1% of GDP in 2006.

Mozambique

Population (millions, 2006)	20
Population growth (avg. annual %, 1997–2006)	2.1
Population density (people per sq. km, 2006)	26
Labor force (millions, 2006)	9.4
Urban population (% of pop., 2006)	35.3
Age dependency ratio	0.89
Surface area (1,000 sq. km, 2006)	802
GNI ($ billions, 2006)	6.9
GNI per capita, Atlas method ($, 2006)	340
GDP growth (avg. annual %, 2002–06)	7.7
Poverty headcount ratio at national poverty line (% of pop., 2004)	30.5

Migration

EMIGRATION, 2005
- Stock of emigrants: **803,261**
- Stock of emigrants as percentage of population: **4.1%**
- Top 10 destination countries: South Africa, Tanzania, Malawi, Portugal, Swaziland, the United Kingdom, Germany, the United States, Zambia, Spain

SKILLED EMIGRATION, 2000
- Emigration rate of tertiary educated: **42.0%**
- Emigration of physicians:
  a) **27** or **5.8%** of physicians trained in the country *(Source: Docquier and Bhargava 2006)*
  b) **1,334** or **75.4%** of physicians trained in the country *(Source: Clemens and Pettersson 2006)*
- Emigration of nurses: **853** or **18.9%** of nurses trained in the country

IMMIGRATION, 2005
- Stock of immigrants: **405,904**
- Stock of immigrants as percentage of population: **2.1%**
- Females as percentage of immigrants: **52.1%**
- Refugees as percentage of immigrants: **0.2%**
- Top 10 source countries: South Africa, Portugal, Zimbabwe, Lesotho, Cape Verde, Tanzania, India, Malawi, Pakistan, Zambia

Remittances

US$ millions	2000	2001	2002	2003	2004	2005	2006	2007
Inward remittance flows	37	42	53	70	58	57	80[a]	80
of which								
Workers' remittances	..	41	29	30	3	6	16	..
Compensation of employees	37	1	24	40	55	51	64	..
Migrants' transfer	..	..	..	0	..	..	..	..
Outward remittance flows	156	64	50	29	20	21	26[b]	..
of which								
Workers' remittances	103	32	16	20	11	11	12	..
Compensation of employees	53	32	34	9	9	10	14	..
Migrants' transfer	..	..	0	0	..	..	..	..

a. 1.1% of GDP in 2006.
b. 0.3% of GDP in 2006.

Myanmar

Population (millions, 2006)	51
Population growth (avg. annual %, 1997–2006)	1.2
Population density (people per sq. km, 2006)	78
Labor force (millions, 2006)	28
Urban population (% of pop., 2006)	31.3
Age dependency ratio	0.51
Surface area (1,000 sq. km, 2006)	677
GNI ($ millions, 2006)	..
GNI per capita, Atlas method ($, 2006)	..
GDP growth (avg. annual %, 2002–06)	8.4
Poverty headcount ratio at national poverty line (% of pop., 2004)	..

Migration

EMIGRATION, 2005
- Stock of emigrants: **426,860**
- Stock of emigrants as percentage of population: **0.8%**
- Top 10 destination countries: Thailand, India, the United States, Australia, the United Kingdom, Japan, Canada, Germany, France, New Zealand

SKILLED EMIGRATION, 2000
- Emigration rate of tertiary educated: **3.4%**
- Emigration of physicians: **625** or **4.2%** of physicians trained in the country

IMMIGRATION, 2005
- Stock of immigrants: **117,435**
- Stock of immigrants as percentage of population: **0.2%**
- Females as percentage of immigrants: **46.1%**
- Refugees as percentage of immigrants: **0.1%**
- Top source countries: China, India, Pakistan, Bangladesh

Remittances

US$ millions	2000	2001	2002	2003	2004	2005	2006	2007
Inward remittance flows	**104**	**117**	**106**	**85**	**117**	**131**	**117**	**125**
of which								
Workers' remittances	77	86	76	59	81	87	66	..
Compensatio n of employees	27	31	30	26	36	44	51	..
Migrants' transfer	..	..	..	..	..	..	..	..
Outward remittance flows	**14**	**14**	**23**	**23**	**25**	**19**	**32**	**..**
of which								
Workers' remittances	14	14	23	23	25	19	32	..
Compensation of employees	..	..	..	..	..	..	..	..
Migrants' transfer	..	..	..	..	..	..	..	..

Namibia

LOWER MIDDLE INCOME

Population (millions, 2006)	2.1
Population growth (avg. annual %, 1997–2006)	1.9
Population density (people per sq. km, 2006)	2
Labor force (thousands, 2006)	656
Urban population (% of pop., 2006)	35.7
Age dependency ratio	0.8
Surface area (1,000 sq. km, 2006)	824
GNI ($ billions, 2006)	6.3
GNI per capita, Atlas method ($, 2006)	3,230
GDP growth (avg. annual %, 2002–06)	5.0
Poverty headcount ratio at national poverty line (% of pop., 2004)	32.8

Migration

EMIGRATION, 2005
- Stock of emigrants: **15,101**
- Stock of emigrants as percentage of population: **0.7%**
- Top 10 destination countries: Mozambique, Tanzania, the United Kingdom, the United States, Germany, Australia, Canada, Zambia, New Zealand, the Netherlands

SKILLED EMIGRATION, 2000
- Emigration rate of tertiary educated: **3.4%**
- Emigration of physicians:
  a) **9** or **1.6%** of physicians trained in the country (*Source: Docquier and Bhargava 2006*)
  b) **382** or **45.0%** of physicians trained in the country (*Source: Clemens and Pettersson 2006*)
- Emigration of nurses: **152** or **5.4%** of nurses trained in the country

IMMIGRATION, 2005
- Stock of immigrants: **143,275**
- Stock of immigrants as percentage of population: **7.1%**
- Females as percentage of immigrants: **47.1%**
- Refugees as percentage of immigrants: **8.9%**
- Top source countries: Angola, South Africa, Zambia, Botswana

Remittances

US$ millions	2000	2001	2002	2003	2004	2005	2006	2007
Inward remittance flows	9	9	7	12	16	19	17[a]	17
of which								
Workers' remittances	4	4	3	5	6	7	7	..
Compensation of employees	5	5	4	7	9	11	10	..
Migrants' transfer	0	0	0	0	1	1	0	..
Outward remittance flows	9	8	8	15	17	19	21[b]	..
of which								
Workers' remittances	3	2	2	4	4	4	4	..
Compensation of employees	6	6	6	11	13	14	16	..
Migrants' transfer	0	0	0	0	0	1	1	..

a. 0.3% of GDP in 2006.
b. 0.3% of GDP in 2006.

Nepal

Population (millions, 2006)	28
Population growth (avg. annual %, 1997–2006)	2.2
Population density (people per sq. km, 2006)	193
Labor force (millions, 2006)	11
Urban population (% of pop., 2006)	16.3
Age dependency ratio	0.73
Surface area (1,000 sq. km, 2006)	147
GNI ($ billions, 2006)	8.2
GNI per capita, Atlas method ($, 2006)	290
GDP growth (avg. annual %, 2002–06)	2.2
Poverty headcount ratio at national poverty line (% of pop., 2004)	24.7

Migration

EMIGRATION, 2005
- Stock of emigrants: **753,662**
- Stock of emigrants as percentage of population: **2.8%**
- Top 10 destination countries: India, Thailand, Saudi Arabia, the United States, the United Kingdom, Brunei, the Republic of Korea, Japan, Germany, Australia

SKILLED EMIGRATION, 2000
- Emigration rate of tertiary educated: **2.7%**
- Emigration of physicians: **19** or **1.6%** of physicians trained in the country

IMMIGRATION, 2005
- Stock of immigrants: **818,582**
- Stock of immigrants as percentage of population: **3.0%**
- Females as percentage of immigrants: **69.1%**
- Refugees as percentage of immigrants: **15.3%**
- Top source countries: India, Bhutan, Pakistan, China, Australia, Sri Lanka, Bangladesh, Maldives, New Zealand

Remittances

US$ millions	2000	2001	2002	2003	2004	2005	2006	2007
Inward remittance flows	111	147	678	771	823	1,211	1,453ᵃ	1,600
of which								
Workers' remittances	111	147	655	744	793	1,126	1,373	..
Compensation of employees	..	..	23	27	30	85	80	..
Migrants' transfer	..	..	..	..	..	..	..	..
Outward remittance flows	17	24	34	26	64	65	79ᵇ	..
of which								
Workers' remittances	17	24	33	25	63	60	69	..
Compensation of employees	..	..	1	1	1	5	10	..
Migrants' transfer	..	..	..	..	..	..	..	..

a. 18.0% of GDP in 2006.
b. 1.0% of GDP in 2006.

Netherlands, The

Population (millions, 2006)	16
Population growth (avg. annual %, 1997–2006)	0.5
Population density (people per sq. km, 2006)	483
Labor force (millions, 2006)	8.7
Urban population (% of pop., 2006)	80.7
Age dependency ratio	0.48
Surface area (1,000 sq. km, 2006)	42
GNI ($ billions, 2006)	682
GNI per capita, Atlas method ($, 2006)	42,670
GDP growth (avg. annual %, 2002–06)	1.1
Poverty headcount ratio at national poverty line (% of pop., 2004)	..

Migration

IMMIGRATION, 2005
- Stock of immigrants: **1,638,104**
- Stock of immigrants as percentage of population: **10.1%**
- Females as percentage of immigrants: **54.4%**
- Refugees as percentage of immigrants: **7.3%**
- Top 10 source countries: Suriname, Turkey, Indonesia, Morocco, Germany, Netherlands Antilles, Serbia and Montenegro, Belgium, the United Kingdom, Iraq

EMIGRATION, 2005
- Stock of emigrants: **812,475**
- Stock of emigrants as percentage of population: **5.0%**
- Top 10 destination countries: Germany, Canada, the United States, Australia, Belgium, Spain, the United Kingdom, France, Turkey, New Zealand

SKILLED EMIGRATION, 2000
- Emigration rate of tertiary educated: **8.9%**
- Emigration of physicians: **3,287** or **6.1%** of physicians trained in the country

Remittances

US$ millions	2000	2001	2002	2003	2004	2005	2006	2007
Inward remittance flows	1,157	1,357	1,215	2,024	2,164	2,227	2,424ᵃ	2,600
of which								
Workers' remittances	..	..	..	..	..	..	..	..
Compensation of employees	426	483	484	1,120	1,251	1,233	1,135	..
Migrants' transfer	731	875	731	904	913	994	1,289	..
Outward remittance flows	3,122	2,850	2,889	4,238	5,032	5,678	6,662ᵇ	..
of which								
Workers' remittances	523	549	613	656	644	849	975	..
Compensation of employees	924	984	1,027	1,812	2,290	2,420	2,832	..
Migrants' transfer	1,675	1,316	1,249	1,770	2,098	2,409	2,855	..

a. 0.4% of GDP in 2006.
b. 1.0% of GDP in 2006.

New Caledonia

Population (thousands, 2006)	238
Population growth (avg. annual %, 1997–2006)	1.9
Population density (people per sq. km, 2006)	13
Labor force (thousands, 2006)	99
Urban population (% of pop., 2006)	64.1
Age dependency ratio	0.51
Surface area (1,000 sq. km, 2006)	19
GNI ($ millions, 2006)	..
GNI per capita, Atlas method ($, 2006)	..
GDP growth (avg. annual %, 2002-06)	..
Poverty headcount ratio at national poverty line (% of pop., 2004)	..

Migration

IMMIGRATION, 2005
- Stock of immigrants: **43,153**
- Stock of immigrants as percentage of population: **18.2%**
- Females as percentage of immigrants: **44.4%**
- Refugees as percentage of immigrants: **0.0%**
- Top source countries: Papua New Guinea, Fiji, the Solomon Islands, French Polynesia, Indonesia, Vietnam, Vanuatu

EMIGRATION, 2005
- Stock of emigrants: **1,622**
- Stock of emigrants as percentage of population: **0.7%**
- Top 10 destination countries: Australia, French Polynesia, New Zealand, the Solomon Islands, Fiji, Vanuatu, the Netherlands, Chile, the Dominican Republic, Bolivia

SKILLED EMIGRATION, 2000
Skilled emigration data are currently not available for this country.

Remittances

US$ millions	2000	2001	2002	2003	2004	2005	2006	2007
Inward remittance flows	..	..	333	449	493	512	535	535
of which								
Workers' remittances	..	..	2	5	8	5	4	..
Compensation of employees	..	..	331	444	485	507	531	..
Migrants' transfer	..	..	..	..	..	..	..	..
Outward remittance flows	..	..	20	21	22	27	50	..
of which								
Workers' remittances	..	..	7	6	7	10	18	..
Compensation of employees	..	..	13	15	15	17	32	..
Migrants' transfer	..	..	..	..	..	..	..	..

New Zealand

Population (millions, 2006)	4.1
Population growth (avg. annual %, 1997–2006)	1.0
Population density (people per sq. km, 2006)	15
Labor force (millions, 2006)	2.2
Urban population (% of pop., 2006)	86.3
Age dependency ratio	0.5
Surface area (1,000 sq. km, 2006)	271
GNI ($ billions, 2006)	106
GNI per capita, Atlas method ($, 2006)	27,250
GDP growth (avg. annual %, 2002–06)	3.1
Poverty headcount ratio at national poverty line (% of pop., 2004)	..

Migration

IMMIGRATION, 2005
- Stock of immigrants: **642,164**
- Stock of immigrants as percentage of population: **15.9%**
- Females as percentage of immigrants: **52.5%**
- Refugees as percentage of immigrants: **0.8%**
- Top 10 source countries: the United Kingdom, Australia, Samoa, China, South Africa, Fiji, the Netherlands, India, Tonga, the Republic of Korea

EMIGRATION, 2005
- Stock of emigrants: **498,006**
- Stock of emigrants as percentage of population: **12.4%**
- Top 10 destination countries: Australia, the United Kingdom, the United States, Canada, Thailand, Japan, the Netherlands, Ireland, Samoa, Germany

SKILLED EMIGRATION, 2000
- Emigration rate of tertiary educated: **15.0%**
- Emigration of physicians: **1,295** or **13.2%** of physicians trained in the country

Remittances

US$ millions	2000	2001	2002	2003	2004	2005	2006	2007
Inward remittance flows	452	1,034	1,381	1,355	1,280	739	650[a]	650
of which								
Workers' remittances	..	..	..	..	..	..	..	..
Compensation of employees	..	..	..	..	..	..	..	..
Migrants' transfer	236	841	1,148	1,065	958	739	650	..
Outward remittance flows	564	126	273	839	1,093	936	865[b]	..
of which								
Workers' remittances	..	..	..	..	..	..	..	..
Compensation of employees	..	..	..	..	..	..	..	..
Migrants' transfer	418	..	..	561	806	936	865	..

a. 0.6% of GDP in 2006.
b. 0.8% of GDP in 2006.

Nicaragua

Latin America and the Caribbean	LOWER MIDDLE INCOME
Population (millions, 2006)	5.2
Population growth (avg. annual %, 1997–2006)	1.4
Population density (people per sq. km, 2006)	43
Labor force (millions, 2006)	2.0
Urban population (% of pop., 2006)	59.4
Age dependency ratio	0.71
Surface area (1,000 sq. km, 2006)	130
GNI ($ billions, 2006)	5.3
GNI per capita, Atlas method ($, 2006)	1,000
GDP growth (avg. annual %, 2002–06)	3.2
Poverty headcount ratio at national poverty line (% of pop., 2004)	44.9

Migration

EMIGRATION, 2005
- Stock of emigrants: **683,520**
- Stock of emigrants as percentage of population: **12.5%**
- Top 10 destination countries: Costa Rica, the United States, Canada, Panama, Guatemala, Spain, Mexico, El Salvador, República Bolivariana de Venezuela, Germany

SKILLED EMIGRATION, 2000
- Emigration rate of tertiary educated: **30.9%**
- Emigration of physicians: **149** or **2.6%** of physicians trained in the country

IMMIGRATION, 2005
- Stock of immigrants: **28,253**
- Stock of immigrants as percentage of population: **0.5%**
- Females as percentage of immigrants: **50.6%**
- Refugees as percentage of immigrants: **1.0%**
- Top 10 source countries: Honduras, Costa Rica, the United States, El Salvador, Guatemala, Mexico, Cuba, Spain, Panama, Russia

Remittances

US$ millions	2000	2001	2002	2003	2004	2005	2006	2007
Inward remittance flows	320	336	377	439	519	600	656ª	715
of which								
Workers' remittances	320	336	377	439	519	600	656	..
Compensation of employees	..	..	..	..	..	..	..	..
Migrants' transfer	..	..	..	..	..	..	..	..
Outward remittance flows	..	..	..	..	..	..	..	..
of which								
Workers' remittances	..	..	..	..	..	..	..	..
Compensation of employees	..	..	..	..	..	..	..	..
Migrants' transfer	..	..	..	..	..	..	..	..

a. 12.2% of GDP in 2006.

Niger

Population (millions, 2006)	14
Population growth (avg. annual %, 1997–2006)	3.4
Population density (people per sq. km, 2006)	11
Labor force (millions, 2006)	6.1
Urban population (% of pop., 2006)	17
Age dependency ratio	1.04
Surface area (1,000 sq. km, 2006)	1,267
GNI ($ billions, 2006)	3.6
GNI per capita, Atlas method ($, 2006)	260
GDP growth (avg. annual %, 2002–06)	3.4
Poverty headcount ratio at national poverty line (% of pop., 2004)	63.8

Migration

EMIGRATION, 2005
- Stock of emigrants: **437,844**
- Stock of emigrants as percentage of population: **3.1%**
- Top 10 destination countries: Côte d'Ivoire, Burkina Faso, Nigeria, Chad, Benin, Togo, France, Italy, Germany, the United States

SKILLED EMIGRATION, 2000
- Emigration rate of tertiary educated: **6.1%**
- Emigration of physicians:
  a) **3** or **0.7%** of physicians trained in the country *(Source: Docquier and Bhargava 2006)*
  b) **37** or **8.7%** of physicians trained in the country *(Source: Clemens and Pettersson 2006)*
- Emigration of nurses: **66** or **2.4%** of nurses trained in the country

IMMIGRATION, 2005
- Stock of immigrants: **123,687**
- Stock of immigrants as percentage of population: **0.9%**
- Females as percentage of immigrants: **52.1%**
- Refugees as percentage of immigrants: **0.3%**
- Top 10 source countries: Nigeria, Mali, Burkina Faso, Benin, Côte d'Ivoire, Ghana, Togo, Senegal, Chad, Sudan

Remittances

US$ millions	2000	2001	2002	2003	2004	2005	2006	2007
Inward remittance flows	14	22	19	26	60	67	67[a]	67
of which								
Workers' remittances	5	14	9	12	43	46	..	..
Compensation of employees	10	8	10	14	17	21	..	..
Migrants' transfer	..	..	..	..	..	..	..	..
Outward remittance flows	12	10	6	9	25	29	29[b]	..
of which								
Workers' remittances	11	9	5	7	22	27	..	..
Compensation of employees	1	2	2	2	3	2	..	..
Migrants' transfer	..	..	..	..	..	..	..	..

a. 1.9% of GDP in 2006.
b. 0.8% of GDP in 2006.

Nigeria

Population (millions, 2006)	145
Population growth (avg. annual %, 1997-2006)	2.6
Population density (people per sq. km, 2006)	159
Labor force (millions, 2006)	53
Urban population (% of pop., 2006)	49
Age dependency ratio	0.89
Surface area (1,000 sq. km, 2006)	924
GNI ($ billions, 2006)	103
GNI per capita, Atlas method ($, 2006)	640
GDP growth (avg. annual %, 2002-06)	6.1
Poverty headcount ratio at national poverty line (% of pop., 2004)	71.2

Migration

EMIGRATION, 2005
- Stock of emigrants: **836,832**
- Stock of emigrants as percentage of population: **0.6%**
- Top 10 destination countries: the United States, Chad, the United Kingdom, Cameroon, Benin, Niger, Italy, Sudan, Germany, Spain

SKILLED EMIGRATION, 2000
- Emigration rate of tertiary educated: **36.1%**
- Emigration of physicians:
  a) **1,548** or **4.3%** of physicians trained in the country *(Source: Docquier and Bhargava 2006)*
  b) **4,856** or **13.6%** of physicians trained in the country *(Source: Clemens and Pettersson 2006)*
- Emigration of nurses: **12,579** or **11.7%** of nurses trained in the country

IMMIGRATION, 2005
- Stock of immigrants: **971,450**
- Stock of immigrants as percentage of population: **0.7%**
- Females as percentage of immigrants: **48.1%**
- Refugees as percentage of immigrants: **0.8%**
- Top 10 source countries: Benin, Ghana, Mali, Togo, Niger, Chad, Cameroon, Liberia, Mauritania, Egypt

Remittances

US$ millions	2000	2001	2002	2003	2004	2005	2006	2007
Inward remittance flows	1,392	1,167	1,209	1,063	2,273	3,329	3,329[a]	3,329
of which								
Workers' remittances	1,392	1,167	1,209	1,063	2,273	3,329	..	..
Compensation of employees	..	..	..	..	..	..	..	..
Migrants' transfer	..	..	..	..	..	..	..	..
Outward remittance flows	1	1	1	12	21	18	18[b]	..
of which								
Workers' remittances	1	1	1	12	21	18	..	..
Compensation of employees	..	..	..	..	..	..	..	..
Migrants' transfer	..	..	..	..	..	..	..	..

a. 2.9% of GDP in 2006.
b. 0.02% of GDP in 2006.

Norway

Population (millions, 2006)	4.6
Population growth (avg. annual %, 1997–2006)	0.6
Population density (people per sq. km, 2006)	15
Labor force (millions, 2006)	2.5
Urban population (% of pop., 2006)	77.5
Age dependency ratio	0.52
Surface area (1,000 sq. km, 2006)	324
GNI ($ billions, 2006)	313
GNI per capita, Atlas method ($, 2006)	66,530
GDP growth (avg. annual %, 2002–06)	2.1
Poverty headcount ratio at national poverty line (% of pop., 2004)	..

Migration

IMMIGRATION, 2005

- Stock of immigrants: **343,929**
- Stock of immigrants as percentage of population: **7.4%**
- Females as percentage of immigrants: **50.9%**
- Refugees as percentage of immigrants: **12.5%**
- Top 10 source countries: Sweden, Denmark, the United States, Iraq, Pakistan, the United Kingdom, Germany, Serbia and Montenegro, Bosnia and Herzegovina, Vietnam

EMIGRATION, 2005

- Stock of emigrants: **180,575**
- Stock of emigrants as percentage of population: **3.9%**
- Top 10 destination countries: Sweden, the United States, Denmark, the United Kingdom, Spain, Germany, Canada, Australia, Turkey, France

SKILLED EMIGRATION, 2000

- Emigration rate of tertiary educated: **5.4%**
- Emigration of physicians: **583** or **3.7%** of physicians trained in the country

Remittances

US$ millions	2000	2001	2002	2003	2004	2005	2006	2007
Inward remittance flows	246	254	302	392	465	506	524[a]	524
of which								
Workers' remittances	..	..	..	..	..	..	..	..
Compensation of employees	270	279	333	392	465	506	524	..
Migrants' transfer	..	..	..	..	..	..	..	..
Outward remittance flows	718	554	658	1,430	1,749	2,170	2,620[b]	..
of which								
Workers' remittances	..	..	..	..	..	..	..	..
Compensation of employees	1,060	1,022	923	1,430	1,749	2,170	2,620	..
Migrants' transfer	..	..	..	..	..	..	..	..

a. 0.2% of GDP in 2006.
b. 0.8% of GDP in 2006.

Oman

UPPER MIDDLE INCOME

Population (millions, 2006)	2.6
Population growth (avg. annual %, 1997–2006)	1.6
Population density (people per sq. km, 2006)	8
Labor force (thousands, 2006)	986
Urban population (% of pop., 2006)	71.5
Age dependency ratio	0.58
Surface area (1,000 sq. km, 2006)	310
GNI ($ billions, 2006)	23
GNI per capita, Atlas method ($, 2006)	9,070
GDP growth (avg. annual %, 2002–06)	2.1
Poverty headcount ratio at national poverty line (% of pop., 2004)	..

Migration

EMIGRATION, 2005
- Stock of emigrants: **6,877**
- Stock of emigrants as percentage of population: **0.3%**
- Top 10 destination countries: the United Kingdom, the United States, Bahrain, Canada, Australia, the Netherlands, Germany, New Zealand, Sudan, Cyprus

SKILLED EMIGRATION, 2000
- Emigration rate of tertiary educated: **0.5%**
- Emigration of physicians: **9** or **0.3%** of physicians trained in the country

IMMIGRATION, 2005
- Stock of immigrants: **627,571**
- Stock of immigrants as percentage of population: **24.5%**
- Females as percentage of immigrants: **20.9%**
- Refugees as percentage of immigrants: **0.0%**
- Top 10 source countries: India, Bangladesh, Pakistan, Egypt, Sri Lanka, the Philippines, Sudan, Jordan, the United Kingdom, the Netherlands

Remittances

US$ millions	2000	2001	2002	2003	2004	2005	2006	2007
Inward remittance flows	39	39	39	39	39	39	39	43
of which								
Workers' remittances	..	..	..	..	..	..	..	..
Compensation of employees	39	39	39	39	39	39	39	..
Migrants' transfer	..	..	..	..	..	..	..	..
Outward remittance flows	1,451	1,532	1,602	1,672	1,826	2,257	2,788	..
of which								
Workers' remittances	1,451	1,532	1,602	1,672	1,826	2,257	2,788	..
Compensation of employees	..	..	..	..	..	..	..	..
Migrants' transfer	..	..	..	..	..	..	..	..

Migration and Remittances Factbook 2008

Pakistan

Population (millions, 2006)	159
Population growth (avg. annual %, 1997–2006)	2.4
Population density (people per sq. km, 2006)	206
Labor force (millions, 2006)	59
Urban population (% of pop., 2006)	35.3
Age dependency ratio	0.71
Surface area (1,000 sq. km, 2006)	796
GNI ($ billions, 2006)	126
GNI per capita, Atlas method ($, 2006)	770
GDP growth (avg. annual %, 2002–06)	5.8
Poverty headcount ratio at national poverty line (% of pop., 2004)	9

Migration

EMIGRATION, 2005

- Stock of emigrants: **3,415,952**
- Stock of emigrants as percentage of population: **2.2%**
- Top 10 destination countries: India, Saudi Arabia, the United Kingdom, the United States, Canada, Oman, Germany, Italy, Spain, Singapore

SKILLED EMIGRATION, 2000

- Emigration rate of tertiary educated: **9.2%**
- Emigration of physicians: **4,359** or **5.0%** of physicians trained in the country

IMMIGRATION, 2005

- Stock of immigrants: **3,254,112**
- Stock of immigrants as percentage of population: **2.1%**
- Females as percentage of immigrants: **44.8%**
- Refugees as percentage of immigrants: **27.3%**

Remittances

US$ millions	2000	2001	2002	2003	2004	2005	2006	2007
Inward remittance flows	1,075	1,461	3,554	3,964	3,945	4,280	5,121[a]	6,100
of which								
Workers' remittances	1,075	1,461	3,554	3,963	3,943	4,277	5,113	..
Compensation of employees	..	..	..	1	2	3	8	..
Migrants' transfer	..	..	..	..	..	..	..	..
Outward remittance flows	2	3	2	5	10	3	2[b]	..
of which								
Workers' remittances	2	3	2	5	9	2	1	..
Compensation of employees	..	..	..	..	1	1	1	..
Migrants' transfer	..	..	..	..	..	..	..	..

a. 4.0% of GDP in 2006.
b. 0.002% of GDP in 2006.

Palau

     UPPER MIDDLE INCOME

Population (thousands, 2006)	20
Population growth (avg. annual %, 1997–2006)	..
Population density (people per sq. km, 2006)	44
Labor force (millions, 2006)	..
Urban population (% of pop., 2006)	69.7
Age dependency ratio	..
Surface area (sq. km, 2006)	460
GNI ($ millions, 2006)	159
GNI per capita, Atlas method ($, 2006)	7,990
GDP growth (avg. annual %, 2002–06)	2.3
Poverty headcount ratio at national poverty line (% of pop., 2004)	..

Migration

EMIGRATION, 2005
- Stock of emigrants: **6,965**
- Stock of emigrants as percentage of population: **34.9%**
- Top 10 destination countries: the United States, Guam, the Philippines, Northern Mariana Islands, Mexico, Fiji, Japan, Australia, Greece, New Zealand

SKILLED EMIGRATION, 2000
- Emigration rate of tertiary educated: **30.0%**
- Emigration of physicians: **0** or **0.0%** of physicians trained in the country

IMMIGRATION, 2005
- Stock of immigrants: **3,036**
- Stock of immigrants as percentage of population: **15.2%**
- Females as percentage of immigrants: **36.6%**
- Refugees as percentage of immigrants: **0.0%**
- Top source countries: the Philippines, the United States, the Federated States of Micronesia, Japan, Guam, Northern Mariana Islands, the Republic of Korea

Remittances

Remittance data are currently not available for this country.

Panama

Latin America and the Caribbean	UPPER MIDDLE INCOME
Population (millions, 2006)	3.3
Population growth (avg. annual %, 1997–2006)	1.9
Population density (people per sq. km, 2006)	44
Labor force (millions, 2006)	1.5
Urban population (% of pop., 2006)	71.6
Age dependency ratio	0.57
Surface area (1,000 sq. km, 2006)	76
GNI ($ billions, 2006)	16
GNI per capita, Atlas method ($, 2006)	4,890
GDP growth (avg. annual %, 2002–06)	5.8
Poverty headcount ratio at national poverty line (% of pop., 2004)	6

Migration

EMIGRATION, 2005
- Stock of emigrants: **215,240**
- Stock of emigrants as percentage of population: **6.7%**
- Top 10 destination countries: the United States, Costa Rica, Spain, Canada, Mexico, Colombia, República Bolivariana de Venezuela, Italy, Chile, the United Kingdom

SKILLED EMIGRATION, 2000
- Emigration rate of tertiary educated: **20.0%**
- Emigration of physicians: **105** or **2.1%** of physicians trained in the country

IMMIGRATION, 2005
- Stock of immigrants: **102,243**
- Stock of immigrants as percentage of population: **3.2%**
- Females as percentage of immigrants: **50.3%**
- Refugees as percentage of immigrants: **1.7%**
- Top 10 source countries: Colombia, China, the Dominican Republic, the United States, Nicaragua, Costa Rica, Peru, Spain, Mexico, India

Remittances

US$ millions	2000	2001	2002	2003	2004	2005	2006	2007
Inward remittance flows	16	73	85	94	105	126	149[a]	280
of which								
Workers' remittances	16	73	85	94	105	124	149	..
Compensation of employees	..	..	..	..	..	..	..	..
Migrants' transfer	..	..	..	..	..	..	..	..
Outward remittance flows	22	42	45	57	72	88	121[b]	..
of which								
Workers' remittances	22	42	45	57	72	88	121	..
Compensation of employees	..	..	..	..	..	..	..	..
Migrants' transfer	..	..	..	..	..	..	..	..

a. 0.9% of GDP in 2006.
b. 0.7% of GDP in 2006.

Papua New Guinea

East Asia and Pacific	LOW INCOME

Population (millions, 2006)	6.0
Population growth (avg. annual %, 1997–2006)	2.2
Population density (people per sq. km, 2006)	13
Labor force (millions, 2006)	2.6
Urban population (% of pop., 2006)	13.5
Age dependency ratio	0.73
Surface area (1,000 sq. km, 2006)	463
GNI ($ billions, 2006)	5.1
GNI per capita, Atlas method ($, 2006)	770
GDP growth (avg. annual %, 2002–06)	2.3
Poverty headcount ratio at national poverty line (% of pop., 2004)	..

Migration

EMIGRATION, 2005

- Stock of emigrants: **51,025**
- Stock of emigrants as percentage of population: **0.9%**
- Top 10 destination countries: Australia, New Caledonia, the United States, the United Kingdom, New Zealand, Fiji, the Solomon Islands, Canada, the Philippines, Switzerland

SKILLED EMIGRATION, 2000

- Emigration rate of tertiary educated: **28.2%**
- Emigration of physicians: **123** or **31.8%** of physicians trained in the country

IMMIGRATION, 2005

- Stock of immigrants: **25,404**
- Stock of immigrants as percentage of population: **0.4%**
- Females as percentage of immigrants: **41.8%**
- Refugees as percentage of immigrants: **30.3%**
- Top 10 source countries: Australia, the United Kingdom, New Zealand, the United States, Germany, Indonesia, the Netherlands, China, India, Japan

Remittances

US$ millions	2000	2001	2002	2003	2004	2005	2006	2007
Inward remittance flows	7	6	11	13	16	13	13[a]	13
of which								
Workers' remittances	..	..	6	4	8	6	..	..
Compensation of employees	..	..	..	3	2	1	..	..
Migrants' transfer	7	6	5	6	6	6	..	..
Outward remittance flows	18	17	62	97	123	135	135[b]	..
of which								
Workers' remittances	11	11	45	41	61	75	..	..
Compensation of employees	..	..	12	50	56	54	..	..
Migrants' transfer	7	6	5	6	6	6	..	..

a. 0.2% of GDP in 2006.
b. 2.4% of GDP in 2006.

Paraguay

LOWER MIDDLE INCOME

Population (millions, 2006)	6.0
Population growth (avg. annual %, 1997–2006)	2.1
Population density (people per sq. km, 2006)	15
Labor force (millions, 2006)	2.8
Urban population (% of pop., 2006)	59.1
Age dependency ratio	0.69
Surface area (1,000 sq. km, 2006)	407
GNI ($ billions, 2006)	9.1
GNI per capita, Atlas method ($, 2006)	1,400
GDP growth (avg. annual %, 2002–06)	3.0
Poverty headcount ratio at national poverty line (% of pop., 2004)	13.6

Migration

EMIGRATION, 2005
- Stock of emigrants: **421,279**
- Stock of emigrants as percentage of population: **6.8%**
- Top 10 destination countries: Argentina, Brazil, the United States, Canada, Spain, Bolivia, Japan, Chile, Uruguay, Germany

SKILLED EMIGRATION, 2000
- Emigration rate of tertiary educated: **2.3%**
- Emigration of physicians: **94** or **1.5%** of physicians trained in the country

IMMIGRATION, 2005
- Stock of immigrants: **168,220**
- Stock of immigrants as percentage of population: **2.7%**
- Females as percentage of immigrants: **48.0%**
- Refugees as percentage of immigrants: **0.0%**
- Top 10 source countries: Brazil, Argentina, Uruguay, Chile, Japan, the Republic of Korea, Germany, Mexico, the United States, Peru

Remittances

US$ millions	2000	2001	2002	2003	2004	2005	2006	2007
Inward remittance flows	**278**	**264**	**202**	**223**	**238**	**269**	**432ª**	**450**
of which								
Workers' remittances	152	140	99	110	132	161	296	..
Compensation of employees	126	124	103	113	106	108	136	..
Migrants' transfer	..	..	..	..	..	..	..	..
Outward remittance flows	..	..	..	..	..	..	..	..
of which								
Workers' remittances	..	..	..	..	..	..	..	..
Compensation of employees	..	..	..	..	..	..	..	..
Migrants' transfer	..	..	..	..	..	..	..	..

a. 4.7% of GDP in 2006.

Peru

LOWER MIDDLE INCOME

Population (millions, 2006)	28
Population growth (avg. annual %, 1997–2006)	1.6
Population density (people per sq. km, 2006)	22
Labor force (millions, 2006)	14
Urban population (% of pop., 2006)	72.8
Age dependency ratio	0.59
Surface area (1,000 sq. km, 2006)	1,285
GNI ($ billions, 2006)	86
GNI per capita, Atlas method ($, 2006)	2,920
GDP growth (avg. annual %, 2002-06)	5.8
Poverty headcount ratio at national poverty line (% of pop., 2004)	10.5

Migration

EMIGRATION, 2005
- Stock of emigrants: **898,829**
- Stock of emigrants as percentage of population: **3.2%**
- Top 10 destination countries: the United States, Spain, Argentina, Italy, Japan, Chile, República Bolivariana de Venezuela, Canada, Germany, Bolivia

SKILLED EMIGRATION, 2000
- Emigration rate of tertiary educated: **6.3%**
- Emigration of physicians: **809** or **2.6%** of physicians trained in the country

IMMIGRATION, 2005
- Stock of immigrants: **41,557**
- Stock of immigrants as percentage of population: **0.2%**
- Females as percentage of immigrants: **52.0%**
- Refugees as percentage of immigrants: **1.9%**
- Top 10 source countries: the United States, Chile, Argentina, China, Spain, Bolivia, Italy, Brazil, Colombia, Japan

Remittances

US$ millions	2000	2001	2002	2003	2004	2005	2006	2007
Inward remittance flows	718	753	705	860	1,123	1,440	1,837[a]	2,000
of which								
Workers' remittances	718	753	705	869	1,133	1,440	1,837	..
Compensation of employees	..	..	..	..	..	..	..	..
Migrants' transfer	..	..	..	..	..	..	..	..
Outward remittance flows	275	175	121	116	113	129	133[b]	..
of which								
Workers' remittances	..	..	..	..	..	..	..	..
Compensation of employees	..	..	..	..	..	..	..	..
Migrants' transfer	275	175	118	116	113	129	133	..

a. 2.0% of GDP in 2006.
b. 0.1% of GDP in 2006.

Philippines, The

Population (millions, 2006)	85
Population growth (avg. annual %, 1997–2006)	1.9
Population density (people per sq. km, 2006)	284
Labor force (millions, 2006)	38
Urban population (% of pop., 2006)	63.4
Age dependency ratio	0.63
Surface area (1,000 sq. km, 2006)	300
GNI ($ billions, 2006)	128
GNI per capita, Atlas method ($, 2006)	1,420
GDP growth (avg. annual %, 2002–06)	5.2
Poverty headcount ratio at national poverty line (% of pop., 2004)	13.5

Migration

EMIGRATION, 2005
- Stock of emigrants: **3,631,405**
- Stock of emigrants as percentage of population: **4.4%**
- Top 10 destination countries: the United States, Saudi Arabia, Malaysia, Canada, Japan, Italy, Australia, Guam, the United Kingdom, the Republic of Korea

SKILLED EMIGRATION, 2000
- Emigration rate of tertiary educated: **14.8%**
- Emigration of physicians: **9,796** or **9.3%** of physicians trained in the country

IMMIGRATION, 2005
- Stock of immigrants: **374,458**
- Stock of immigrants as percentage of population: **0.5%**
- Females as percentage of immigrants: **49.1%**
- Refugees as percentage of immigrants: **0.0%**
- Top 10 source countries: the United States, China, the United Kingdom, Bahrain, Japan, Antigua and Barbuda, Indonesia, India, Brazil, Angola

Remittances

US$ millions	2000	2001	2002	2003	2004	2005	2006	2007
Inward remittance flows	6,212	6,164	9,735	10,243	11,471	13,566	15,250ª	17,000
of which								
Workers' remittances	5,161	6,328	7,167	7,681	8,617	10,668	12,481	..
Compensation of employees	1,763	2,432	2,568	2,558	2,851	2,893	2,758	..
Migrants' transfer	37	9	..	4	3	5	11	..
Outward remittance flows	93	56	58	18	17	15	20ᵇ	..
of which								
Workers' remittances	..	..	..	..	..	..	..	..
Compensation of employees	..	..	..	..	..	..	..	..
Migrants' transfer	21	24	21	18	17	15	20	..

a. 13.0% of GDP in 2006.
b. 0.02% of GDP in 2006.

Poland

UPPER MIDDLE INCOME

Population (millions, 2006)	38
Population growth (avg. annual %, 1997–2006)	-0.1
Population density (people per sq. km, 2006)	124
Labor force (millions, 2006)	17
Urban population (% of pop., 2006)	62.2
Age dependency ratio	0.41
Surface area (1,000 sq. km, 2006)	313
GNI ($ billions, 2006)	325
GNI per capita, Atlas method ($, 2006)	8,190
GDP growth (avg. annual %, 2002–06)	4.0
Poverty headcount ratio at national poverty line	0.1

Migration

EMIGRATION, 2005
- Stock of emigrants: **2,316,438**
- Stock of emigrants as percentage of population: **6.0%**
- Top 10 destination countries: the United States, Germany, Belarus, Canada, France, Israel, the United Kingdom, Australia, Italy, Austria

SKILLED EMIGRATION, 2000
- Emigration rate of tertiary educated: **12.3%**
- Emigration of physicians: **3,973** or **4.5%** of physicians trained in the country

IMMIGRATION, 2005
- Stock of immigrants: **702,808**
- Stock of immigrants as percentage of population: **1.8%**
- Females as percentage of immigrants: **59.9%**
- Refugees as percentage of immigrants: **0.4%**
- Top 10 source countries: Ukraine, Belarus, Germany, Lithuania, Russia, France, the United States, the Czech Republic, Austria, Italy

Remittances

US$ millions	2000	2001	2002	2003	2004	2005	2006	2007
Inward remittance flows	**1,726**	**1,995**	**1,989**	**2,655**	**2,710**	**3,549**	**4,370**[a]	**5,000**
of which								
Workers' remittances	1,534	1,802	1,725	2,288	2,347	3,092	3,786	..
Compensation of employees	192	193	264	367	359	446	574	..
Migrants' transfer	..	..	..	..	4	11	10	..
Outward remittance flows	**311**	**345**	**353**	**325**	**460**	**602**	**800**[b]	..
of which								
Workers' remittances	99	95	86	33	16	13	13	..
Compensation of employees	212	250	267	292	438	571	774	..
Migrants' transfer	..	..	..	..	6	18	13	..

a. 1.3% of GDP in 2006.
b. 0.2% of GDP in 2006.

Migration and Remittances Factbook 2008

Portugal

Population (millions, 2006)	11
Population growth (avg. annual %, 1997–2006)	0.5
Population density (people per sq. km, 2006)	116
Labor force (millions, 2006)	5.6
Urban population (% of pop., 2006)	58.2
Age dependency ratio	0.49
Surface area (1,000 sq. km, 2006)	92
GNI ($ billions, 2006)	189
GNI per capita, Atlas method ($, 2006)	18,100
GDP growth (avg. annual %, 2002–06)	0.5
Poverty headcount ratio at national poverty line (% of pop., 2004)	..

Migration

IMMIGRATION, 2005
- Stock of immigrants: **763,668**
- Stock of immigrants as percentage of population: **7.3%**
- Females as percentage of immigrants: **52.0%**
- Refugees as percentage of immigrants: **0.0%**
- Top 10 source countries: Angola, France, Mozambique, Brazil, Cape Verde, Germany, República Bolivariana de Venezuela, Guinea-Bissau, Spain, Switzerland

EMIGRATION, 2005
- Stock of emigrants: **1,950,486**
- Stock of emigrants as percentage of population: **18.6%**
- Top 10 destination countries: France, the United States, Brazil, Germany, Canada, Spain, Switzerland, Mozambique, República Bolivariana de Venezuela, Luxembourg

SKILLED EMIGRATION, 2000
- Emigration rate of tertiary educated: **13.8%**
- Emigration of physicians: **722** or **2.1%** of physicians trained in the country

Remittances

US$ millions	2000	2001	2002	2003	2004	2005	2006	2007
Inward remittance flows	**3,406**	**3,566**	**2,858**	**3,042**	**3,305**	**3,102**	**3,329ᵃ**	**3,750**
of which								
Workers' remittances	3,179	3,340	2,664	2,752	3,032	2,826	3,045	..
Compensation of employees	241	221	201	237	230	235	260	..
Migrants' transfer	75	86	66	53	43	41	24	..
Outward remittance flows	**454**	**706**	**792**	**936**	**1,164**	**1,306**	**1,386ᵇ**	..
of which								
Workers' remittances	173	366	412	529	604	695	777	..
Compensation of employees	203	250	257	259	378	436	444	..
Migrants' transfer	78	90	123	148	182	175	165	..

a. 1.7% of GDP in 2006.
b. 0.7% of GDP in 2006.

Qatar

Population (thousands, 2006)	828
Population growth (avg. annual %, 1997–2006)	4.3
Population density (people per sq. km, 2006)	75
Labor force (thousands, 2006)	481
Urban population (% of pop., 2006)	95.5
Age dependency ratio	0.3
Surface area (1,000 sq. km, 2006)	11
GNI ($ millions, 2006)	..
GNI per capita, Atlas method ($, 2006)	..
GDP growth (avg. annual %, 2002–06)	9.4
Poverty headcount ratio at national poverty line (% of pop., 2004)	..

Migration

IMMIGRATION, 2005
- Stock of immigrants: **636,751**
- Stock of immigrants as percentage of population: **78.3%**
- Females as percentage of immigrants: **25.8%**
- Refugees as percentage of immigrants: **0.0%**

EMIGRATION, 2005
- Stock of emigrants: **5,783**
- Stock of emigrants as percentage of population: **0.7%**
- Top 10 destination countries: the United States, Canada, the United Kingdom, Australia, France, Bahrain, Germany, Ireland, Italy, Sudan

SKILLED EMIGRATION, 2000
- Emigration rate of tertiary educated: **2.9%**
- Emigration of physicians: **37** or **3.1%** of physicians trained in the country

Remittances

Remittance data are currently not available for this country.

Romania

| UPPER MIDDLE INCOME

Population (millions, 2006)	22
Population growth (avg. annual %, 1997–2006)	-0.5
Population density (people per sq. km, 2006)	94
Labor force (millions, 2006)	10
Urban population (% of pop., 2006)	53.9
Age dependency ratio	0.43
Surface area (1,000 sq. km, 2006)	238
GNI ($ billions, 2006)	118
GNI per capita, Atlas method ($, 2006)	4,850
GDP growth (avg. annual %, 2002–06)	6.1
Poverty headcount ratio at national poverty line (% of pop., 2004)	1.1

Migration

EMIGRATION, 2005
- Stock of emigrants: **1,244,052**
- Stock of emigrants as percentage of population: **5.7%**
- Top 10 destination countries: Israel, Hungary, the United States, Spain, Italy, Germany, Canada, Austria, France, Greece

SKILLED EMIGRATION, 2000
- Emigration rate of tertiary educated: **14.1%**
- Emigration of physicians: **2,296** or **5.1%** of physicians trained in the country

IMMIGRATION, 2005
- Stock of immigrants: **133,441**
- Stock of immigrants as percentage of population: **0.6%**
- Females as percentage of immigrants: **50.7%**
- Refugees as percentage of immigrants: **1.1%**
- Top 10 source countries: Moldova, Bulgaria, Ukraine, Russia, Syria, Hungary, Greece, Turkey, Italy, Germany

Remittances

US$ millions	2000	2001	2002	2003	2004	2005	2006	2007
Inward remittance flows	96	116	143	124	132	4,733	6,707[a]	6,800
of which								
Workers' remittances	2	4	7	14	18	3,754	5,506	..
Compensation of employees	94	112	136	110	113	954	1,157	..
Migrants' transfer	..	..	..	..	1	25	44	..
Outward remittance flows	6	5	7	8	8	34	56[b]	..
of which								
Workers' remittances	1	1	..	1	1	4	6	..
Compensation of employees	5	4	6	7	5	24	42	..
Migrants' transfer	..	..	1	..	2	6	8	..

a. 5.5% of GDP in 2006.
b. 0.05% of GDP in 2006.

Russian Federation, The

Population (millions, 2006)	142
Population growth (avg. annual %, 1997–2006)	-0.4
Population density (people per sq. km, 2006)	9
Labor force (millions, 2006)	73
Urban population (% of pop., 2006)	72.9
Age dependency ratio	0.4
Surface area (1,000 sq. km, 2006)	17,098
GNI ($ billions, 2006)	958
GNI per capita, Atlas method ($, 2006)	5,780
GDP growth (avg. annual %, 2002–06)	6.5
Poverty headcount ratio at national poverty line (% of pop., 2004)	0.3

Migration

EMIGRATION, 2005
- Stock of emigrants: **11,480,137**
- Stock of emigrants as percentage of population: **8.0%**
- Top 10 destination countries: Ukraine, Kazakhstan, Belarus, Israel, Uzbekistan, the United States, Latvia, Germany, Moldova, Estonia

SKILLED EMIGRATION, 2000
- Emigration rate of tertiary educated: **1.3%**
- Emigration of physicians: **1,875** or **0.3%** of physicians trained in the country

IMMIGRATION, 2005
- Stock of immigrants: **12,079,626**
- Stock of immigrants as percentage of population: **8.4%**
- Females as percentage of immigrants: **57.8%**
- Refugees as percentage of immigrants: **0.0%**
- Top 10 source countries: Ukraine, Kazakhstan, Belarus, Uzbekistan, Azerbaijan, Georgia, Armenia, the Kyrgyz Republic, Tajikistan, Moldova

Remittances

US$ millions	2000	2001	2002	2003	2004	2005	2006	2007
Inward remittance flows	1,275	1,403	1,359	1,453	2,495	2,918	3,091ª	4,000
of which								
Workers' remittances	..	363	232	300	925	621	766	..
Compensation of employees	500	624	704	814	1,206	1,714	1,647	..
Migrants' transfer	775	416	423	339	364	583	678	..
Outward remittance flows	1,101	1,823	2,226	3,233	5,188	6,989	11,438ᵇ	..
of which								
Workers' remittances	..	421	788	1,306	2,672	3,051	4,587	..
Compensation of employees	232	493	507	958	1,464	2,921	6,038	..
Migrants' transfer	867	908	931	969	1,052	1,017	813	..

a. 0.3% of GDP in 2006.
b. 1.2% of GDP in 2006.

Rwanda

Population (millions, 2006)	9.2
Population growth (avg. annual %, 1997–2006)	4.9
Population density (people per sq. km, 2006)	375
Labor force (millions, 2006)	4.3
Urban population (% of pop., 2006)	20.2
Age dependency ratio	0.84
Surface area (1,000 sq. km, 2006)	26
GNI ($ billions, 2006)	2.5
GNI per capita, Atlas method ($, 2006)	250
GDP growth (avg. annual %, 2002–06)	5.1
Poverty headcount ratio at national poverty line (% of pop., 2004)	58.8

Migration

EMIGRATION, 2005
- Stock of emigrants: **196,104**
- Stock of emigrants as percentage of population: **2.2%**
- Top 10 destination countries: Uganda, Tanzania, Belgium, Canada, France, the United Kingdom, the United States, Germany, Italy, the Netherlands

SKILLED EMIGRATION, 2000
- Emigration rate of tertiary educated: **19.0%**
- Emigration of physicians:
  - a) **15** or **8.8%** of physicians trained in the country *(Source: Docquier and Bhargava 2006)*
  - b) **118** or **43.2%** of physicians trained in the country *(Source: Clemens and Pettersson 2006)*
- Emigration of nurses: **292** or **13.9%** of nurses trained in the country

IMMIGRATION, 2005
- Stock of immigrants: **121,183**
- Stock of immigrants as percentage of population: **1.3%**
- Females as percentage of immigrants: **47.0%**
- Refugees as percentage of immigrants: **48.5%**
- Top source countries: the Democratic Republic of Congo, Burundi, Uganda, Tanzania, India, Belgium

Remittances

US$ millions	2000	2001	2002	2003	2004	2005	2006	2007
Inward remittance flows	7	8	7	9	10	21	21[a]	21
of which								
Workers' remittances	4	5	7	9	10	9	17	..
Compensation of employees	3	2	..	0	0	12	4	..
Migrants' transfer	..	..	..	..	..	..	..	..
Outward remittance flows	28	33	32	30	31	35	47[b]	..
of which								
Workers' remittances	16	16	18	15	15	14	17	..
Compensation of employees	12	17	14	14	16	21	30	..
Migrants' transfer	..	..	0	..	..	..	..	..

a. 0.8% of GDP in 2006.
b. 1.9% of GDP in 2006.

Samoa

East Asia and Pacific **LOWER MIDDLE INCOME**

Population (thousands, 2006)	186
Population growth (avg. annual %, 1997–2006)	0.9
Population density (people per sq. km, 2006)	66
Labor force (thousands, 2006)	65
Urban population (% of pop., 2006)	22.6
Age dependency ratio	0.82
Surface area (1,000 sq. km, 2006)	3
GNI ($ millions, 2006)	417
GNI per capita, Atlas method ($, 2006)	2,270
GDP growth (avg. annual %, 2002–06)	3.4
Poverty headcount ratio at national poverty line (% of pop., 2004)	..

Migration

EMIGRATION, 2005
- Stock of emigrants: **100,982**
- Stock of emigrants as percentage of population: **54.6%**
- Top 10 destination countries: New Zealand, the United States, American Samoa, Australia, Fiji, Kiribati, Italy, the United Kingdom, Canada, Tonga

SKILLED EMIGRATION, 2000
- Emigration rate of tertiary educated: **66.6%**
- Emigration of physicians: **0** or **0.0%** of physicians trained in the country

IMMIGRATION, 2005
- Stock of immigrants: **9,196**
- Stock of immigrants as percentage of population: **5.0%**
- Females as percentage of immigrants: **48.0%**
- Refugees as percentage of immigrants: **0.0%**
- Top 10 source countries: American Samoa, New Zealand, the United States, Australia, Fiji, Tonga, China, Japan, Papua New Guinea, Germany

Remittances

US$ millions	2000	2001	2002	2003	2004	2005	2006	2007
Inward remittance flows	45	45	1	1	1	1	1ᵃ	1
of which								
Workers' remittances	..	..	..	..	..	..	..	..
Compensation of employees	..	..	..	..	1	1	1	..
Migrants' transfer	..	..	..	..	..	..	..	..
Outward remittance flows	..	..	..	..	11	11	2ᵇ	..
of which								
Workers' remittances	..	..	..	..	..	..	..	..
Compensation of employees	..	..	..	..	11	11	2	..
Migrants' transfer	..	..	..	..	..	..	..	..

a. 0.2% of GDP in 2006.
b. 0.5% of GDP in 2006.

Migration and Remittances Factbook 2008

San Marino

Population (thousands, 2006)	29
Population growth (avg. annual %, 1997–2006)	..
Population density (people per sq. km, 2006)	477
Labor force (millions, 2006)	..
Urban population (% of pop., 2006)	97.5
Age dependency ratio	..
Surface area (sq. km, 2006)	60
GNI ($ millions, 2006)	..
GNI per capita, Atlas method ($, 2006)	..
GDP growth (avg. annual %, 2002–06)	2.3
Poverty headcount ratio at national poverty line (% of pop., 2004)	..

Migration

IMMIGRATION, 2005
- Stock of immigrants: **9,424**
- Stock of immigrants as percentage of population: **33.5%**
- Females as percentage of immigrants: **53.5%**
- Refugees as percentage of immigrants: **0.0%**

EMIGRATION, 2005
- Stock of emigrants: **7,451**
- Stock of emigrants as percentage of population: **26.5%**
- Top 10 destination countries: Italy, the United States, France, Germany, Switzerland, Canada, Spain, Belgium, the United Kingdom, Greece

SKILLED EMIGRATION, 2000
- Emigration rate of tertiary educated: **29.9%**
- Emigration of physicians: **0** or **0.0%** of physicians trained in the country

Remittances
Remittance data are currently not available for this country.

São Tomé and Principe

Population (thousands, 2006)	160
Population growth (avg. annual %, 1997–2006)	2.1
Population density (people per sq. km, 2006)	167
Labor force (thousands, 2006)	51
Urban population (% of pop., 2006)	58.8
Age dependency ratio	0.77
Surface area (sq. km, 2006)	960
GNI ($ millions, 2006)	120
GNI per capita, Atlas method ($, 2006)	780
GDP growth (avg. annual %, 2002–06)	7.1
Poverty headcount ratio at national poverty line (% of pop., 2004)	..

Migration

EMIGRATION, 2005
- Stock of emigrants: **21,264**
- Stock of emigrants as percentage of population: **13.6%**
- Top 10 destination countries: Portugal, Cape Verde, France, Spain, the Netherlands, the United Kingdom, the United States, Germany, Switzerland, Italy

SKILLED EMIGRATION, 2000
- Emigration rate of tertiary educated: **35.6%**
- Emigration of physicians:
  a) **53** or **43.4%** of physicians trained in the country *(Source: Docquier and Bhargava 2006)*
  b) **97** or **60.6%** of physicians trained in the country *(Source: Clemens and Pettersson 2006)*
- Emigration of nurses: **149** or **46.4%** of nurses trained in the country

IMMIGRATION, 2005
- Stock of immigrants: **7,499**
- Stock of immigrants as percentage of population: **4.8%**
- Females as percentage of immigrants: **46.8%**
- Refugees as percentage of immigrants: **0.0%**
- Top 10 source countries: Angola, Cape Verde, Portugal, Gabon, Equatorial Guinea, Mozambique, Guinea-Bissau, Russia, France, the Republic of Congo

Remittances

US$ millions	2000	2001	2002	2003	2004	2005	2006	2007
Inward remittance flows	1	1	1	1	1	1	1[a]	1
of which								
Workers' remittances	0	1	1	2	..	..	..	..
Compensation of employees	..	..	..	..	..	..	..	..
Migrants' transfer	..	..	..	..	..	..	..	..
Outward remittance flows	1	1	1	1	1	1	1[b]	..
of which								
Workers' remittances	..	..	..	..	..	..	..	..
Compensation of employees	1	1	0	1	..	..	..	..
Migrants' transfer	..	..	..	..	..	..	..	..

a. 0.8% of GDP in 2006.
b. 0.8% of GDP in 2006.

Saudi Arabia

Population (millions, 2006)	24
Population growth (avg. annual %, 1997–2006)	2.2
Population density (people per sq. km, 2006)	12
Labor force (millions, 2006)	7.7
Urban population (% of pop., 2006)	81.2
Age dependency ratio	0.66
Surface area (1,000 sq. km, 2006)	2,000
GNI ($ billions, 2006)	310
GNI per capita, Atlas method ($, 2006)	12,510
GDP growth (avg. annual %, 2002–06)	4.9
Poverty headcount ratio at national poverty line (% of pop., 2004)	..

Migration

IMMIGRATION, 2005
- Stock of immigrants: **6,360,730**
- Stock of immigrants as percentage of population: **25.9%**
- Females as percentage of immigrants: **30.1%**
- Refugees as percentage of immigrants: **3.8%**
- Top 10 source countries: India, Egypt, Pakistan, the Philippines, Bangladesh, the Republic of Yemen, Indonesia, Sudan, Jordan, Sri Lanka

EMIGRATION, 2005
- Stock of emigrants: **80,705**
- Stock of emigrants as percentage of population: **0.3%**
- Top 10 destination countries: the United States, Canada, the United Kingdom, Bahrain, India, Turkey, Australia, France, República Bolivariana de Venezuela, Germany

SKILLED EMIGRATION, 2000
- Emigration rate of tertiary educated: **0.7%**
- Emigration of physicians: **209** or **0.7%** of physicians trained in the country

Remittances

US$ millions	2000	2001	2002	2003	2004	2005	2006	2007
Inward remittance flows	..	..	..	..	..	..	..	..
of which								
Workers' remittances	..	..	..	..	..	..	..	..
Compensation of employees	..	..	..	..	..	..	..	..
Migrants' transfer	..	..	..	..	..	..	..	..
Outward remittance flows	**15,390**	**15,120**	**15,854**	**14,783**	**13,555**	**13,996**	**15,611**[a]	..
of which								
Workers' remittances	15,390	15,120	15,854	14,783	13,555	13,996	15,611	..
Compensation of employees	..	..	..	..	..	..	..	..
Migrants' transfer	..	..	..	..	..	..	..	..

a. 5.0% of GDP in 2006.

Senegal

Population (millions, 2006)	12
Population growth (avg. annual %, 1997–2006)	2.4
Population density (people per sq. km, 2006)	62
Labor force (millions, 2006)	4.7
Urban population (% of pop., 2006)	41.9
Age dependency ratio	0.83
Surface area (1,000 sq. km, 2006)	197
GNI ($ billions, 2006)	8.9
GNI per capita, Atlas method ($, 2006)	750
GDP growth (avg. annual %, 2002–06)	4.3
Poverty headcount ratio at national poverty line (% of pop., 2004)	13.1

Migration

EMIGRATION, 2005
- Stock of emigrants: **463,403**
- Stock of emigrants as percentage of population: **4.0%**
- Top 10 destination countries: the Gambia, France, Italy, Mauritania, Spain, Gabon, the United States, the Republic of Congo, Guinea-Bissau, Nigeria

SKILLED EMIGRATION, 2000
- Emigration rate of tertiary educated: **24.1%**
- Emigration of physicians:
  a) **27** or **2.8%** of physicians trained in the country *(Source: Docquier and Bhargava 2006)*
  b) **678** or **51.4%** of physicians trained in the country *(Source: Clemens and Pettersson 2006)*
- Emigration of nurses: **695** or **26.9%** of nurses trained in the country

IMMIGRATION, 2005
- Stock of immigrants: **325,940**
- Stock of immigrants as percentage of population: **2.8%**
- Females as percentage of immigrants: **40.2%**
- Refugees as percentage of immigrants: **6.4%**
- Top 10 source countries: Guinea, Mauritania, Guinea-Bissau, Mali, France, Cape Verde, the Gambia, Morocco, Syria, the United States

Remittances

US$ millions	2000	2001	2002	2003	2004	2005	2006	2007
Inward remittance flows	233	305	344	511	633	633	633[a]	874
of which								
Workers' remittances	179	260	297	448	563	..	..	..
Compensation of employees	54	45	48	63	70	..	..	..
Migrants' transfer	..	..	..	..	..	..	..	..
Outward remittance flows	55	51	39	57	77	77	77[b]	..
of which								
Workers' remittances	48	43	34	48	67	..	..	..
Compensation of employees	7	9	5	9	10	..	..	..
Migrants' transfer	..	..	..	..	..	..	..	..

a. 7.1% of GDP in 2006.
b. 0.9% of GDP in 2006.

Serbia and Montenegro

Europe and Central Asia	UPPER MIDDLE INCOME

Population (millions, 2006)	8.0
Population growth (avg. annual %, 1997–2006)	-0.6
Population density (people per sq. km, 2006)	79
Labor force (millions, 2006)	..
Urban population (% of pop., 2006)	..
Age dependency ratio	..
Surface area (1,000 sq. km, 2006)	102
GNI ($ billions, 2006)	34
GNI per capita, Atlas method ($, 2006)	7,770
GDP growth (avg. annual %, 2002–06)	9.2
Poverty headcount ratio at national poverty line (% of pop., 2004)	..

Migration

EMIGRATION, 2005
- Stock of emigrants: **2,298,352**
- Stock of emigrants as percentage of population: **21.9%**
- Top 10 destination countries: Germany, Austria, Switzerland, the United States, Turkey, Croatia, Sweden, Italy, Canada, Australia

SKILLED EMIGRATION, 2000
- Emigration rate of tertiary educated: **17.4%**
- Emigration of physicians: **1,794** or **7.3%** of physicians trained in the country

IMMIGRATION, 2005
- Stock of immigrants: **512,336**
- Stock of immigrants as percentage of population: **4.9%**
- Females as percentage of immigrants: **57.0%**
- Refugees as percentage of immigrants: **52.6%**

Remittances

US$ millions	2000	2001	2002	2003	2004	2005	2006	2007
Inward remittance flows	1,132	1,698	2,089	2,661	4,129	4,650	4,703[a]	4,910
of which								
Workers' remittances	..	..	..	..	..	..	..	..
Compensation of employees	..	..	..	..	..	..	..	..
Migrants' transfer	..	..	..	..	..	..	..	..
Outward remittance flows	..	..	..	..	..	..	..	..
of which								
Workers' remittances	..	..	..	..	..	..	..	..
Compensation of employees	..	..	..	..	..	..	..	..
Migrants' transfer	..	..	..	..	..	..	..	..

a. 13.8% of GDP in 2006.

Seychelles, The

Population (thousands, 2006)	86
Population growth (avg. annual %, 1997-2006)	1.1
Population density (people per sq. km, 2006)	186
Labor force (millions, 2006)	..
Urban population (% of pop., 2006)	53.4
Age dependency ratio	..
Surface area (sq. km, 2006)	460
GNI ($ millions, 2006)	711
GNI per capita, Atlas method ($, 2006)	8,650
GDP growth (avg. annual %, 2002-06)	-0.4
Poverty headcount ratio at national poverty line (% of pop., 2004)	..

Migration

EMIGRATION, 2005

- Stock of emigrants: **11,841**
- Stock of emigrants as percentage of population: **14.7%**
- Top 10 destination countries: the United Kingdom, Australia, Canada, Tanzania, Italy, the United States, France, Germany, Switzerland, the Netherlands

SKILLED EMIGRATION, 2000

- Emigration rate of tertiary educated: **58.6%**
- Emigration of physicians:
  a) **5** or **4.6%** of physicians trained in the country *(Source: Docquier and Bhargava 2006)*
  b) **50** or **29.4%** of physicians trained in the country *(Source: Clemens and Pettersson 2006)*
- Emigration of nurses: **175** or **29.3%** of nurses trained in the country

IMMIGRATION, 2005

- Stock of immigrants: **4,932**
- Stock of immigrants as percentage of population: **6.1%**
- Females as percentage of immigrants: **40.2%**
- Refugees as percentage of immigrants: **0.0%**

Remittances

US$ millions	2000	2001	2002	2003	2004	2005	2006	2007
Inward remittance flows	3	2	2	5	7	12	14[a]	15
of which								
Workers' remittances	3	2	2	5	7	12	14	..
Compensation of employees	0	0	0	0	0	0	0	..
Migrants' transfer	..	..	..	..	..	..	..	..
Outward remittance flows	13	11	15	7	8	10	18[b]	..
of which								
Workers' remittances	8	3	1	2	3	4	10	..
Compensation of employees	3	2	3	5	5	6	8	..
Migrants' transfer	..	..	..	..	..	..	..	..

a. 1.9% of GDP in 2006.
b. 2.4% of GDP in 2006.

Sierra Leone

Population (millions, 2006)	5.6
Population growth (avg. annual %, 1997-2006)	3.0
Population density (people per sq. km, 2006)	79
Labor force (millions, 2006)	2.4
Urban population (% of pop., 2006)	41.4
Age dependency ratio	0.86
Surface area (1,000 sq. km, 2006)	72
GNI ($ billions, 2006)	1.4
GNI per capita, Atlas method ($, 2006)	240
GDP growth (avg. annual %, 2002-06)	11.7
Poverty headcount ratio at national poverty line (% of pop., 2004)	56.9

Migration

EMIGRATION, 2005
- Stock of emigrants: **78,516**
- Stock of emigrants as percentage of population: **1.4%**
- Top 10 destination countries: the United States, the United Kingdom, Germany, Liberia, Nigeria, Spain, the Netherlands, the Gambia, Canada, Italy

SKILLED EMIGRATION, 2000
- Emigration rate of tertiary educated: **41.0%**
- Emigration of physicians:
  - a) **26** or **6.7%** of physicians trained in the country *(Source: Docquier and Bhargava 2006)*
  - b) **249** or **42.4%** of physicians trained in the country *(Source: Clemens and Pettersson 2006)*
- Emigration of nurses: **1,457** or **48.9%** of nurses trained in the country

IMMIGRATION, 2005
- Stock of immigrants: **119,162**
- Stock of immigrants as percentage of population: **2.2%**
- Females as percentage of immigrants: **42.7%**
- Refugees as percentage of immigrants: **56.8%**
- Top 10 source countries: Guinea, Gabon, Liberia, Lebanon, Nigeria, Mali, Ghana, Senegal, the United Kingdom, the United States

Remittances

US$ millions	2000	2001	2002	2003	2004	2005	2006	2007
Inward remittance flows	7	7	22	26	25	2	34[a]	38
of which								
Workers' remittances	7	6	7	26	25	2	30	..
Compensation of employees	..	..	14	0	0	0	4	..
Migrants' transfer	..	0	..	..	..	..	..	..
Outward remittance flows	..	0	3	3	2	2	36[b]	..
of which								
Workers' remittances	..	0	0	1	0	0	34	..
Compensation of employees	..	..	2	2	2	2	2	..
Migrants' transfer	..	0	..	..	..	..	..	..

a. 2.4% of GDP in 2006.
b. 2.5% of GDP in 2006.

Singapore

Population (millions, 2006)	4.4
Population growth (avg. annual %, 1997–2006)	1.8
Population density (people per sq. km, 2006)	6,376
Labor force (millions, 2006)	2.2
Urban population (% of pop., 2006)	100
Age dependency ratio	0.38
Surface area (sq. km, 2006)	699
GNI ($ billions, 2006)	128
GNI per capita, Atlas method ($, 2006)	29,320
GDP growth (avg. annual %, 2002–06)	6.1
Poverty headcount ratio at national poverty line (% of pop., 2004)	..

Migration

IMMIGRATION, 2005
- Stock of immigrants: **1,842,953**
- Stock of immigrants as percentage of population: **42.6%**
- Females as percentage of immigrants: **50.3%**
- Refugees as percentage of immigrants: **0.0%**
- Top 10 source countries: Malaysia, China, India, Indonesia, Pakistan, Bangladesh, the United States, Sri Lanka, Hong Kong (China), Canada

EMIGRATION, 2005
- Stock of emigrants: **230,007**
- Stock of emigrants as percentage of population: **5.3%**
- Top 10 destination countries: Malaysia, the United Kingdom, Australia, the United States, Canada, India, New Zealand, the Netherlands, Brunei, Thailand

SKILLED EMIGRATION, 2000
- Emigration rate of tertiary educated: **15.2%**
- Emigration of physicians: **607** or **9.7%** of physicians trained in the country

Remittances
Remittance data are currently not available for this country.

Slovak Republic, The

     UPPER MIDDLE INCOME

Population (millions, 2006)	5.4
Population growth (avg. annual %, 1997–2006)	0.02
Population density (people per sq. km, 2006)	112
Labor force (millions, 2006)	2.7
Urban population (% of pop., 2006)	56.3
Age dependency ratio	0.39
Surface area (1,000 sq. km, 2006)	49
GNI ($ billions, 2006)	54
GNI per capita, Atlas method ($, 2006)	9,870
GDP growth (avg. annual %, 2002–06)	5.6
Poverty headcount ratio at national poverty line (% of pop., 2004)	..

Migration

EMIGRATION, 2005
- Stock of emigrants: **520,962**
- Stock of emigrants as percentage of population: **9.6%**
- Top 10 destination countries: the Czech Republic, Hungary, the United States, Germany, Austria, Canada, Israel, the United Kingdom, Italy, France

SKILLED EMIGRATION, 2000
- Emigration rate of tertiary educated: **15.3%**
- Emigration of physicians: **733** or **4.0%** of physicians trained in the country

IMMIGRATION, 2005
- Stock of immigrants: **124,464**
- Stock of immigrants as percentage of population: **2.3%**
- Females as percentage of immigrants: **56.0%**
- Refugees as percentage of immigrants: **0.3%**
- Top 10 source countries: the Czech Republic, Hungary, Ukraine, Poland, Romania, Russia, Serbia and Montenegro, France, Bulgaria, the United States

Remittances

US$ millions	2000	2001	2002	2003	2004	2005	2006	2007
Inward remittance flows	18	24	24	424	424	424	424[a]	424
of which								
Workers' remittances	..	..	..	..	..	..	..	..
Compensation of employees	18	..	24	425	..	..	..	..
Migrants' transfer	0	..	0	(1)	..	..	..	..
Outward remittance flows	8	8	11	16	16	16	16[b]	..
of which								
Workers' remittances	..	..	..	..	..	..	..	..
Compensation of employees	7	..	11	16	..	..	..	..
Migrants' transfer	1	..	0	0	..	..	..	..

a. 0.8% of GDP in 2006.
b. 0.03% of GDP in 2006.

Slovenia

Population (millions, 2006)	2.0
Population growth (avg. annual %, 1997–2006)	0.03
Population density (people per sq. km, 2006)	99
Labor force (millions, 2006)	1.0
Urban population (% of pop., 2006)	51.2
Age dependency ratio	0.42
Surface area (1,000 sq. km, 2006)	20
GNI ($ billions, 2006)	37
GNI per capita, Atlas method ($, 2006)	18,890
GDP growth (avg. annual %, 2002–06)	4.0
Poverty headcount ratio at national poverty line (% of pop., 2004)	..

Migration

IMMIGRATION, 2005
- Stock of immigrants: **167,330**
- Stock of immigrants as percentage of population: **8.5%**
- Females as percentage of immigrants: **45.6%**
- Refugees as percentage of immigrants: **0.1%**
- Top 10 source countries: Bosnia and Herzegovina, Croatia, Serbia and Montenegro, FYR Macedonia, Ukraine, Germany, Russia, Italy, Austria, Romania

EMIGRATION, 2005
- Stock of emigrants: **133,965**
- Stock of emigrants as percentage of population: **6.8%**
- Top 10 destination countries: Germany, Austria, Croatia, Canada, France, Italy, the United States, Australia, Switzerland, the United Kingdom

SKILLED EMIGRATION, 2000
- Emigration rate of tertiary educated: **11.0%**
- Emigration of physicians: **80** or **1.8%** of physicians trained in the country

Remittances

US$ millions	2000	2001	2002	2003	2004	2005	2006	2007
Inward remittance flows	205	201	217	238	266	264	283[a]	300
of which								
Workers' remittances	14	17	17	13	12	7	6	..
Compensation of employees	188	182	196	217	249	254	274	..
Migrants' transfer	3	2	4	8	5	3	3	..
Outward remittance flows	29	29	46	66	80	95	129[b]	..
of which								
Workers' remittances	0	..	0	0	1	1	1	..
Compensation of employees	27	27	45	65	78	90	127	..
Migrants' transfer	2	2	1	1	2	4	1	..

a. 0.8% of GDP in 2006.
b. 0.3% of GDP in 2006.

Solomon Islands, The

Population (thousands, 2006)	489
Population growth (avg. annual %, 1997–2006)	2.7
Population density (people per sq. km, 2006)	17
Labor force (thousands, 2006)	200
Urban population (% of pop., 2006)	17.3
Age dependency ratio	0.75
Surface area (1,000 sq. km, 2006)	29
GNI ($ millions, 2006)	338
GNI per capita, Atlas method ($, 2006)	680
GDP growth (avg. annual %, 2002–06)	4.6
Poverty headcount ratio at national poverty line (% of pop., 2004)	..

Migration

EMIGRATION, 2005
- Stock of emigrants: **4,324**
- Stock of emigrants as percentage of population: **0.9%**
- Top 10 destination countries: New Caledonia, Australia, New Zealand, the United Kingdom, the United States, Fiji, Canada, Samoa, Greece, Japan

SKILLED EMIGRATION, 2000
- Emigration rate of tertiary educated: **3.7%**
- Emigration of physicians: **0** or **0.0%** of physicians trained in the country

IMMIGRATION, 2005
- Stock of immigrants: **3,279**
- Stock of immigrants as percentage of population: **0.7%**
- Females as percentage of immigrants: **41.9%**
- Refugees as percentage of immigrants: **0.0%**
- Top 10 source countries: Papua New Guinea, Kiribati, Australia, China, Fiji, the Philippines, New Zealand, the United States, Malaysia, New Caledonia

Remittances

US$ millions	2000	2001	2002	2003	2004	2005	2006	2007
Inward remittance flows	4	5	4	4	9	7	21[a]	21
of which								
Workers' remittances	..	..	1	1	2	3	10	..
Compensation of employees	4	5	2	3	7	4	9	..
Migrants' transfer	..	..	1	..	..	..	2	..
Outward remittance flows	6	2	2	2	2	2	3[b]	..
of which								
Workers' remittances	3	1	0	0	0	0	1	..
Compensation of employees	3	2	1	1	2	2	2	..
Migrants' transfer	..	0	0	0	0	0	0	..

a. 6.3% of GDP in 2006.
b. 0.9% of GDP in 2006.

Somalia

LOW INCOME

Population (millions, 2006)	8.5
Population growth (avg. annual %, 1997–2006)	2.9
Population density (people per sq. km, 2006)	14
Labor force (millions, 2006)	3.6
Urban population (% of pop., 2006)	35.7
Age dependency ratio	0.88
Surface area (1,000 sq. km, 2006)	638
GNI ($ millions, 2006)	..
GNI per capita, Atlas method ($, 2006)	..
GDP growth (avg. annual %, 2002–06)	..
Poverty headcount ratio at national poverty line (% of pop., 2004)	..

Migration

EMIGRATION, 2005

- Stock of emigrants: **441,417**
- Stock of emigrants as percentage of population: **5.4%**
- Top 10 destination countries: Ethiopia, the United Kingdom, the United States, Saudi Arabia, the Netherlands, Canada, Sweden, Denmark, Italy, Norway

SKILLED EMIGRATION, 2000

- Emigration rate of tertiary educated: **58.6%**
- Emigration of physicians:
  a) **116** or **25.0%** of physicians trained in the country *(Source: Docquier and Bhargava 2006)*
  b) **151** or **32.8%** of physicians trained in the country *(Source: Clemens and Pettersson 2006)*
- Emigration of nurses: **164** or **9.9%** of nurses trained in the country

IMMIGRATION, 2005

- Stock of immigrants: **281,702**
- Stock of immigrants as percentage of population: **3.4%**
- Females as percentage of immigrants: **46.5%**
- Refugees as percentage of immigrants: **0.1%**

Remittances

Remittance data are currently not available for this country.

South Africa

Population (millions, 2006)	47
Population growth (avg. annual %, 1997–2006)	1.7
Population density (people per sq. km, 2006)	39
Labor force (millions, 2006)	20
Urban population (% of pop., 2006)	59.8
Age dependency ratio	0.58
Surface area (1,000 sq. km, 2006)	1,219
GNI ($ billions, 2006)	250
GNI per capita, Atlas method ($, 2006)	5,390
GDP growth (avg. annual %, 2002–06)	4.3
Poverty headcount ratio at national poverty line (% of pop., 2004)	8.6

Migration

EMIGRATION, 2005
- Stock of emigrants: **713,104**
- Stock of emigrants as percentage of population: **1.5%**
- Top 10 destination countries: the United Kingdom, Mozambique, Australia, the United States, Canada, Namibia, New Zealand, Portugal, Swaziland, the Netherlands

SKILLED EMIGRATION, 2000
- Emigration rate of tertiary educated: **5.4%**
- Emigration of physicians:
  a) **4,412** or **13.2%** of physicians trained in the country (Source: Docquier and Bhargava 2006)
  b) **7,363** or **21.1%** of physicians trained in the country (Source: Clemens and Pettersson 2006)
- Emigration of nurses: **4,844** or **5.1%** of nurses trained in the country

IMMIGRATION, 2005
- Stock of immigrants: **1,106,214**
- Stock of immigrants as percentage of population: **2.3%**
- Females as percentage of immigrants: **41.4%**
- Refugees as percentage of immigrants: **2.6%**
- Top source countries: Zimbabwe, Mozambique, Lesotho, Swaziland, Botswana, Malawi, Australia, New Zealand

Remittances

US$ millions	2000	2001	2002	2003	2004	2005	2006	2007
Inward remittance flows	344	297	288	435	523	658	735[a]	735
of which								
Workers' remittances	..	..	..	..	..	..	..	..
Compensation of employees	325	282	268	391	468	614	692	..
Migrants' transfer	19	16	20	44	55	44	43	..
Outward remittance flows	685	568	541	706	937	1,055	1,067[b]	..
of which								
Workers' remittances	..	..	..	..	..	..	..	..
Compensation of employees	614	521	506	706	935	1,041	1,055	..
Migrants' transfer	71	47	35	..	2	14	12	..

a. 0.3% of GDP in 2006.
b. 0.4% of GDP in 2006.

Spain

Population (millions, 2006)	44
Population growth (avg. annual %, 1997–2006)	1.0
Population density (people per sq. km, 2006)	87
Labor force (millions, 2006)	21
Urban population (% of pop., 2006)	76.8
Age dependency ratio	0.45
Surface area (1,000 sq. km, 2006)	505
GNI ($ billions, 2006)	1,201
GNI per capita, Atlas method ($, 2006)	27,570
GDP growth (avg. annual %, 2002–06)	3.2
Poverty headcount ratio at national poverty line (% of pop., 2004)	..

Migration

IMMIGRATION, 2005
- Stock of immigrants: **4,790,074**
- Stock of immigrants as percentage of population: **11.1%**
- Females as percentage of immigrants: **47.4%**
- Refugees as percentage of immigrants: **0.1%**
- Top 10 source countries: Morocco, Ecuador, Colombia, France, Germany, the United Kingdom, Argentina, República Bolivariana de Venezuela, Romania, Portugal

EMIGRATION, 2005
- Stock of emigrants: **1,323,373**
- Stock of emigrants as percentage of population: **3.1%**
- Top 10 destination countries: France, Germany, Argentina, the United States, República Bolivariana de Venezuela, Switzerland, the United Kingdom, Brazil, Italy, Andorra

SKILLED EMIGRATION, 2000
- Emigration rate of tertiary educated: **2.6%**
- Emigration of physicians: **4,961** or **3.7%** of physicians trained in the country

Remittances

US$ millions	2000	2001	2002	2003	2004	2005	2006	2007
Inward remittance flows	4,517	4,720	5,178	6,072	7,528	7,960	8,863[a]	8,863
of which								
Workers' remittances	3,417	3,665	3,959	4,718	5,196	5,343	6,057	..
Compensation of employees	697	763	826	1,013	1,157	1,318	1,503	..
Migrants' transfer	745	666	798	838	1,175	1,299	1,303	..
Outward remittance flows	2,059	2,470	2,914	5,139	6,977	8,136	11,004[b]	..
of which								
Workers' remittances	1,325	1,987	2,697	3,939	5,211	6,123	8,570	..
Compensation of employees	842	836	841	925	1,341	1,545	1,864	..
Migrants' transfer	319	252	251	275	425	468	570	..

a. 0.7% of GDP in 2006.
b. 0.9% of GDP in 2006.

Sri Lanka

Population (millions, 2006)	20
Population growth (avg. annual %, 1997–2006)	0.8
Population density (people per sq. km, 2006)	306
Labor force (millions, 2006)	8.5
Urban population (% of pop., 2006)	15.1
Age dependency ratio	0.45
Surface area (1,000 sq. km, 2006)	66
GNI ($ billions, 2006)	27
GNI per capita, Atlas method ($, 2006)	1,300
GDP growth (avg. annual %, 2002–06)	5.8
Poverty headcount ratio at national poverty line (% of pop., 2004)	3.3

Migration

EMIGRATION, 2005
- Stock of emigrants: **935,599**
- Stock of emigrants as percentage of population: **4.5%**
- Top 10 destination countries: India, Saudi Arabia, Canada, the United Kingdom, Germany, Italy, Australia, Oman, the United States, France

SKILLED EMIGRATION, 2000
- Emigration rate of tertiary educated: **27.5%**
- Emigration of physicians: **1,663** or **17.4%** of physicians trained in the country

IMMIGRATION, 2005
- Stock of immigrants: **368,228**
- Stock of immigrants as percentage of population: **1.8%**
- Females as percentage of immigrants: **53.4%**
- Refugees as percentage of immigrants: **0.0%**
- Top 10 source countries: India, Australia, France, the United Kingdom, China, Sweden, Malaysia, Germany, the United States, Pakistan

Remittances

US$ millions	2000	2001	2002	2003	2004	2005	2006	2007
Inward remittance flows	1,166	1,185	1,309	1,438	1,590	1,990	2,350[a]	2,700
of which								
Workers' remittances	1,142	1,155	1,287	1,414	1,564	1,968	2,326	..
Compensation of employees	12	14	9	10	10	7	6	..
Migrants' transfer	12	15	13	14	16	15	18	..
Outward remittance flows	20	194	209	230	237	257	283[b]	..
of which								
Workers' remittances	..	172	190	209	214	233	258	..
Compensation of employees	14	17	13	15	16	16	17	..
Migrants' transfer	6	5	6	6	7	8	8	..

a. 8.7% of GDP in 2006.
b. 1.0% of GDP in 2006.

St. Kitts and Nevis

Population (thousands, 2006)	48
Population growth (avg. annual %, 1997–2006)	1.7
Population density (people per sq. km, 2006)	134
Labor force (millions, 2006)	..
Urban population (% of pop., 2006)	32.2
Age dependency ratio	..
Surface area (sq. km, 2006)	360
GNI ($ millions, 2006)	426
GNI per capita, Atlas method ($, 2006)	8,840
GDP growth (avg. annual %, 2002–06)	3.8
Poverty headcount ratio at national poverty line (% of pop., 2004)	..

Migration

EMIGRATION, 2005
- Stock of emigrants: **0**
- Stock of emigrants as percentage of population: **0.0%**

SKILLED EMIGRATION, 2000
- Emigration rate of tertiary educated: **71.8%**
- Emigration of physicians: **14** or **21.2%** of physicians trained in the country

IMMIGRATION, 2005
- Stock of immigrants: **4,446**
- Stock of immigrants as percentage of population: **10.4%**
- Females as percentage of immigrants: **49.7%**
- Refugees as percentage of immigrants: **0.0%**

Remittances

US$ millions	2000	2001	2002	2003	2004	2005	2006	2007
Inward remittance flows	4	4	3	3	3	3	3ª	3
of which								
Workers' remittances	..	..	..	..	..	..	..	..
Compensation of employees	1	1	0	0	0	0	..	..
Migrants' transfer	3	3	3	3	3	3	..	..
Outward remittance flows	3	4	3	4	3	3	3ᵇ	..
of which								
Workers' remittances	..	..	..	..	..	..	..	..
Compensation of employees	3	4	3	4	3	3	..	..
Migrants' transfer	0	0	0	0	0	0	..	..

a. 0.6% of GDP in 2006.
b. 0.6% of GDP in 2006.

St. Lucia

UPPER MIDDLE INCOME

Population (thousands, 2006)	166
Population growth (avg. annual %, 1997–2006)	1.2
Population density (people per sq. km, 2006)	272
Labor force (thousands, 2006)	80
Urban population (% of pop., 2006)	27.7
Age dependency ratio	0.55
Surface area (sq. km, 2006)	620
GNI ($ millions, 2006)	841
GNI per capita, Atlas method ($, 2006)	5,110
GDP growth (avg. annual %, 2002–06)	4.4
Poverty headcount ratio at national poverty line (% of pop., 2004)	23.7

Migration

EMIGRATION, 2005
- Stock of emigrants: **0**
- Stock of emigrants as percentage of population: **0.0%**

SKILLED EMIGRATION, 2000
- Emigration rate of tertiary educated: **36.0%**
- Emigration of physicians: **158** or **66.1%** of physicians trained in the country

IMMIGRATION, 2005
- Stock of immigrants: **8,674**
- Stock of immigrants as percentage of population: **5.4%**
- Females as percentage of immigrants: **51.7%**
- Refugees as percentage of immigrants: **0.0%**

Remittances

US$ millions	2000	2001	2002	2003	2004	2005	2006	2007
Inward remittance flows	3	3	2	2	2	2	2[a]	2
of which								
Workers' remittances	..	..	..	..	..	..	..	..
Compensation of employees	0	0	0	0	0	0	..	..
Migrants' transfer	3	3	2	2	2	2	..	..
Outward remittance flows	1	1	1	1	1	1	1[b]	..
of which								
Workers' remittances	..	..	..	..	..	..	..	..
Compensation of employees	..	..	..	..	..	..	..	..
Migrants' transfer	1	1	1	1	1	1	..	..

a. 0.2% of GDP in 2006.
b. 0.1% of GDP in 2006.

St. Vincent and the Grenadines

Latin America and the Caribbean	UPPER MIDDLE INCOME
Population (thousands, 2006)	120
Population growth (avg. annual %, 1997–2006)	0.5
Population density (people per sq. km, 2006)	307
Labor force (thousands, 2006)	58
Urban population (% of pop., 2006)	46.3
Age dependency ratio	0.55
Surface area (sq. km, 2006)	390
GNI ($ millions, 2006)	466
GNI per capita, Atlas method ($, 2006)	3,930
GDP growth (avg. annual %, 2002–06)	3.7
Poverty headcount ratio at national poverty line (% of pop., 2004)	..

Migration

EMIGRATION, 2005
- Stock of emigrants: **0**
- Stock of emigrants as percentage of population: **0.0%**

SKILLED EMIGRATION, 2000
- Emigration rate of tertiary educated: **56.8%**
- Emigration of physicians: **0** or **0.0%** of physicians trained in the country

IMMIGRATION, 2005
- Stock of immigrants: **10,342**
- Stock of immigrants as percentage of population: **8.7%**
- Females as percentage of immigrants: **51.7%**
- Refugees as percentage of immigrants: **0.0%**

Remittances

US$ millions	2000	2001	2002	2003	2004	2005	2006	2007
Inward remittance flows	3	3	4	4	5	5	5[a]	5
of which								
Workers' remittances	..	..	..	..	..	..	..	..
Compensation of employees	0	0	1	1	1	1	..	..
Migrants' transfer	3	3	3	3	4	4	..	..
Outward remittance flows	1	1	1	1	1	2	2[b]	..
of which								
Workers' remittances	..	..	..	..	..	..	..	..
Compensation of employees	..	..	..	..	..	1	..	..
Migrants' transfer	1	1	1	1	1	1	..	..

a. 1.1% of GDP in 2006.
b. 0.4% of GDP in 2006.

Sudan

Sub-Saharan Africa **LOW INCOME**

Population (millions, 2006)	37
Population growth (avg. annual %, 1997–2006)	2.1
Population density (people per sq. km, 2006)	16
Labor force (millions, 2006)	11
Urban population (% of pop., 2006)	41.7
Age dependency ratio	0.74
Surface area (1,000 sq. km, 2006)	2,506
GNI ($ billions, 2006)	34
GNI per capita, Atlas method ($, 2006)	810
GDP growth (avg. annual %, 2002-06)	7.6
Poverty headcount ratio at national poverty line (% of pop., 2004)	..

Migration

EMIGRATION, 2005
- Stock of emigrants: **587,120**
- Stock of emigrants as percentage of population: **1.6%**
- Top 10 destination countries: Saudi Arabia, Uganda, Chad, the United States, the United Kingdom, Oman, Ethiopia, Canada, Germany, Australia

SKILLED EMIGRATION, 2000
- Emigration rate of tertiary educated: **5.6%**
- Emigration of physicians:
   a) **410** or **7.6%** of physicians trained in the country *(Source: Docquier and Bhargava 2006)*
   b) **758** or **13.2%** of physicians trained in the country *(Source: Clemens and Pettersson 2006)*
- Emigration of nurses: **166** or **0.6%** of nurses trained in the country

IMMIGRATION, 2005
- Stock of immigrants: **638,596**
- Stock of immigrants as percentage of population: **1.8%**
- Females as percentage of immigrants: **48.3%**
- Refugees as percentage of immigrants: **22.4%**
- Top 10 source countries: Eritrea, Ethiopia, Chad, Nigeria, Egypt, the Republic of Yemen, India, West Bank and Gaza, the Democratic Republic of Congo, Somalia

Remittances

US$ millions	2000	2001	2002	2003	2004	2005	2006	2007
Inward remittance flows	641	740	978	1,223	1,403	1,016	1,157[a]	1,157
of which								
Workers' remittances	638	730	970	1,218	1,401	1,014	1,155	..
Compensation of employees	3	9	8	5	2	2	2	..
Migrants' transfer	..	..	..	..	..	..	..	..
Outward remittance flows	4	2	4	1	2	2	2[b]	..
of which								
Workers' remittances	..	..	..	..	..	..	..	..
Compensation of employees	4	2	4	1	2	2	2	..
Migrants' transfer	..	..	..	..	..	..	..	..

a. 3.1% of GDP in 2006.
b. 0.01% of GDP in 2006.

Suriname

Population (thousands, 2006)	452
Population growth (avg. annual %, 1997–2006)	0.8
Population density (people per sq. km, 2006)	3
Labor force (thousands, 2006)	154
Urban population (% of pop., 2006)	74.2
Age dependency ratio	0.57
Surface area (1,000 sq. km, 2006)	163
GNI ($ billions, 2006)	1.5
GNI per capita, Atlas method ($, 2006)	3,200
GDP growth (avg. annual %, 2002-06)	5.4
Poverty headcount ratio at national poverty line (% of pop., 2004)	..

Migration

EMIGRATION, 2005

- Stock of emigrants: **250,628**
- Stock of emigrants as percentage of population: **55.8%**
- Top 10 destination countries: the Netherlands, French Guiana, the United States, Netherlands Antilles, Canada, Belgium, Guyana, the United Kingdom, France, Brazil

SKILLED EMIGRATION, 2000

- Emigration rate of tertiary educated: **89.9%**
- Emigration of physicians: **11** or **5.2%** of physicians trained in the country

IMMIGRATION, 2005

- Stock of immigrants: **5,297**
- Stock of immigrants as percentage of population: **1.2%**
- Females as percentage of immigrants: **47.2%**
- Refugees as percentage of immigrants: **0.0%**

Remittances

US$ millions	2000	2001	2002	2003	2004	2005	2006	2007
Inward remittance flows	..	..	15	23	9	4	2[a]	2
of which								
Workers' remittances	..	0	13	21	7	2	0	..
Compensation of employees	..	..	2	2	2	2	2	..
Migrants' transfer	..	..	..	0	..	..	..	..
Outward remittance flows	2	2	22	28	14	9	5[b]	..
of which								
Workers' remittances	1	1	21	23	9	5	2	..
Compensation of employees	1	1	1	5	5	4	3	..
Migrants' transfer	..	..	..	0	..	..	..	..

a. 0.1% of GDP in 2006.
b. 0.3% of GDP in 2006.

Swaziland

LOWER MIDDLE INCOME

Population (millions, 2006)	1.1
Population growth (avg. annual %, 1997–2006)	1.9
Population density (people per sq. km, 2006)	65
Labor force (thousands, 2006)	338
Urban population (% of pop., 2006)	24.4
Age dependency ratio	0.79
Surface area (1,000 sq. km, 2006)	17
GNI ($ billions, 2006)	2.7
GNI per capita, Atlas method ($, 2006)	2,430
GDP growth (avg. annual %, 2002–06)	2.5
Poverty headcount ratio at national poverty line (% of pop., 2004)	46.7

Migration

EMIGRATION, 2005
- Stock of emigrants: **95,608**
- Stock of emigrants as percentage of population: **9.3%**
- Top 10 destination countries: South Africa, Mozambique, the United Kingdom, the United States, Tanzania, Canada, Australia, Portugal, the Netherlands, Germany

SKILLED EMIGRATION, 2000
- Emigration rate of tertiary educated: **5.8%**
- Emigration of physicians:
  a) **0** or **0.0%** of physicians trained in the country *(Source: Docquier and Bhargava 2006)*
  b) **53** or **28.5%** of physicians trained in the country *(Source: Clemens and Pettersson 2006)*
- Emigration of nurses: **96** or **2.8%** of nurses trained in the country

IMMIGRATION, 2005
- Stock of immigrants: **45,459**
- Stock of immigrants as percentage of population: **4.4%**
- Females as percentage of immigrants: **47.0%**
- Refugees as percentage of immigrants: **1.6%**
- Top source countries: Mozambique, South Africa

Remittances

US$ millions	2000	2001	2002	2003	2004	2005	2006	2007
Inward remittance flows	57	53	45	65	83	95	98[a]	98
of which								
Workers' remittances	..	..	..	..	1	1	1	..
Compensation of employees	57	53	44	65	82	94	94	..
Migrants' transfer	0	0	1	..	..	0	3	..
Outward remittance flows	21	27	21	39	5	6	16[b]	..
of which								
Workers' remittances	21	26	21	37	0	3	1	..
Compensation of employees	..	..	..	2	4	5	15	..
Migrants' transfer	..	0	0	..	1	0	0	..

a. 3.7% of GDP in 2006.
b. 0.6% of GDP in 2006.

Sweden

Population (millions, 2006)	9.0
Population growth (avg. annual %, 1997-2006)	0.2
Population density (people per sq. km, 2006)	22
Labor force (millions, 2006)	4.7
Urban population (% of pop., 2006)	84.3
Age dependency ratio	0.53
Surface area (1,000 sq. km, 2006)	450
GNI ($ billions, 2006)	384
GNI per capita, Atlas method ($, 2006)	43,580
GDP growth (avg. annual %, 2002-06)	2.9
Poverty headcount ratio at national poverty line (% of pop., 2004)	..

Migration

IMMIGRATION, 2005
- Stock of immigrants: **1,117,286**
- Stock of immigrants as percentage of population: **12.4%**
- Females as percentage of immigrants: **52.1%**
- Refugees as percentage of immigrants: **5.3%**
- Top 10 source countries: Finland, Serbia and Montenegro, Iraq, Bosnia and Herzegovina, the Islamic Republic of Iran, Norway, Poland, Denmark, Germany, Turkey

EMIGRATION, 2005
- Stock of emigrants: **300,771**
- Stock of emigrants as percentage of population: **3.3%**
- Top 10 destination countries: the United States, Norway, Finland, Germany, the United Kingdom, Spain, Denmark, France, Canada, Switzerland

SKILLED EMIGRATION, 2000
- Emigration rate of tertiary educated: **4.4%**
- Emigration of physicians: **933** or **3.3%** of physicians trained in the country

Remittances

US$ millions	2000	2001	2002	2003	2004	2005	2006	2007
Inward remittance flows	**510**	**543**	**540**	**578**	**420**	**372**	**336ª**	**336**
of which								
Workers' remittances	161	185	190	203	..	..	..	..
Compensation of employees	304	329	319	336	377	329	336	..
Migrants' transfer	46	29	31	39	43	43	..	..
Outward remittance flows	**545**	**589**	**590**	**600**	**646**	**532**	**589ᵇ**	..
of which								
Workers' remittances	34	31	35	24	..	..	..	..
Compensation of employees	488	543	537	554	621	507	589	..
Migrants' transfer	23	16	18	22	25	25	..	..

a. 0.1% of GDP in 2006.
b. 0.2% of GDP in 2006.

Switzerland

Population (millions, 2006)	7.4
Population growth (avg. annual %, 1997–2006)	0.5
Population density (people per sq. km, 2006)	186
Labor force (millions, 2006)	4.2
Urban population (% of pop., 2006)	75.6
Age dependency ratio	0.48
Surface area (1,000 sq. km, 2006)	41
GNI ($ billions, 2006)	410
GNI per capita, Atlas method ($, 2006)	57,230
GDP growth (avg. annual %, 2002–06)	1.3
Poverty headcount ratio at national poverty line (% of pop., 2004)	..

Migration

IMMIGRATION, 2005
- Stock of immigrants: **1,659,686**
- Stock of immigrants as percentage of population: **22.9%**
- Females as percentage of immigrants: **49.7%**
- Refugees as percentage of immigrants: **2.8%**
- Top 10 source countries: Italy, Germany, Serbia and Montenegro, Portugal, France, Spain, Turkey, Austria, Bosnia and Herzegovina, FYR Macedonia

EMIGRATION, 2005
- Stock of emigrants: **481,060**
- Stock of emigrants as percentage of population: **6.6%**
- Top 10 destination countries: Spain, France, the United States, Germany, Italy, Canada, the United Kingdom, Portugal, Austria, Turkey

SKILLED EMIGRATION, 2000
- Emigration rate of tertiary educated: **9.1%**
- Emigration of physicians: **1,255** or **4.7%** of physicians trained in the country

Remittances

US$ millions	2000	2001	2002	2003	2004	2005	2006	2007
Inward remittance flows	**1,119**	**1,301**	**1,372**	**1,706**	**1,889**	**1,828**	**1,859**[a]	**1,950**
of which								
Workers' remittances	125	125	147	173	194	202	209	..
Compensation of employees	995	1,176	1,225	1,533	1,695	1,626	1,650	..
Migrants' transfer	..	..	..	..	..	..	..	..
Outward remittance flows	**7,591**	**8,380**	**9,223**	**11,411**	**12,839**	**13,200**	**13,805**[b]	..
of which								
Workers' remittances	1,704	1,820	2,045	2,661	3,003	3,171	3,356	..
Compensation of employees	5,888	6,561	7,178	8,750	9,836	10,029	10,449	..
Migrants' transfer	..	..	..	..	..	..	..	..

a. 0.5% of GDP in 2006.
b. 3.6% of GDP in 2006.

Syrian Arab Republic, The

Middle East and North Africa	LOWER MIDDLE INCOME
Population (millions, 2006)	19
Population growth (avg. annual %, 1997–2006)	2.5
Population density (people per sq. km, 2006)	106
Labor force (millions, 2006)	7.9
Urban population (% of pop., 2006)	50.8
Age dependency ratio	0.66
Surface area (1,000 sq. km, 2006)	185
GNI ($ billions, 2006)	34
GNI per capita, Atlas method ($, 2006)	1,570
GDP growth (avg. annual %, 2002–06)	4.0
Poverty headcount ratio at national poverty line (% of pop., 2004)	..

Migration

EMIGRATION, 2005
- Stock of emigrants: **480,708**
- Stock of emigrants as percentage of population: **2.5%**
- Top 10 destination countries: Saudi Arabia, the United States, Germany, West Bank and Gaza, Libya, Canada, Sweden, Israel, France, República Bolivariana de Venezuela

SKILLED EMIGRATION, 2000
- Emigration rate of tertiary educated: **5.2%**
- Emigration of physicians: **2,283** or **9.5%** of physicians trained in the country

IMMIGRATION, 2005
- Stock of immigrants: **984,587**
- Stock of immigrants as percentage of population: **5.2%**
- Females as percentage of immigrants: **48.9%**
- Refugees as percentage of immigrants: **43.7%**
- Top source country: West Bank and Gaza

Remittances

US$ millions	2000	2001	2002	2003	2004	2005	2006	2007
Inward remittance flows	180	170	135	889	855	823	795[a]	824
of which								
Workers' remittances	..	..	..	743	690	763	770	..
Compensation of employees	180	170	135	146	165	60	25	..
Migrants' transfer	..	..	..	..	..	..	..	..
Outward remittance flows	29	30	35	40	42	40	235[b]	..
of which								
Workers' remittances	..	..	..	..	1	2	160	..
Compensation of employees	29	30	35	40	41	38	75	..
Migrants' transfer	..	..	..	..	..	..	..	..

a. 2.3% of GDP in 2006.
b. 0.7% of GDP in 2006.

Tajikistan

LOW INCOME

Population (millions, 2006)	6.7
Population growth (avg. annual %, 1997–2006)	1.3
Population density (people per sq. km, 2006)	47
Labor force (millions, 2006)	2.2
Urban population (% of pop., 2006)	24.6
Age dependency ratio	0.73
Surface area (1,000 sq. km, 2006)	143
GNI ($ billions, 2006)	2.7
GNI per capita, Atlas method ($, 2006)	390
GDP growth (avg. annual %, 2002–06)	8.7
Poverty headcount ratio at national poverty line (% of pop., 2004)	7

Migration

EMIGRATION, 2005
- Stock of emigrants: **796,593**
- Stock of emigrants as percentage of population: **12.2%**
- Top 10 destination countries: Russia, Uzbekistan, Ukraine, Israel, Kazakhstan, the Kyrgyz Republic, Latvia, the United States, Germany, Lithuania

SKILLED EMIGRATION, 2000
- Emigration rate of tertiary educated: **0.7%**
- Emigration of physicians: **3** or **0.03%** of physicians trained in the country

IMMIGRATION, 2005
- Stock of immigrants: **306,433**
- Stock of immigrants as percentage of population: **4.7%**
- Females as percentage of immigrants: **57.8%**
- Refugees as percentage of immigrants: **1.1%**
- Top source countries: Uzbekistan, Russia, the Kyrgyz Republic

Remittances

US$ millions	2000	2001	2002	2003	2004	2005	2006	2007
Inward remittance flows	..	..	79	146	252	466	1,019[a]	1,250
of which								
Workers' remittances	..	..	78	146	252	465	1,015	..
Compensation of employees	..	..	0	0	0	1	4	..
Migrants' transfer	..	..	..	..	..	..	..	..
Outward remittance flows	..	..	13	64	119	145	395[b]	..
of which								
Workers' remittances	..	..	13	64	119	144	393	..
Compensation of employees	..	..	0	0	0	1	2	..
Migrants' transfer	..	..	..	..	..	..	..	..

a. **36.2% of GDP in 2006.**
b. **14.0% of GDP in 2006.**

Tanzania

Population (millions, 2006)	39
Population growth (avg. annual %, 1997–2006)	2.5
Population density (people per sq. km, 2006)	45
Labor force (millions, 2006)	20
Urban population (% of pop., 2006)	24.6
Age dependency ratio	0.84
Surface area (1,000 sq. km, 2006)	945
GNI ($ billions, 2006)	13
GNI per capita, Atlas method ($, 2006)	350
GDP growth (avg. annual %, 2002–06)	6.5
Poverty headcount ratio at national poverty line (% of pop., 2004)	50.9

Migration

EMIGRATION, 2005
- Stock of emigrants: **188,789**
- Stock of emigrants as percentage of population: **0.5%**
- Top 10 destination countries: Uganda, the United Kingdom, Canada, Mozambique, Malawi, the United States, Australia, Rwanda, Germany, the Netherlands

SKILLED EMIGRATION, 2000
- Emigration rate of tertiary educated: **15.8%**
- Emigration of physicians:
  a) **81** or **8.8%** of physicians trained in the country *(Source: Docquier and Bhargava 2006)*
  b) **1,356** or **51.8%** of physicians trained in the country *(Source: Clemens and Pettersson 2006)*
- Emigration of nurses: **953** or **3.5%** of nurses trained in the country

IMMIGRATION, 2005
- Stock of immigrants: **792,328**
- Stock of immigrants as percentage of population: **2.1%**
- Females as percentage of immigrants: **52.3%**
- Refugees as percentage of immigrants: **73.1%**
- Top 10 source countries: Burundi, Mozambique, Kenya, the Republic of Congo, Rwanda, Zambia, Uganda, Malawi, India, the United States

Remittances

US$ millions	2000	2001	2002	2003	2004	2005	2006	2007
Inward remittance flows	8	15	12	9	11	18	14[a]	14
of which								
Workers' remittances	..	5	5	2	3	8	8	..
Compensation of employees	8	10	7	7	8	10	6	..
Migrants' transfer	..	..	..	..	..	..	..	..
Outward remittance flows	20	31	27	27	34	31	29[b]	..
of which								
Workers' remittances	..	8	6	5	6	6	6	..
Compensation of employees	20	22	21	22	28	25	23	..
Migrants' transfer	..	..	..	..	..	..	..	..

a. 0.1% of GDP in 2006.
b. 0.2% of GDP in 2006.

Thailand

East Asia and Pacific	LOWER MIDDLE INCOME
Population (millions, 2006)	65
Population growth (avg. annual %, 1997–2006)	0.9
Population density (people per sq. km, 2006)	127
Labor force (millions, 2006)	36
Urban population (% of pop., 2006)	32.6
Age dependency ratio	0.44
Surface area (1,000 sq. km, 2006)	513
GNI ($ billions, 2006)	202
GNI per capita, Atlas method ($, 2006)	2,990
GDP growth (avg. annual %, 2002–06)	5.6
Poverty headcount ratio at national poverty line (% of pop., 2004)	0.1

Migration

EMIGRATION, 2005
- Stock of emigrants: **758,180**
- Stock of emigrants as percentage of population: **1.2%**
- Top 10 destination countries: the United States, Cambodia, Malaysia, Germany, Japan, Australia, Saudi Arabia, the United Kingdom, the Republic of Korea, Sweden

SKILLED EMIGRATION, 2000
- Emigration rate of tertiary educated: **2.2%**
- Emigration of physicians: **630** or **3.3%** of physicians trained in the country

IMMIGRATION, 2005
- Stock of immigrants: **1,050,459**
- Stock of immigrants as percentage of population: **1.6%**
- Females as percentage of immigrants: **56.8%**
- Refugees as percentage of immigrants: **11.6%**
- Top 10 source countries: China, Myanmar, Lao PDR, Cambodia, Nepal, Sri Lanka, Japan, India, Vietnam, the United States

Remittances

US$ millions	2000	2001	2002	2003	2004	2005	2006	2007
Inward remittance flows	1,697	1,252	1,380	1,607	1,622	1,187	1,333[a]	1,707
of which								
Workers' remittances	..	..	..	..	..	..	..	..
Compensation of employees	1,697	1,252	1,380	1,607	1,622	1,187	1,333	..
Migrants' transfer	..	..	..	..	..	..	..	..
Outward remittance flows	..	..	..	..	..	..	..	..
of which								
Workers' remittances	..	..	..	..	..	..	..	..
Compensation of employees	..	..	..	..	..	..	..	..
Migrants' transfer	..	..	..	..	..	..	..	..

a. 0.6% of GDP in 2006.

Timor-Leste

East Asia and Pacific **LOW INCOME**

Population (millions, 2006)	1.0
Population growth (avg. annual %, 1997–2006)	2.9
Population density (people per sq. km, 2006)	69
Labor force (thousands, 2006)	422
Urban population (% of pop., 2006)	26.9
Age dependency ratio	0.78
Surface area (1,000 sq. km, 2006)	15
GNI ($ millions, 2006)	848
GNI per capita, Atlas method ($, 2006)	840
GDP growth (avg. annual %, 2002–06)	-2.1
Poverty headcount ratio at national poverty line (% of pop., 2004)	..

Migration

EMIGRATION, 2005
- Stock of emigrants: **15,310**
- Stock of emigrants as percentage of population: **1.6%**
- Top 10 destination countries: Australia, Portugal, the Philippines, Canada, New Zealand, the Netherlands, Greece, República Bolivariana de Venezuela, the Czech Republic, France

SKILLED EMIGRATION, 2000
- Emigration rate of tertiary educated: **n/a**.
- Emigration of physicians: **8** or **16.3%** of physicians trained in the country

IMMIGRATION, 2005
- Stock of immigrants: **6,127**
- Stock of immigrants as percentage of population: **0.7%**
- Females as percentage of immigrants: **47.6%**
- Refugees as percentage of immigrants: **2.3%**

Remittances

Remittance data are currently not available for this country.

Togo

Population (millions, 2006)	6.3
Population growth (avg. annual %, 1997–2006)	3.0
Population density (people per sq. km, 2006)	116
Labor force (millions, 2006)	2.5
Urban population (% of pop., 2006)	40.8
Age dependency ratio	0.86
Surface area (1,000 sq. km, 2006)	57
GNI ($ billions, 2006)	2.2
GNI per capita, Atlas method ($, 2006)	350
GDP growth (avg. annual %, 2002–06)	2.5
Poverty headcount ratio at national poverty line (% of pop., 2004)	..

Migration

EMIGRATION, 2005
- Stock of emigrants: **222,008**
- Stock of emigrants as percentage of population: **3.6%**
- Top 10 destination countries: Nigeria, Benin, Germany, France, Gabon, the United States, the Republic of Congo, Niger, Italy, Canada

SKILLED EMIGRATION, 2000
- Emigration rate of tertiary educated: **13.6%**
- Emigration of physicians:
  a) **36** or **11.5%** of physicians trained in the country *(Source: Docquier and Bhargava 2006)*
  b) **180** or **40.4%** of physicians trained in the country *(Source: Clemens and Pettersson 2006)*
- Emigration of nurses: **186** or **19.2%** of nurses trained in the country

IMMIGRATION, 2005
- Stock of immigrants: **183,304**
- Stock of immigrants as percentage of population: **3.0%**
- Females as percentage of immigrants: **50.4%**
- Refugees as percentage of immigrants: **5.9%**
- Top source countries: Benin, Ghana, Nigeria, Niger, France, Mali, Lebanon, Germany, the United States

Remittances

US$ millions	2000	2001	2002	2003	2004	2005	2006	2007
Inward remittance flows	34	69	104	148	179	192	192[a]	192
of which								
Workers' remittances	16	52	87	128	153	164	..	..
Compensation of employees	19	17	17	20	26	28	..	..
Migrants' transfer	..	..	..	..	..	..	..	..
Outward remittance flows	7	5	17	28	34	36	36[b]	..
of which								
Workers' remittances	4	5	17	27	33	35	..	..
Compensation of employees	3	0	0	1	1	1	..	..
Migrants' transfer	..	..	..	..	..	..	..	..

a. 8.7% of GDP in 2006.
b. 1.6% of GDP in 2006.

Tonga

Population (thousands, 2006)	102
Population growth (avg. annual %, 1997–2006)	0.5
Population density (people per sq. km, 2006)	142
Labor force (thousands, 2006)	40
Urban population (% of pop., 2006)	24.3
Age dependency ratio	0.71
Surface area (sq. km, 2006)	750
GNI ($ millions, 2006)	223
GNI per capita, Atlas method ($, 2006)	2,170
GDP growth (avg. annual %, 2002–06)	2.4
Poverty headcount ratio at national poverty line (% of pop., 2004)	..

Migration

EMIGRATION, 2005
- Stock of emigrants: **51,570**
- Stock of emigrants as percentage of population: **50.4%**
- Top 10 destination countries: the United States, New Zealand, Australia, American Samoa, Chile, Fiji, Kiribati, France, the United Kingdom, Samoa

SKILLED EMIGRATION, 2000
- Emigration rate of tertiar y educated: **74.2%**
- Emigration of physicians: **0** or **0.0%** of physicians trained in the country

IMMIGRATION, 2005
- Stock of immigrants: **1,163**
- Stock of immigrants as percentage of population: **1.1%**
- Females as percentage of immigrants: **46.3%**
- Refugees as percentage of immigrants: **0.0%**
- Top source countries: Fiji, Samoa, India, China, Japan

Remittances

US$ millions	2000	2001	2002	2003	2004	2005	2006	2007
Inward remittance flows	..	**53**	**66**	**55**	**67**	**67**	**72[a]**	**77**
of which								
Workers' remittances	..	53	62	52	64	62	69	..
Compensation of employees	..	..	4	3	3	4	3	..
Migrants' transfer	..	..	0	0	0	0	0	..
Outward remittance flows	..	**11**	**16**	**9**	**10**	**12**	**12[b]**	..
of which								
Workers' remittances	..	11	15	8	10	12	12	..
Compensation of employees	..	..	1	1	0	..	..	..
Migrants' transfer	..	..	0	0	0	0	0	..

a. 32.3% of GDP in 2006.
b. 5.4% of GDP in 2006.

Trinidad and Tobago

Population (millions, 2006)	1.3
Population growth (avg. annual %, 1997–2006)	0.3
Population density (people per sq. km, 2006)	255
Labor force (thousands, 2006)	634
Urban population (% of pop., 2006)	12.5
Age dependency ratio	0.4
Surface area (1,000 sq. km, 2006)	5
GNI ($ billions, 2006)	19
GNI per capita, Atlas method ($, 2006)	13,340
GDP growth (avg. annual %, 2002–06)	9.7
Poverty headcount ratio at national poverty line (% of pop., 2004)	1.1

Migration

EMIGRATION, 2005
- Stock of emigrants: **361,596**
- Stock of emigrants as percentage of population: **27.7%**
- Top 10 destination countries: the United States, Canada, the United Kingdom, República Bolivariana de Venezuela, Barbados, Virgin Islands (U.S.), Australia, Germany, the Netherlands, Antigua and Barbuda

SKILLED EMIGRATION, 2000
- Emigration rate of tertiary educated: **78.4%**
- Emigration of physicians: **40** or **3.8%** of physicians trained in the country

IMMIGRATION, 2005
- Stock of immigrants: **37,564**
- Stock of immigrants as percentage of population: **2.9%**
- Females as percentage of immigrants: **53.6%**
- Refugees as percentage of immigrants: **0.0%**
- Top source countries: Grenada, Guyana, the United States, the United Kingdom, Barbados, República Bolivariana de Venezuela, India

Remittances

US$ millions	2000	2001	2002	2003	2004	2005	2006	2007
Inward remittance flows	38	41	79	87	87	92	92[a]	92
of which								
Workers' remittances	38	41	79	87	87	92	..	..
Compensation of employees	..	..	..	..	..	..	..	..
Migrants' transfer	..	..	..	..	..	..	..	..
Outward remittance flows	..	..	..	..	..	..	..	..
of which								
Workers' remittances	..	..	..	..	..	..	..	..
Compensation of employees	..	..	..	..	..	..	..	..
Migrants' transfer	..	..	..	..	..	..	..	..

a. 0.5% of GDP in 2006.

Tunisia

Middle East and North Africa | **LOWER MIDDLE INCOME**

Population (millions, 2006)	10
Population growth (avg. annual %, 1997–2006)	1.1
Population density (people per sq. km, 2006)	65
Labor force (millions, 2006)	4.0
Urban population (% of pop., 2006)	65.7
Age dependency ratio	0.46
Surface area (1,000 sq. km, 2006)	164
GNI ($ billions, 2006)	29
GNI per capita, Atlas method ($, 2006)	2,970
GDP growth (avg. annual %, 2002–06)	4.5
Poverty headcount ratio at national poverty line (% of pop., 2004)	0.2

Migration

EMIGRATION, 2005
- Stock of emigrants: **623,221**
- Stock of emigrants as percentage of population: **6.2%**
- Top 10 destination countries: France, Libya, Germany, Israel, Saudi Arabia, Italy, the United States, Switzerland, Canada, Belgium

SKILLED EMIGRATION, 2000
- Emigration rate of tertiary educated: **9.6%**
- Emigration of physicians:
  a) **296** or **4.2%** of physicians trained in the country *(Source: Docquier and Bhargava 2006)*
  b) **3,192** or **33.1%** of physicians trained in the country *(Source: Clemens and Pettersson 2006)*
- Emigration of nurses: **1,478** or **5.3%** of nurses trained in the country

IMMIGRATION, 2005
- Stock of immigrants: **37,858**
- Stock of immigrants as percentage of population: **0.4%**
- Females as percentage of immigrants: **48.7%**
- Refugees as percentage of immigrants: **0.2%**
- Top source countries: Algeria, Morocco, France, Italy, Libya

Remittances

US$ millions	2000	2001	2002	2003	2004	2005	2006	2007
Inward remittance flows	796	927	1,071	1,250	1,432	1,393	1,510[a]	1,669
of which								
Workers' remittances	796	927	1,071	1,250	1,432	1,393	1,510	..
Compensation of employees	..	..	..	..	..	..	..	..
Migrants' transfer	..	..	..	..	..	..	..	..
Outward remittance flows	27	24	20	24	19	16	16[b]	..
of which								
Workers' remittances	21	21	13	17	13	16	16	..
Compensation of employees	..	..	..	..	..	..	..	..
Migrants' transfer	6	3	8	7	6	..	..	..

a. 5.0% of GDP in 2006.
b. 0.1% of GDP in 2006.

Turkey

Population (millions, 2006)	73
Population growth (avg. annual %, 1997–2006)	1.5
Population density (people per sq. km, 2006)	95
Labor force (millions, 2006)	27
Urban population (% of pop., 2006)	67.8
Age dependency ratio	0.52
Surface area (1,000 sq. km, 2006)	784
GNI ($ billions, 2006)	402
GNI per capita, Atlas method ($, 2006)	5,400
GDP growth (avg. annual %, 2002–06)	7.2
Poverty headcount ratio at national poverty line (% of pop., 2004)	3.2

Migration

EMIGRATION, 2005
- Stock of emigrants: **4,402,914**
- Stock of emigrants as percentage of population: **6.0%**
- Top 10 destination countries: Germany, France, the Netherlands, Austria, the United States, Saudi Arabia, Bulgaria, Greece, Switzerland, the United Kingdom

SKILLED EMIGRATION, 2000
- Emigration rate of tertiary educated: **4.6%**
- Emigration of physicians: **1,986** or **2.3%** of physicians trained in the country

IMMIGRATION, 2005
- Stock of immigrants: **1,328,405**
- Stock of immigrants as percentage of population: **1.8%**
- Females as percentage of immigrants: **52.6%**
- Refugees as percentage of immigrants: **0.3%**
- Top 10 source countries: Bulgaria, Germany, Serbia and Montenegro, Greece, FYR Macedonia, the Netherlands, Romania, Russia, the United Kingdom, Azerbaijan

Remittances

US$ millions	2000	2001	2002	2003	2004	2005	2006	2007
Inward remittance flows	4,560	2,786	1,936	729	804	851	1,111[a]	1,200
of which								
Workers' remittances	4,560	2,786	1,936	729	804	851	1,111	..
Compensation of employees	..	..	..	..	..	..	..	..
Migrants' transfer	..	..	..	..	..	..	..	..
Outward remittance flows	..	..	..	..	..	96	107[b]	..
of which								
Workers' remittances	..	..	..	..	..	..	..	..
Compensation of employees	..	..	..	..	..	96	107	..
Migrants' transfer	..	..	..	..	..	..	..	..

a. 0.3% of GDP in 2006.
b. 0.03% of GDP in 2006.

Turkmenistan

LOWER MIDDLE INCOME

Population (millions, 2006)	4.9
Population growth (avg. annual %, 1997–2006)	1.4
Population density (people per sq. km, 2006)	10
Labor force (millions, 2006)	2.3
Urban population (% of pop., 2006)	46.6
Age dependency ratio	0.55
Surface area (1,000 sq. km, 2006)	488
GNI ($ billions, 2006)	9.9
GNI per capita, Atlas method ($, 2006)	..
GDP growth (avg. annual %, 2002–06)	..
Poverty headcount ratio at national poverty line (% of pop., 2004)	4.7

Migration

EMIGRATION, 2005
- Stock of emigrants: **260,345**
- Stock of emigrants as percentage of population: **5.4%**
- Top 10 destination countries: Russia, Ukraine, Israel, Latvia, Turkey, Germany, Armenia, the United States, Kazakhstan, the Islamic Republic of Iran

SKILLED EMIGRATION, 2000
- Emigration rate of tertiary educated: **0.1%**
- Emigration of physicians: **2** or **0.01%** of physicians trained in the country

IMMIGRATION, 2005
- Stock of immigrants: **223,732**
- Stock of immigrants as percentage of population: **4.6%**
- Females as percentage of immigrants: **57.8%**
- Refugees as percentage of immigrants: **5.9%**
- Top source countries: Uzbekistan, Russia, Kazakhstan, Azerbaijan, Armenia, Ukraine

Remittances
Remittance data are currently not available for this country.

Uganda

Population (millions, 2006)	30
Population growth (avg. annual %, 1997–2006)	3.3
Population density (people per sq. km, 2006)	152
Labor force (millions, 2006)	12
Urban population (% of pop., 2006)	12.7
Age dependency ratio	1.12
Surface area (1,000 sq. km, 2006)	241
GNI ($ billions, 2006)	9.2
GNI per capita, Atlas method ($, 2006)	300
GDP growth (avg. annual %, 2002–06)	5.7
Poverty headcount ratio at national poverty line (% of pop., 2004)	82.6

Migration

EMIGRATION, 2005
- Stock of emigrants: **154,747**
- Stock of emigrants as percentage of population: **0.5%**
- Top 10 destination countries: the United Kingdom, Tanzania, the United States, Canada, Rwanda, Sweden, Germany, Australia, Zambia, Denmark

SKILLED EMIGRATION, 2000
- Emigration rate of tertiary educated: **21.6%**
- Emigration of physicians:
  a) **218** or **19.0%** of physicians trained in the country *(Source: Docquier and Bhargava 2006)*
  b) **1,837** or **43.1%** of physicians trained in the country *(Source: Clemens and Pettersson 2006)*
- Emigration of nurses: **1,122** or **10.2%** of nurses trained in the country

IMMIGRATION, 2005
- Stock of immigrants: **518,158**
- Stock of immigrants as percentage of population: **1.8%**
- Females as percentage of immigrants: **49.4%**
- Refugees as percentage of immigrants: **50.3%**
- Top 10 source countries: Sudan, Rwanda, Burundi, the Democratic Republic of Congo, Tanzania, Kenya, the United Kingdom, the United States, Canada, Australia

Remittances

US$ millions	2000	2001	2002	2003	2004	2005	2006	2007
Inward remittance flows	238	342	421	306	371	423	814ª	856
of which								
Workers' remittances	238	342	421	306	371	423	814	..
Compensation of employees	..	..	..	..	..	..	..	..
Migrants' transfer	..	..	..	..	..	..	..	..
Outward remittance flows	353	355	401	259	235	359	322ᵇ	..
of which								
Workers' remittances	308	304	355	212	181	307	301	..
Compensation of employees	45	51	46	47	54	52	21	..
Migrants' transfer	..	..	..	..	..	..	..	..

a. **8.7% of GDP in 2006.**
b. **3.5% of GDP in 2006.**

Ukraine

LOWER MIDDLE INCOME

Population (millions, 2006)	47
Population growth (avg. annual %, 1997–2006)	-0.9
Population density (people per sq. km, 2006)	80
Labor force (millions, 2006)	22
Urban population (% of pop., 2006)	68
Age dependency ratio	0.44
Surface area (1,000 sq. km, 2006)	604
GNI ($ billions, 2006)	104
GNI per capita, Atlas method ($, 2006)	1,950
GDP growth (avg. annual %, 2002–06)	7.3
Poverty headcount ratio at national poverty line (% of pop., 2004)	0.2

Migration

EMIGRATION, 2005
- Stock of emigrants: **6,081,890**
- Stock of emigrants as percentage of population: **13.1%**
- Top 10 destination countries: Russia, the United States, Poland, Israel, Kazakhstan, Moldova, Germany, Belarus, Canada, Spain

SKILLED EMIGRATION, 2000
- Emigration rate of tertiary educated: **6.0%**
- Emigration of physicians: **1,581** or **1.1%** of physicians trained in the country

IMMIGRATION, 2005
- Stock of immigrants: **6,833,198**
- Stock of immigrants as percentage of population: **14.7%**
- Females as percentage of immigrants: **57.8%**
- Refugees as percentage of immigrants: **0.0%**
- Top 10 source countries: Russia, Belarus, Kazakhstan, Uzbekistan, Moldova, Azerbaijan, Georgia, Armenia, Tajikistan, the Kyrgyz Republic

Remittances

US$ millions	2000	2001	2002	2003	2004	2005	2006	2007
Inward remittance flows	33	141	209	330	411	595	829[a]	944
of which								
Workers' remittances	..	84	133	185	193	236	289	..
Compensation of employees	33	56	74	145	218	359	540	..
Migrants' transfer	..	1	2	..	..	..	..	..
Outward remittance flows	10	5	15	29	20	34	30[b]	..
of which								
Workers' remittances	..	..	..	..	..	2	2	..
Compensation of employees	2	..	4	4	6	10	9	..
Migrants' transfer	8	5	11	25	14	22	19	..

a. 0.8% of GDP in 2006.
b. 0.03% of GDP in 2006.

Migration and Remittances Factbook 2008

United Arab Emirates, The

HIGH INCOME

Population (millions, 2006)	4.6
Population growth (avg. annual %, 1997–2006)	6.2
Population density (people per sq. km, 2006)	55
Labor force (millions, 2006)	2.8
Urban population (% of pop., 2006)	76.7
Age dependency ratio	0.29
Surface area (1,000 sq. km, 2006)	84
GNI ($ billions, 2006)	105
GNI per capita, Atlas method ($, 2006)	23,950
GDP growth (avg. annual %, 2002–06)	8.2
Poverty headcount ratio at national poverty line (% of pop., 2004)	..

Migration

IMMIGRATION, 2005
- Stock of immigrants: **3,211,749**
- Stock of immigrants as percentage of population: **71.4%**
- Females as percentage of immigrants: **27.8%**
- Refugees as percentage of immigrants: **0.0%**
- Top source country: India

EMIGRATION, 2005
- Stock of emigrants: **41,287**
- Stock of emigrants as percentage of population: **0.9%**
- Top 10 destination countries: India, the United States, Canada, the United Kingdom, Australia, Germany, Bahrain, France, Sweden, the Netherlands

SKILLED EMIGRATION, 2000
- Emigration rate of tertiary educated: **1.2%**
- Emigration of physicians: **253** or **3.8%** of physicians trained in the country

Remittances
Remittance data are currently not available for this country.

United Kingdom, The

Population (millions, 2006)	60
Population growth (avg. annual %, 1997–2006)	0.3
Population density (people per sq. km, 2006)	249
Labor force (millions, 2006)	31
Urban population (% of pop., 2006)	89.8
Age dependency ratio	0.51
Surface area (1,000 sq. km, 2006)	244
GNI ($ billions, 2006)	2,385
GNI per capita, Atlas method ($, 2006)	40,180
GDP growth (avg. annual %, 2002–06)	2.5
Poverty headcount ratio at national poverty line (% of pop., 2004)	..

Migration

IMMIGRATION, 2005
- Stock of immigrants: **5,408,118**
- Stock of immigrants as percentage of population: **9.1%**
- Females as percentage of immigrants: **54.3%**
- Refugees as percentage of immigrants: **5.5%**
- Top 10 source countries: Ireland, India, Pakistan, Germany, the United States, Bangladesh, Jamaica, South Africa, Kenya, Australia

EMIGRATION, 2005
- Stock of emigrants: **4,158,909**
- Stock of emigrants as percentage of population: **7.0%**
- Top 10 destination countries: Australia, the United States, Canada, Ireland, Spain, New Zealand, Germany, France, the Netherlands, Italy

SKILLED EMIGRATION, 2000
- Emigration rate of tertiary educated: **16.7%**
- Emigration of physicians: **12,160** or **9.4%** of physicians trained in the country

Remittances

US$ millions	2000	2001	2002	2003	2004	2005	2006	2007
Inward remittance flows	**3,614**	**4,825**	**4,485**	**5,029**	**6,350**	**6,302**	**6,954**[a]	**7,000**
of which								
Workers' remittances	..	..	..	..	..	..	..	..
Compensation of employees	1,552	1,562	1,695	1,825	2,142	1,772	1,931	..
Migrants' transfer	2,062	3,263	2,790	3,204	4,208	4,530	5,023	..
Outward remittance flows	**2,044**	**3,342**	**2,439**	**2,624**	**2,957**	**3,877**	**4,526**[b]	..
of which								
Workers' remittances	..	..	..	..	..	..	..	..
Compensation of employees	1,336	1,472	1,582	1,728	2,015	2,876	3,295	..
Migrants' transfer	708	1,870	858	896	942	1,001	1,231	..

a. 0.3% of GDP in 2006.
b. 0.2% of GDP in 2006.

Migration and Remittances Factbook 2008

United States, The

Population (millions, 2006)	299
Population growth (avg. annual %, 1997–2006)	1.0
Population density (people per sq. km, 2006)	33
Labor force (millions, 2006)	157
Urban population (% of pop., 2006)	81.1
Age dependency ratio	0.49
Surface area (1,000 sq. km, 2006)	9,632
GNI ($ billions, 2006)	13,232
GNI per capita, Atlas method ($, 2006)	44,970
GDP growth (avg. annual %, 2002–06)	3.0
Poverty headcount ratio at national poverty line (% of pop., 2004)	..

Migration

IMMIGRATION, 2005
- Stock of immigrants: **38,354,709**
- Stock of immigrants as percentage of population: **12.9%**
- Females as percentage of immigrants: **50.2%**
- Refugees as percentage of immigrants: **1.1%**
- Top 10 source countries: Mexico, the Philippines, Germany, India, China, Vietnam, Canada, Cuba, El Salvador, the United Kingdom

EMIGRATION, 2005
- Stock of emigrants: **2,261,443**
- Stock of emigrants as percentage of population: **0.8%**
- Top 10 destination countries: Mexico, Canada, the United Kingdom, Germany, Italy, Japan, Australia, West Bank and Gaza, Spain, the Republic of Korea

SKILLED EMIGRATION, 2000
- Emigration rate of tertiary educated: **0.5%**
- Emigration of physicians: **1,867** or **0.2%** of physicians trained in the country

Remittances

US$ millions	2000	2001	2002	2003	2004	2005	2006	2007
Inward remittance flows	2,835	2,931	2,811	2,813	2,822	2,890	2,880ª	3,000
of which								
Workers' remittances	..	..	..	..	..	..	..	..
Compensation of employees	2,835	2,879	2,811	2,813	2,822	2,890	2,880	..
Migrants' transfer	..	..	..	..	..	..	..	..
Outward remittance flows	30,961	34,592	36,126	36,545	39,347	40,635	42,222ᵇ	..
of which								
Workers' remittances	23,442	26,506	27,746	28,033	30,384	31,345	32,810	..
Compensation of employees	7,519	8,086	8,380	8,512	8,963	9,290	9,412	..
Migrants' transfer	..	..	..	..	..	..	..	..

a. 0.02% of GDP in 2006.
b. 0.3% of GDP in 2006.

Uruguay

UPPER MIDDLE INCOME

Population (millions, 2006)	3.3
Population growth (avg. annual %, 1997–2006)	0.2
Population density (people per sq. km, 2006)	19
Labor force (millions, 2006)	1.7
Urban population (% of pop., 2006)	92.1
Age dependency ratio	0.6
Surface area (1,000 sq. km, 2006)	176
GNI ($ billions, 2006)	19
GNI per capita, Atlas method ($, 2006)	5,310
GDP growth (avg. annual %, 2002–06)	3.3
Poverty headcount ratio at national poverty line (% of pop., 2004)	..

Migration

EMIGRATION, 2005
- Stock of emigrants: **288,480**
- Stock of emigrants as percentage of population: **8.3%**
- Top 10 destination countries: Argentina, Spain, the United States, Brazil, Australia, Canada, República Bolivariana de Venezuela, Paraguay, Chile, Sweden

SKILLED EMIGRATION, 2000
- Emigration rate of tertiary educated: **8.6%**
- Emigration of physicians: **155** or **1.3%** of physicians trained in the country

IMMIGRATION, 2005
- Stock of immigrants: **84,114**
- Stock of immigrants as percentage of population: **2.4%**
- Females as percentage of immigrants: **54.2%**
- Refugees as percentage of immigrants: **0.1%**
- Top 10 source countries: Argentina, Spain, Brazil, Italy, Chile, Germany, Paraguay, Poland, the United States, France

Remittances

US$ millions	2000	2001	2002	2003	2004	2005	2006	2007
Inward remittance flows	..	..	36	62	70	77	89[a]	100
of which								
Workers' remittances	..	..	36	62	70	77	89	..
Compensation of employees	..	..	0	..	0	0	..	..
Migrants' transfer	..	..	..	..	..	..	..	..
Outward remittance flows	..	..	..	1	2	2	3[b]	..
of which								
Workers' remittances	..	..	..	1	2	2	3	..
Compensation of employees	..	..	..	..	..	..	..	..
Migrants' transfer	..	..	..	..	..	..	..	..

a. 0.5% of GDP in 2006.
b. 0.02% of GDP in 2006.

Uzbekistan

Population (millions, 2006)	27
Population growth (avg. annual %, 1997–2006)	1.3
Population density (people per sq. km, 2006)	62
Labor force (millions, 2006)	12
Urban population (% of pop., 2006)	36.7
Age dependency ratio	0.59
Surface area (1,000 sq. km, 2006)	447
GNI ($ billions, 2006)	17
GNI per capita, Atlas method ($, 2006)	610
GDP growth (avg. annual %, 2002–06)	6.0
Poverty headcount ratio at national poverty line (% of pop., 2004)	0

Migration

EMIGRATION, 2005
- Stock of emigrants: **2,185,539**
- Stock of emigrants as percentage of population: **8.2%**
- Top 10 destination countries: Russia, Ukraine, Tajikistan, Kazakhstan, the Kyrgyz Republic, Turkmenistan, Israel, Latvia, the United States, Germany

SKILLED EMIGRATION, 2000
- Emigration rate of tertiary educated: **1.0%**
- Emigration of physicians: **10** or **0.01%** of physicians trained in the country

IMMIGRATION, 2005
- Stock of immigrants: **1,267,839**
- Stock of immigrants as percentage of population: **4.8%**
- Females as percentage of immigrants: **57.8%**
- Refugees as percentage of immigrants: **3.5%**
- Top source countries: Russia, Tajikistan, Kazakhstan

Remittances
Remittance data are currently not available for this country.

Vanuatu

Population (thousands, 2006)	215
Population growth (avg. annual %, 1997-2006)	2.0
Population density (people per sq. km, 2006)	18
Labor force (thousands, 2006)	109
Urban population (% of pop., 2006)	23.9
Age dependency ratio	0.75
Surface area (1,000 sq. km, 2006)	12
GNI ($ millions, 2006)	358
GNI per capita, Atlas method ($, 2006)	1,710
GDP growth (avg. annual %, 2002-06)	2.7
Poverty headcount ratio at national poverty line (% of pop., 2004)	..

Migration

EMIGRATION, 2005
- Stock of emigrants: **3,092**
- Stock of emigrants as percentage of population: **1.5%**
- Top 10 destination countries: Australia, France, New Caledonia, New Zealand, the United Kingdom, the United States, Spain, Fiji, Samoa, Switzerland

SKILLED EMIGRATION, 2000
- Emigration rate of tertiary educated: **5.0%**
- Emigration of physicians: **0** or **0.0%** of physicians trained in the country

IMMIGRATION, 2005
- Stock of immigrants: **1,042**
- Stock of immigrants as percentage of population: **0.5%**
- Females as percentage of immigrants: **46.6%**
- Refugees as percentage of immigrants: **0.0%**
- Top 10 source countries: Australia, France, New Zealand, the United Kingdom, Fiji, New Caledonia, Papua New Guinea, the Solomon Islands

Remittances

US$ millions	2000	2001	2002	2003	2004	2005	2006	2007
Inward remittance flows	35	53	8	9	10	11	11[a]	11
of which								
Workers' remittances	11	16	0	0	0	0	0	..
Compensation of employees	3	3	4	4	5	5	5	..
Migrants' transfer	21	34	4	5	5	6	6	..
Outward remittance flows	73	78	15	17	18	18	18[b]	..
of which								
Workers' remittances	15	14	0	0	0	0	0	..
Compensation of employees	3	2	2	3	3	3	3	..
Migrants' transfer	55	62	13	14	15	15	15	..

a. 2.8% of GDP in 2006.
b. 4.6% of GDP in 2006.

Venezuela, República Bolivariana de

Latin America and the Caribbean	UPPER MIDDLE INCOME
Population (millions, 2006)	27
Population growth (avg. annual %, 1997–2006)	1.8
Population density (people per sq. km, 2006)	31
Labor force (millions, 2006)	13
Urban population (% of pop., 2006)	93.7
Age dependency ratio	0.56
Surface area (1,000 sq. km, 2006)	912
GNI ($ billions, 2006)	180
GNI per capita, Atlas method ($, 2006)	6,070
GDP growth (avg. annual %, 2002–06)	4.5
Poverty headcount ratio at national poverty line (% of pop., 2004)	18.7

Migration

EMIGRATION, 2005
- Stock of emigrants: **463,759**
- Stock of emigrants as percentage of population: **1.7%**
- Top 10 destination countries: Spain, the United States, Colombia, Portugal, Canada, the Dominican Republic, Italy, Chile, Germany, the United Kingdom

SKILLED EMIGRATION, 2000
- Emigration rate of tertiary educated: **3.3%**
- Emigration of physicians: **505** or **1.1%** of physicians trained in the country

IMMIGRATION, 2005
- Stock of immigrants: **1,010,148**
- Stock of immigrants as percentage of population: **3.8%**
- Females as percentage of immigrants: **50.0%**
- Refugees as percentage of immigrants: **0.0%**
- Top 10 source countries: Colombia, Spain, Portugal, Italy, Peru, Ecuador, Chile, the Dominican Republic, Syria, Cuba

Remittances

US$ millions	2000	2001	2002	2003	2004	2005	2006	2007
Inward remittance flows	17	19	19	21	20	148	165ᵃ	165
of which								
Workers' remittances	..	..	..	187	123	128	145	..
Compensation of employees	17	19	19	21	20	20	20	..
Migrants' transfer	..	..	..	..	..	..	..	..
Outward remittance flows	331	406	383	209	214	211	253ᵇ	..
of which								
Workers' remittances	302	379	360	179	186	183	225	..
Compensation of employees	29	27	23	30	28	28	28	..
Migrants' transfer	..	..	..	..	..	..	..	..

a. 0.1% of GDP in 2006.
b. 0.1% of GDP in 2006.

Vietnam

Population (millions, 2006)	84
Population growth (avg. annual %, 1997–2006)	1.2
Population density (people per sq. km, 2006)	271
Labor force (millions, 2006)	45
Urban population (% of pop., 2006)	26.9
Age dependency ratio	0.52
Surface area (1,000 sq. km, 2006)	329
GNI ($ billions, 2006)	59
GNI per capita, Atlas method ($, 2006)	690
GDP growth (avg. annual %, 2002–06)	7.8
Poverty headcount ratio at national poverty line (% of pop., 2004)	0.6

Migration

EMIGRATION, 2005
- Stock of emigrants: **2,225,413**
- Stock of emigrants as percentage of population: **2.6%**
- Top 10 destination countries: the United States, Canada, Cambodia, Australia, France, Germany, the Republic of Korea, the United Kingdom, Japan, Thailand

SKILLED EMIGRATION, 2000
- Emigration rate of tertiary educated: **39.0%**
- Emigration of physicians: **2,443** or **5.6%** of physicians trained in the country

IMMIGRATION, 2005
- Stock of immigrants: **21,105**
- Stock of immigrants as percentage of population: **0.03%**
- Females as percentage of immigrants: **46.2%**
- Refugees as percentage of immigrants: **4.4%**

Remittances

US$ millions	2000	2001	2002	2003	2004	2005	2006	2007
Inward remittance flows	..	2,000	2,714	2,700	3,200	4,000	4,800[a]	5,000
of which								
Workers' remittances	..	..	..	..	..	..	..	..
Compensation of employees	..	..	..	..	..	..	..	..
Migrants' transfer	..	..	..	..	..	..	..	..
Outward remittance flows	..	..	..	..	..	..	..	..
of which								
Workers' remittances	..	..	..	..	..	..	..	..
Compensation of employees	..	..	..	..	..	..	..	..
Migrants' transfer	..	..	..	..	..	..	..	..

a. 7.9% of GDP in 2006.

West Bank and Gaza

Population (millions, 2006)	3.7
Population growth (avg. annual %, 1997–2006)	4.0
Population density (people per sq. km, 2006)	621
Labor force (thousands, 2006)	794
Urban population (% of pop., 2006)	71.7
Age dependency ratio	0.93
Surface area (1,000 sq. km, 2006)	6
GNI ($ billions, 2006)	4.2
GNI per capita, Atlas method ($, 2006)	1,230
GDP growth (avg. annual %, 2002–06)	2.0
Poverty headcount ratio at national poverty line (% of pop., 2004)	..

Migration

EMIGRATION, 2005
- Stock of emigrants: **954,924**
- Stock of emigrants as percentage of population: **25.8%**
- Top 10 destination countries: Syria, Saudi Arabia, Libya, Canada, the United Kingdom, Australia, Sudan, Sweden, Chile, France

SKILLED EMIGRATION, 2000
- Emigration rate of tertiary educated:
- Emigration of physicians: **60** or **2.8%** of physicians trained in the country

IMMIGRATION, 2005
- Stock of immigrants: **1,680,142**
- Stock of immigrants as percentage of population: **45.4%**
- Females as percentage of immigrants: **43.4%**
- Refugees as percentage of immigrants: **100.0%**
- Top 10 source countries: Israel, Jordan, Egypt, the United States, Syria, Lebanon, the Republic of Yemen, Tunisia

Remittances

US$ millions	2000	2001	2002	2003	2004	2005	2006	2007
Inward remittance flows	859	409	344	472	455	598	598[a]	598
of which								
Workers' remittances	65	29	25	40	35	45	..	..
Compensation of employees	777	362	301	403	401	486	..	..
Migrants' transfer	17	18	17	29	19	66	..	..
Outward remittance flows	23	10	9	13	13	16	16[b]	..
of which								
Workers' remittances	22	9	8	13	12	15	..	..
Compensation of employees	1	1	1	1	1	1	..	..
Migrants' transfer	..	..	..	..	..	..	..	..

a. 14.7% of GDP in 2006.
b. 0.4% of GDP in 2006.

Yemen, The Republic of

LOW INCOME

Population (millions, 2006)	22
Population growth (avg. annual %, 1997–2006)	3.1
Population density (people per sq. km, 2006)	41
Labor force (millions, 2006)	6.2
Urban population (% of pop., 2006)	27.7
Age dependency ratio	0.93
Surface area (1,000 sq. km, 2006)	528
GNI ($ billions, 2006)	18
GNI per capita, Atlas method ($, 2006)	760
GDP growth (avg. annual %, 2002–06)	3.8
Poverty headcount ratio at national poverty line (% of pop., 2004)	7.2

Migration

EMIGRATION, 2005
- Stock of emigrants: **593,137**
- Stock of emigrants as percentage of population: **2.8%**
- Top 10 destination countries: Saudi Arabia, Israel, the United States, the United Kingdom, West Bank and Gaza, Sudan, Germany, France, Bahrain, Canada

SKILLED EMIGRATION, 2000
- Emigration rate of tertiary educated: **5.7%**
- Emigration of physicians: **68** or **1.9%** of physicians trained in the country

IMMIGRATION, 2005
- Stock of immigrants: **264,842**
- Stock of immigrants as percentage of population: **1.3%**
- Females as percentage of immigrants: **31.8%**
- Refugees as percentage of immigrants: **26.0%**

Remittances

US$ millions	2000	2001	2002	2003	2004	2005	2006	2007
Inward remittance flows	1,288	1,295	1,294	1,270	1,283	1,283	1,283[a]	1,283
of which								
Workers' remittances	1,288	1,295	1,294	1,270	1,283	1,283	1,283	..
Compensation of employees	..	..	..	..	..	..	..	..
Migrants' transfer	..	..	..	..	..	..	..	..
Outward remittance flows	61	64	64	60	108	109	121[b]	..
of which								
Workers' remittances	61	64	64	60	36	37	41	..
Compensation of employees	..	..	..	..	72	72	80	..
Migrants' transfer	..	..	..	..	..	..	..	..

a. 6.7% of GDP in 2006.
b. 0.6% of GDP in 2006.

Zambia

Population (millions, 2006)	12
Population growth (avg. annual %, 1997–2006)	1.9
Population density (people per sq. km, 2006)	16
Labor force (millions, 2006)	5.0
Urban population (% of pop., 2006)	35.1
Age dependency ratio	0.95
Surface area (1,000 sq. km, 2006)	753
GNI ($ billions, 2006)	10
GNI per capita, Atlas method ($, 2006)	630
GDP growth (avg. annual %, 2002–06)	5.0
Poverty headcount ratio at national poverty line (% of pop., 2004)	60

Migration

EMIGRATION, 2005
- Stock of emigrants: **150,281**
- Stock of emigrants as percentage of population: **1.3%**
- Top 10 destination countries: Tanzania, the United Kingdom, Malawi, Namibia, the United States, Mozambique, Australia, Canada, the Netherlands, New Zealand

SKILLED EMIGRATION, 2000
- Emigration rate of tertiary educated: **10.0%**
- Emigration of physicians:
  a) **89** or **11.5%** of physicians trained in the country *(Source: Docquier and Bhargava 2006)*
  b) **883** or **56.9%** of physicians trained in the country *(Source: Clemens and Pettersson 2006)*
- Emigration of nurses: **1,110** or **9.2%** of nurses trained in the country

IMMIGRATION, 2005
- Stock of immigrants: **274,842**
- Stock of immigrants as percentage of population: **2.4%**
- Females as percentage of immigrants: **50.4%**
- Refugees as percentage of immigrants: **55.4%**
- Top 10 source countries: Angola, the Democratic Republic of Congo, Zimbabwe, Malawi, India, the Republic of Congo, South Africa, the United Kingdom, Mozambique, the United States

Remittances

US$ millions	2000	2001	2002	2003	2004	2005	2006	2007
Inward remittance flows	..	..	..	36	48	53	58[a]	58
of which								
Workers' remittances	..	..	..	36	48	53	58	..
Compensation of employees	..	..	..	..	..	..	..	..
Migrants' transfer	..	..	..	..	..	..	..	..
Outward remittance flows	24	24	24	71	76	94	116[b]	..
of which								
Workers' remittances	18	20	20	54	64	77	93	..
Compensation of employees	6	8	18	17	12	17	23	..
Migrants' transfer	..	..	..	..	..	..	..	..

a. 0.5% of GDP in 2006.
b. 1.1% of GDP in 2006.

Zimbabwe

LOW INCOME

Population (millions, 2006)	13
Population growth (avg. annual %, 1997–2006)	0.9
Population density (people per sq. km, 2006)	34
Labor force (millions, 2006)	5.8
Urban population (% of pop., 2006)	36.4
Age dependency ratio	0.76
Surface area (1,000 sq. km, 2006)	391
GNI ($ billions, 2006)	3.2
GNI per capita, Atlas method ($, 2006)	340
GDP growth (avg. annual %, 2002–06)	-5.7
Poverty headcount ratio at national poverty line (% of pop., 2004)	61.9

Migration

EMIGRATION, 2005
- Stock of emigrants: **761,226**
- Stock of emigrants as percentage of population: **5.9%**
- Top 10 destination countries: South Africa, the United Kingdom, Mozambique, Zambia, Malawi, the United States, Australia, Canada, Tanzania, New Zealand

SKILLED EMIGRATION, 2000
- Emigration rate of tertiary educated: **7.6%**
- Emigration of physicians:
  a) **192** or **16.0%** of physicians trained in the country *(Source: Docquier and Bhargava 2006)*
  b) **1,602** or **51.1%** of physicians trained in the country *(Source: Clemens and Pettersson 2006)*
- Emigration of nurses: **3,723** or **24.2%** of nurses trained in the country

IMMIGRATION, 2005
- Stock of immigrants: **510,637**
- Stock of immigrants as percentage of population: **3.9%**
- Females as percentage of immigrants: **37.8%**
- Refugees as percentage of immigrants: **1.0%**

Remittances
Remittance data are currently not available for this country.

Glossary

Age dependency ratio (dependents to working-age population) is the ratio of dependents—people younger than 15 or older than 64—to the working-age population, those within ages 15 to 64. For example, 0.7 means there are 7 dependents for every 10 working-age people (World Bank).

Compensation of employees comprises wages, salaries, and other benefits (in cash or in kind) earned by individuals—in economies other than those in which they are residents—for work performed for and paid for by residents of those economies. Employees, in this context, include seasonal or other short-term workers (less than one year) and border workers who have centers of economic interest in their own economies (IMF).

Emigration rate of tertiary educated is the stock of emigrants with at least tertiary education as a fraction of the total tertiary educated in the country. Tertiary education refers to more than high school or 13 years of education (Docquier and Marfouk, 2004).

Labor force comprises people who meet the International Labour Organization (ILO) definition of the economically active population: all people who supply labor for the production of goods and services during a specified period. It includes both the employed and the unemployed. While national practices vary in the treatment of such groups as the armed forces and seasonal or part-time workers, in general the labor force includes the armed forces, the unemployed, and first-time job-seekers, but excludes homemakers and other unpaid caregivers and workers in the informal sector (ILO, using World Bank population estimates).

Migrants are persons who move to a country other than that of their usual residence for a period of at least a year, so that the country of destination effectively becomes their new country of usual residence (UNPD).

Migrants' transfers are contra-entries to flows of goods and changes in financial items that arise from migration (change of residence for at least a year) of individuals from one economy to another. The transfers to be recorded are thus equal to the net worth of the migrants (IMF).

Poverty headcount ratio at national poverty line is the percentage of the population living below the national poverty line. Since its 1990 World Development Report, the World Bank's "global" poverty measures have usually been based on an international poverty line of about $1 a day; more precisely, the line is $32.74 per month, at 1993 international purchasing power parity (World Bank).

Refugees are individuals who, owing to a well-founded fear of being persecuted for reasons of race, religion, nationality, or membership of a particular social group or political opinion, are outside the country of their nationality and are unable or, owing to such fear, are unwilling to avail themselves of the protection of that country; or who, not having a nationality and being outside the country of their former habitual residence as a result of such events, are unable or, owing to such fear, are unwilling to return to it. The estimates of refugee population as of mid-year 2005 were prepared by the UN Population Division (UNPD).

Remittances are defined as the sum of workers' remittances, compensation of employees, and migrants' transfers (World Bank).

Workers' remittances are current transfers by migrants who are considered residents in the destination country (IMF).